14 DAY BOOK
This book is due on or before
the latest date stamped below

D1517620

Elections and Voters in Post-communist Russia

STUDIES OF COMMUNISM IN TRANSITION

General Editor: Ronald J. Hill

*Professor of Comparative Government
and Fellow of Trinity College
Dublin, Ireland*

Studies of Communism in Transition is an important series which applies academic analysis and clarity of thought to the recent traumatic events in Eastern and Central Europe. As many of the preconceptions of the past half century are cast aside, newly independent and autonomous sovereign states are being forced to address long-term, organic problems which had been suppressed by, or appeased within, the Communist system of rule.

The series is edited under the sponsorship of Lorton House, an independent charitable association which exists to promote the academic study of communism and related concepts.

Elections and Voters in Post-communist Russia

Edited by

Matthew Wyman
Keele University, UK

Stephen White
University of Glasgow, UK

Sarah Oates
University of Glasgow, UK

STUDIES OF COMMUNISM IN TRANSITION

Edward Elgar
Cheltenham, UK • Northampton, MA, USA

Published by
Edward Elgar Publishing Limited
Glensanda House
Montpellier Parade
Cheltenham
Glos GL50 1UA
UK

Edward Elgar Publishing, Inc.
6 Market Street
Northampton
Massachusetts 01060
USA

A catalogue record for this book
is available from the British Library

Library of Congress Cataloguing in Publication Data

Elections and voters in post-communist Russia / edited by Matthew
    Wyman, Stephen White, Sarah Oates.
        (Studies of communism in transition)
        Includes bibliographical references and index.
        1. Elections—Russia (Federation)—History. 2. Russia
    (Federation)—Politics and government—1991–   I. Wyman, Matthew,
    1967–   . II. White, Stephen, 1945–   . III. Oates, Sarah.
    IV. Series.
    JN6699.A5E438 1998
    324.947'086—dc21   98–27696
                                                                             CIP

ISBN 1 85898 743 1

Electronic typesetting by Lorton Hall
Printed and bound in Great Britain by
Biddles Ltd, Guildford and King's Lynn

Contents

Figures

Tables

ix

Contributors

Ralph S. Clem (PhD, Columbia University) is Professor of International Relations at Florida International University, Miami. He is the author, co-author, or editor of several books and numerous articles dealing with ethnicity and demography in the former Soviet Union. More recently, he has worked on the electoral geography of Russia, publishing several pieces on that subject. Professor Clem is also editor of the journal *Post-Soviet Geography and Economics*.

Timothy J. Colton is Morris and Anna Feldberg Professor of Government and Russian Studies and Director of the Davis Center for Russian Studies at Harvard University. He is the author of *Moscow: Governing the Socialist Metropolis* (1995) and co-editor, with Jerry F. Hough, of *Growing Pains: Perspectives on the Russian Election of 1993* (1998). He is completing a book on voting in post-Soviet Russia.

Peter R. Craumer is Associate Professor of Geography in the Department of International Relations at Florida International University in Miami. He has written numerous articles on the social and economic geography of the former Soviet Union, most recently focussing on the electoral geography of Russia.

Evelyn Davidheiser received her PhD from Duke University and is the Assistant Director of the Institute of International Studies at the University of Minnesota in Minneapolis. She is the author of 'Left and Right in the Hard Opposition', in Timothy Colton and Jerry F. Hough (eds), *Growing Pains: Perspectives on the Russian Election of 1993* (1998), and co-author, with Jerry F. Hough and Susan Goodrich Lehman, of *The 1996 Russian Presidential Election* (1996).

Geoffrey Evans is a Fellow of Nuffield College, Oxford. He has published numerous articles on electoral behaviour and the sociology of politics. He is co-author of *Understanding Political Change* (1991) and has recently edited *The End of Class Politics: Class Voting in*

Comparative Context. Since 1992 he has (with Stephen Whitefield) conducted studies of social and political change in 13 post-communist societies.

Vicki L. Hesli is Associate Professor at the University of Iowa. Her publications include 'The Sources of Support for Separatism: Public Opinion in Three Soviet Republics' *Nations and Nationalism* (1997) and 'Political Party Development in Divided Societies: The Case of Ukraine', *Electoral Studies* (1998) (both articles co-authored with Arthur H. Miller and William M. Reisinger), and the chapter, 'Political Institutions and Democratic Governance in Divided Societies', in R.D. Grey (ed.), *Democratic Theory and Post-Communist Change*, Prentice-Hall (1997).

Jerry F. Hough is James B. Duke Professor of Political Science, Duke University, and Senior Fellow of the Brookings Institution. His most recent books are *The 1996 Russian Presidential Election* (with Evelyn Davidheiser and Susan Goodrich Lehmann) (1996), *Democratization and Revolution in the USSR, 1985–91* (1997), and *Growing Pains: Perspectives on The Russian Election of 1993* (co-edited with Timothy J. Colton) (1998).

Susan Goodrich Lehmann is an Assistant Professor of Sociology at Columbia University, New York. Her most recent publications include 'Islam and Ethnicity in the Republics of Russia', *Post-Soviet Affairs* (1997), and 'From "Soviet" to "European" Yaroslavl: Changing Neighborhood Preference in a Post-Soviet Russian City', *Urban Studies* (1997) (co-authored with Blair Ruble). In addition to further forthcoming articles, she is completing a book on Russian Orthodox and Islamic revival in post-Soviet Russia.

Ian McAllister is Director of the Research School of Social Sciences at The Australian National University, Canberra. Previously he has held appointments at the University of New South Wales, the University of Strathclyde and the University of Manchester. He is the author of *Political Behaviour* (1992), *Dimensions of Australian Society* (1995, co-author), *The Australian Political System* (1995, co-author) and *How Russia Votes* (1996, co-author). His research interests are in the areas of comparative political behaviour, political parties, voters and electoral systems.

Arthur H. Miller (PhD, University of Michigan, 1971), is Professor of Political Science and Director of the Iowa Social Science Institute at The University of Iowa. He has an international reputation for his research and writing on politics and public opinion in the United States, Europe and the Former Soviet Union. His recent books include *Public Opinion and Regime Change: The New Politics of Post-Soviet Societies* (1992), and *Presidential Campaigns and American Self Images* (1993).

Sarah Oates, a lecturer in the Politics Department at the University of Glasgow, received her PhD from Emory University in 1998. She has published articles on Russian voting and public opinion, including 'Party Platforms: Towards a Definition of the Russian Political Spectrum', in *The Journal of Communist Studies and Transition Politics* (1998). She is working on a book on post-communist parties and voters.

William M. Reisinger is Professor of Political Science at the University of Iowa. His research focuses on democratization in the former communist states, post-Soviet public opinion, and Russian legal orientations. He is the author of *Energy and the Soviet Bloc: Alliance Politics Since Stalin* (1993), and co-author of *Can Democracy Take Root in Post-Soviet Russia?* (1998); he is co-editor of *Constitutional Dialogues in Comparative Perspective* (1998), and has published numerous articles on Soviet and post-Soviet politics.

Leonid Sedov is a chief analyst for the All-Russia Centre for the Study of Public Opinion in Moscow. In addition to designing surveys and directing research, he has published numerous articles analysing Russian voting behaviour.

Stephen White is Professor of Politics and a member of the Institute of Russian and East European Studies at the University of Glasgow. A leading authority on Soviet and post-Soviet politics, his numerous publications include *How Russia Votes* (1997), co-authored with Richard Rose and Ian McAllister, and *Values and Political Change in Post-communist Europe* (1998), in collaboration with William L. Miller and Paul Heywood.

Stephen Whitefield is Fellow in Politics at Pembroke College in Oxford. He is the author of *Industrial Power and the Soviet State* (1993) and has co-authored numerous articles with Geoffrey Evans on economic experience, democratic commitment and partisanship in post-communist Europe including 'Identifying the Bases of Party Competition in Eastern Europe', 'The Politics and Economics of Democratic Commitment', and 'Political Culture versus Rational Choice: The Case of the Czech Republic and Slovakia', all published in the *British Journal of Political Science*.

Matthew Wyman is Lecturer in Politics at Keele University. He is the author of *Public Opinion in Postcommunist Russia* (1997), and of a number of articles in the field of Russian politics, in particular on party development, elections and voting behaviour and mass attitudes. He is working on a monograph on Russian electoral trends and writing a textbook about post-communist Russia.

1. Elections and Voters in the New Russia

Matthew Wyman, Stephen White and Sarah Oates

Elections have quite a long history in Russia. Town councils and regional assemblies have been elected more or less regularly since 1861, and an elected parliament has existed with only brief interruptions since 1905. What Russia does not enjoy is a history of free elections. In the tsarist period, voting was limited to a privileged few. Universal suffrage was introduced following the revolution of February 1917, but after the abortive elections to the Constituent Assembly that November, elections were without choice. Voters could merely accept or reject official, Communist Party-approved candidates, and the consequences of rejection could be severe indeed.[1] In any case, both before and after the revolution, the elections were to relatively unimportant, weak political institutions.

The analyst of the Russian electoral process therefore has only a short series of votes upon which to draw: the partially free votes permitted by Mikhail Gorbachev to Soviet and Russian parliaments in 1989 and 1990, and his referendum on the preservation of the Soviet Union of 1991; the two Russian presidential elections of 1991 and 1996; elections to the new State Duma (parliament) in 1993 and 1995; elections to the Federal Assembly and the referendum on the new

1. Stephen White, Richard Rose and Ian McAllister, *How Russia Votes* (Chatham, NJ: Chatham House, 1997), Ch. 1; Victor Zaslavsky and Robert J. Brym, 'The Functions of Elections in the USSR', *Soviet Studies*, Vol. 30, No. 3 (July 1978), pp. 363–71; Georg Brunner, 'Elections in the Soviet Union', in Robert K. Furtak (ed.), *Elections in Socialist States* (Hemel Hempstead: Harvester-Wheatsheaf, 1990).

Constitution in 1993; and, since 1992, the elections of regional governors and regional and local legislative assemblies (see Appendix A1).

These nine years have seen another development highly beneficial to
the student of the Russian electoral process: the possibility of conducting reliable sample surveys of the Russian electorate.[2] As well as
just counting votes, and observing electoral patterns and trends, this
means that the analyst can explore the relationship among social
position, ideological views, political attitudes and voting decisions.

The study of elections by political scientists has up to the recent
period mostly been about voting in stable, long-established democracies. This means that politics is occurring in the context of relative
economic prosperity and a predominantly market economy, in a situation in which the experience over a long period of time has been of
democratic politics, and where there exist parties and other political
organizations with deep roots in society. Increasingly since the 1970s,
the societies in which elections are fought have become post-industrial
ones, no longer dominated by the manual working class but by a prosperous middle class, with attendant consequences for outcomes.[3]

The context of recent Russian elections has been very different.
They have occurred against the background of an economy in precipi-
tous decline, in a society in which a significant section of the population
lives below the poverty line. The political context is quite different, too.
Politics has been characterized less by compromise and building support within society, and more by the striving for domination and the
complete defeat of opponents. Russian political traditions have been of
a *strong state* and a *weak society*, with the institutions of civil society,
such as political parties, interest groups and social movements of all
kinds, being notably weak and unable to influence the governing
authorities.

How well, then, do established theories about electoral outcomes
and electoral behaviour work in the Russian context? This was one of
the themes of the conference on *Party Politics in Postcommunist
Russia*, held at the University of Glasgow in May 1997 and bringing

2. Matthew Wyman, *Public Opinion in Postcommunist Russia* (Basingstoke:
Macmillan, 1997).
3. Ivor Crewe, 'Voters, Parties and Leaders Thirty Years On: Western Electoral
Studies and the New Democracies of Eastern Europe', in Ian Budge and David
McKay (eds), *Developing Democracy* (London: Sage, 1994), Ch. 4; John Kenneth
Galbraith, *The Culture of Contentment* (Harmondsworth: Penguin, 1993).

together an outstanding set of experts from the West and from Russia itself. Our discussions focused on a series of related questions, among which the following stood out:[4]

- Who votes?
- What is the social basis of voting in Russia?
- What is the nature of partisanship in post-communist Russia?
- Is it meaningful to speak about a left–right division?
- What have been the most important short-term influences on voting behaviour?
- Why have communist successor parties been unable to capitalize on the economic devastation of the post-1991 period?

Contributions to this volume cover each of these important questions, the theoretical context of all of which merits brief discussion.

An active and informed citizenry is of course one of the prerequisites of classical democratic theory. Mass participation is held to give the elites more incentive to take account of popular wishes in their actions. However, the reality of democratic systems is that participation is far from being universal, and that levels of participation vary greatly across countries, over time, and among different social groups and regions. Approaches to explaining levels of political participation fall into two broad groups: the sociological–cultural and the institutional. The former stresses the existence of cultural norms which motivate people to participate in the electoral process. These might include the belief that one's individual political actions can and will make a difference, and also a psychological attachment to elements of the existing political system, such as affiliation to individual parties. The sociological element is that positive beliefs about voting are more likely to come about among higher social status groups – that is, the richer and the better educated – and among the elderly, who are more likely to have come to terms with the status quo.

Some institutional explanations are concerned with more practical

---

4. Our discussions on parties themselves, on party organization and the party system, can be found in a companion volume, edited by John Löwenhardt, *Party Politics in Post-communist Russia* (London: Cass, 1998), which originally appeared as a special issue of *The Journal of Communist Studies and Transition Politics* (Vol.14, Nos 1–2). For convenience, the table of contents is included in Appendix A2 in the present volume.

reasons for why voters do not go to the polls. These include barriers to registering as a voter – a rather complex process in some parts of the world, and a relatively simple, passive activity in others. They also relate to the nature of the electoral system, with the chances of an individual vote making a difference often held to be an explanation for why, on the whole, proportional electoral systems experience higher participation than non-proportional ones. The nature of the party system also matters: well-organized parties are effective in mobilizing potential support which otherwise would have stayed at home. Where there is a party of the poor and excluded, these groups are much more likely to enter the political stage in large numbers.[5]

In Russia, of course, voters have many reasons for cynicism about the likely impact of their participation. Historically, the Russian state has hardly been responsive to popular pressure, and there are so far no examples of a peaceful transfer of power coming about as a result of elections. At every election there are accusations of falsification, coming from various quarters. Scarcely have Russians grown used to one method for conducting elections than the electoral law is again changed, often for purposes of party advantage. It is perhaps unsurprising, then, that overall participation has been relatively low in comparison to Western Europe, ranging from a low of 54.8 per cent for the 1993 State Duma elections and referendum to a high of 69.8 per cent for the first round of the 1996 presidential vote.

In Chapter 2, Ian McAllister and Stephen White analyse turnout in the State Duma elections of 1993 and 1995. Using logistic regression analysis, they explicitly test these various hypotheses about likely influences on the decision to participate in elections, basing their argument on evidence from sample surveys carried out before and after the two elections. They find some elements of truth in each of the above explanations, with the variables they investigate for the 1993 vote being able to explain just under half of the variation in turnout. The most important influence identified is party identification. Social attributes can explain only a small part of the variation, and economic circumstances none at all. External efficacy – measured as the belief on the part of the government that elections, parties, or both, make a difference to what happens, accompanied by support for the idea of

5. Sidney Verba, Norman Nie and Jae-On Kim, *Participation and Political Equality: A Seven-Nation Comparison* (Cambridge: Cambridge University Press, 1978).

democracy – is significant. This is, of course, relevant to institutional explanations of participation, in which citizens vote if there is a clear purpose in so doing, in particular if they believe that their vote can make an impact on the course of events. The finding that the strongest motivation for voting is identification with a specific political party is a significant one for the future of Russian democracy. Active participation is likely to grow to the extent that a party system emerges and stabilizes.

Chapter 3, by Ralph S. Clem and Peter R. Craumer, adds another layer to the explanation by considering the geography of voter turnout. As the authors point out, since most of the discussion of political participation has been cross-national, there has been a tendency to ignore location as an explanatory variable in the political science literature. However, the neighbourhood in which political activity takes place may well be just as important a context as social group identity and interests, and have an equally great influence on attitudes and behaviour. Furthermore, institutional barriers to participation are likely to vary somewhat in different parts of Russia. In a careful examination of trends in electoral participation in Russia's 89 regions in national elections since 1993, they find that electoral participation has consistently been higher in southern and south-western Russia. Clem and Craumer find that the most consistent, important correlates of regional turnout are organizational penetration by parties, in particular the Communist Party of the Russian Federation, and a range of socioeconomic features of regions: age (a positive correlation), education (negative), and the proportion of the work-force employed in agriculture (positive). Economic conditions in a region, however, were not found to be useful in explaining turnout. Of course, as the authors point out, these are data based on regional aggregates, from which it may be rash to generalize about individual behaviour. None the less, their analysis raises some pertinent questions for future investigation.

We then move on to look at factors underlying the voting decision itself. The intellectual context of these chapters is very much the literature on voting behaviour in well-established democracies, out of which we can identify three broad, albeit not mutually exclusive, traditions. First, there is the sociological tradition, relating voting patterns to the underlying social structure of the nation. Second is the social–psychological, which proposes that partisanship, or party identification, rather than group identity or group self-interest, is the key variable determining voter choice – although partisanship itself tends to be a product of group identity and early socialization. Finally, there is the idea of rational choice, positing that voting is strongly related to the rational self-interest of the electorate, most commonly to the short-term perspective or to retrospective economic conditions.

Each of these traditions raises important theoretical questions for analysts of the Russian electoral process. If it is the case that underlying social cleavages are the basis for voting, from where have group identities emerged, given the relatively low level of social self-organization, and the low level of mobilization by political parties in Russian conditions? In addition, how can the relative homogeneity and lack of social stratification of post-communist society be incorporated into the analysis? Is it the case that high levels of electoral volatility make it misleading to talk about cleavage structures dividing the Russian electorate?[6]

Seeing voting as a result of party identification would be, to say the least, eccentric in Russian conditions. For a number of interrelated reasons, many of them characteristic of recently democratized countries, strong parties have so far failed to emerge. Those parties that do exist are primarily elite-based, or in Duverger's term 'internally created', organizations which bring together elite groups, rather than externally orientated ones based on a network of grass-roots organizations.[7] Following Katz and Mair, we can see that there may be compelling reasons why party leaders do not pay attention to building a party organization. Access to state funding or links with business interests or the mass media provide alternative means to keep the organization viable, and indeed mass membership may prove to be a nuisance that excessively constrains leaders.[8] Party membership is not a precondition for a political career. The lack of strong parties is likely to mean low levels of partisanship for years to come.

Given the problems with these ways of approaching voting in Russia, most commentators have argued that, at least in the short term, the main characteristic is likely to be high levels of electoral volatility,

---

6. Peter Mair, 'What Is Different About Post-communist Party Systems?', *Studies in Public Policy*, No. 259 (Glasgow: University of Strathclyde, 1996).
7. Maurice Duverger, *Political Parties* (London: Methuen, 1954).
8. Richard S. Katz and Peter Mair, 'Changing Models of Party Organization and Party Democracy: The Emergence of the Cartel Party', *Party Politics*, Vol. 1, No. 1 (1995), pp. 5–28.

with decisions made according to choices on the basis of likely immediate costs and benefits and perceived long-term consequences. Thus,
White and his collaborators find that attitudes, rather than social
characteristics, have been consistently the better predictors of vote
choice, although it must be noted that social context precedes attitude.[9]
Herbert Kitschelt has argued that party systems may hinge on the
divisions between winners and losers in the new market economy, and
elsewhere that they are likely to be strongly based on charismatic or
clientelistic parties.[10]

In Chapter 4, Stephen Whitefield and Geoffrey Evans make a strong
case for the importance of underlying cleavage structures for the understanding of Russian electoral behaviour. They argue that, contrary to
conventional wisdom, there are compelling reasons for analysts to
expect post-communist electorates in general and the Russian electorate
in particular to be divided along clearly identifiable lines. First, there
are issues such as the demonstrable ideological divisions within society
over the extent and pace of economic transition; institutional design and
the amount of political liberalization; the collapse of the Soviet Union;
and political rights based on ethnicity. Second, against those who argue
for the homogeneity of post-communist societies, there often exist clear
divisions along such cleavages as religion, ethnicity and class, and these
may reinforce the ideological divisions. The absence of strong parties
or institutions of civil society should by no means be expected to
prevent such divisions from emerging, as ordinary people are quite
capable of identifying their interests on the basis of experience and peer
group contacts without being mobilized by elites. In the Russian case,
the authors argue that the main division is likely to be in terms of
economic differences, which will also manifest themselves in value
differences, because religious organizations are weak, non-Russian
minorities make up a relatively small percentage of the population, and
class positions remain uncertain. They also speculate that voters may
behave differently in parliamentary and presidential arenas, or vary
their behaviour according to the presence of particular parties that are
able to mobilize certain kinds of voters.

9. White, Rose and McAllister, *How Russia Votes*, passim.
10. Herbert Kitschelt, 'The Formation of Party Systems in East Central Europe',
    Politics and Society, Vol. 20, No.1 (1992), pp. 7–50; 'Formation of Party
    Cleavages in Post-communist Democracies', *Party Politics*, Vol. 1, No. 4 (1995),
    pp. 447–73.

The evidence for these propositions derives from an analysis of three surveys of public opinion commissioned by the authors and carried out in 1993, 1995 and 1996. Whitefield and Evans use a form of multivariate statistical analysis – discriminant analysis – that is particularly suited to identifying from a series of predictors (that is, all the factors which they argue may serve to differentiate various groups) those factors that in fact help to identify voters for the various individuals and parties. Thus because they are using data from three separate points in time, rather than using a cross-sectional method, they are able to track the dynamics of changes in cleavage structures as they occur in Russia.

The evidence of their analysis is clear. Views about economic reform are by far the most important division. At times, views about the Soviet Union also allowed a distinctive section of the electorate to be identified, but this did not hold for all their surveys. There was little evidence of different patterns emerging in parliamentary votes, in presidential votes or for specific parties. As the authors point out, the fact that electoral competition is primarily along fairly simple dividing lines – between supporters and opponents of a market economy – makes for political conflict which is by its nature resolvable. If the cleavages were best defined by, for example, ethnicity or basic questions of identity, this would make the divisions within the society less subject to resolution. Their findings are good news for the future of democracy in Russia.

Whitefield and Evans's discussion was not concerned with subjective identifications, but with objective characteristics and attitudes. In Chapter 5, Arthur H. Miller, William M. Reisinger and Vicki L. Hesli approach the explanation of voting from a somewhat different perspective. Their dependent variable is the subjective sense among voters interviewed in early 1997 that there exists a party to which they feel close. Encouragingly for the formation of a healthy party system in Russia, a rising proportion of the electorate does indeed feel close to a party. But what underlies the party preference? Is it a function of group identity, views on pressing issues, or leadership identification? The authors make a strong case for the last of these explanations. Asked directly why they feel close to a particular party, Russians are likely to say that it is because it represents their interests or they like its platform. However, it is well known that in responses to survey instruments, respondents tend not to be terribly introspective about their views, preferring instead to offer conventional and familiar explanations. However, the mere fact that people will not admit to it does not mean that their views about the personal qualities of individual political leaders are unimportant. Indeed, when one investigates the relative importance of personal qualities such as decisiveness, concern for others or trustworthiness, one finds that they appear to be strongly associated with feeling close to a party. This is confirmed by the authors in a concluding multiple regression analysis in which they examine the relative importance of views about leaders, social background, attitudes towards democracy and marketization, alongside ideological position. Their conclusion is that, in fact, subjective feelings about leaders were substantially the best predictor of attachment to a party. This is not as damaging as has been assumed by those who are concerned about the possible danger of charismatic parties, or the danger of party identification being stymied as voters identify with a leader, rather than a particular party. For a start, voter assessment of whether an individual does have the personal qualities that make him or her suitable for a leadership role is important for the democratic system to operate effectively.

Chapter 6, by the same authors, is a detailed and subtle account of the political behaviour of various sections of the Russian population, based on evidence from the same 1997 survey. Reisinger, Miller and Hesli map the location of parties and social groups in an ideological space defined by the positions of respondents and parties on scales composed of attitudes towards marketization and attitudes towards the preference for a strong state. The construction of the scales includes the sense of a Russia that is much more influential over the republics of the former Soviet Union than was the case in 1997, as well as trust in the institutions of state security and legality, the armed forces and the police, feelings of patriotism and a preference for a strong national defence.

Their findings are, reassuringly, very consistent with those of Whitefield and Evans in Chapter 4, namely that the Russian electorate is indeed distributed along these two dimensions, as are Russian political parties. As the authors point out, in order to consolidate and win votes reliably in election after election, parties must necessarily be able to identify and campaign among targeted and distinct sections of the electorate with messages that are not too dissonant with popular beliefs.

It is interesting in this respect to note the relative absence of parties and of sections of the electorate representing two of the four logically possible positions in the ideological space defined above: support for both a market and strong state power, and hostility to a market economy and to strong state power. It is important to consider the cause of this phenomenon. Is it that the positions are rarely associated, since those who adopt a more *laissez-faire* attitude in economic matters are also likely to do so with respect to the role of the state, and vice versa? Or is it that the failure of significant sections of the electorate to articulate these positions reflects the failure of the political elite themselves cogently to articulate such points of view? The lack of success of parties such as the Ivan Rybkin bloc and Women of Russia tends to imply the first explanation.

In Chapter 7, by Timothy J. Colton, we move on to consider another aspect of the nature of the Russian electorate, namely the extent to which it is useful to approach its study using concepts of 'left' and 'right'. In established democracies, as well as identifying the social divisions and views about particular issues, scholars have also been concerned with the importance of underlying ways of structuring opinions through ideological beliefs. However, there has been a tendency among scholars of post-communist Russia to dismiss the possibility that ideology might be of any analytic value in the current period. This is partly due to the confusion over what counts as 'left' and 'right'. For example, the communists have moved from being seen as conservative defenders of the status quo to being the leftist opponents of the present government. Conventional wisdom also holds that there is a degree of exhaustion with ideological discussion – indeed with politics in general – among ordinary Russians, and that therefore ideological categories are irrelevant. A further complication is that it is somewhat difficult to place some of Russia's political actors on a conventional left–right scale, leaving some to give up the ideological exercise altogether.

Colton argues that this dismissal of the relevance of the notions of left and right is somewhat gratuitous, and raises the question of whether it is indeed the case. Basing his analysis on a three-wave panel study conducted around the parliamentary and presidential elections of 1995 and 1996, Colton looks at the ways in which Russians actually understand the terms 'left' and 'right'. In general, he finds that a substantial proportion of the electorate – some 11 out of every 20 –

were capable of placing themselves on a left–right scale, indicating that the concepts had some meaning to them. Although this is a lower proportion than is found in the United States or Western Europe, the salience of the left–right scale is hardly non-existent for Russian voters.

The chapter goes on to analyse what the terms 'left' and 'right' meant to respondents. Respondents were asked to locate various prominent politicians on a left–right scale, and were asked, in an open-ended, unstructured question, to describe how they understood the terms. The author also investigated the extent to which self-location on a left–right scale corresponded with issue positions. Colton's analyses here reinforced his general conclusion: although 'left' and 'right' are not terms used in the political discourse of every Russian, they are none the less not completely meaningless, and should not be dismissed by analysts. A concluding regression analysis seeks to confirm the proposition by assessing whether left–right positioning helps to contribute to an understanding of voting for Gennadii Zyuganov in the 1996 presidential vote. The evidence is that for those sections of the electorate who are more politically aware and interested, it does indeed contribute to an explanation of the communist vote.

Jerry F. Hough and Susan Goodrich Lehmann, in their contribution, 'The Mystery of Opponents of Economic Reform among the Yeltsin Voters', tackle head-on one of the central questions for analysts of the Russian electorate: how was it possible that Boris Yeltsin was re-elected for a second term in office when his policies had only minority support? They point to the striking fact that only about a quarter of the Russian electorate and four out of ten of Yeltsin's second-round voters were actually supporters of the president's reform programme. Astonishingly high numbers of people who disagreed fundamentally with what was happening in Russia, or who had personally suffered greatly in the post-1991 period, were nevertheless willing to cast their votes for Yeltsin. Thus, the key question for analysts becomes, what were the other components of Yeltsin's willing coalition, beyond those who were in favour of economic marketization?

The second section of the chapter discusses the nature of public opinion at the time of the 1996 presidential vote. This analysis reinforces what has been established elsewhere, namely that there was no social consensus in the electorate around radical economic reforms. In fact, the majority of Russians were both economically and socially conservative. The authors then go on to discuss a problem too often neglected by analysts of survey data on Russian elections, namely the consistent over-reporting of the proportions who have voted, especially the proportions who claim to have voted for pro-establishment candidates. They provocatively argue that it is appropriate to separate out for analytical purposes those sections of the electorate who had a previous record of non-voting, or who could not remember for whom they had voted in the past, since doing this will give a more accurate reflection of genuine Yeltsin and Zyuganov voters. This is because it is generally found in surveys that these categories are most likely to misreport their voting behaviour.

Hough and Lehmann then detail the characteristics of opponents of reform among Yeltsin's voters. As observed earlier, these are extra-ordinarily similar –in both their social background and their attitudes – to Zyuganov's voters, and very dissimilar to supporters of economic reform among the Yeltsin electorate. Various explanations for this are offered. First of all, there is the possibility of electoral falsification. However, this scarcely explains why conservative survey respondents should also claim to have voted for the president. A second explanation relates to presidential patronage: a fear of the consequences of not supporting Yeltsin – withdrawal of subsidies, economic punishment of the locality and so forth. While they argue that there is probably an element of truth in this explanation, they instead stress a third cause. They assert that the Yeltsin electorate included supporters of economic liberalization *as well as* a significant section whose views were politi-cally authoritarian. This authoritarian group was attracted by actions which the liberal component of his supporters were inclined to attribute to the negative side of Yeltsin's personality: his humiliation of defeated opponents (in particular Mikhail Gorbachev), his use of patronage, the nature of 'court' politics in the Kremlin, and Yeltsin's attempt to act the role of 'good tsar'. All of this reflects Russian social atomization, including the weakness of social institutions such as an independent media, political parties, interest groups and social movements which can anchor individuals more securely in their social environment. Indeed, it is characteristic of the kind of society which many have identified as the breeding-ground for dangerous forms of political authoritarianism. As the authors point out, the different sides of Yeltsin attract two distinct groups: one that Westerners would consider liberal, the other with a distinctly more authoritarian flavour.

Chapter 9 is by Leonid Sedov of the All-Russia Centre for Public Opinion Research (VTsIOM) in Moscow. Sedov continues our discussion of the 1996 presidential election and is concerned with some more general characteristics of the Russian electorate. Using some of the array of poll evidence that VTsIOM has accumulated in the decade since its formation, Sedov is able to track the movement of voters between the 1995 Duma election, and the first and second rounds of the 1996 vote. He can thus establish with some confidence the nature of the constituencies constructed by presidential candidates for the 1996 elections. His data also provide a striking illustration of the extent of volatility of the Russian electorate, which Sedov describes as being in a state of Brownian motion, flitting randomly from one party or candidate to another and from abstention to participation and back again. According to Sedov, there are very few voters who consistently support a single political force, and these disproportionately consist of opponents of democracy and supporters of parties that are by no means committed to open political competition.

The final chapter, by Evelyn Davidheiser, addresses a key puzzle of the 1996 presidential election: why did the Communist Party of the Russian Federation (CPRF), following an overwhelming victory in the parliamentary elections of 1995, prove unable to get its candidate, Gennadii Zyuganov, elected as President of Russia in 1996? The central underlying cause of this, she argues, is that the CPRF adopted a less extreme platform in the parliamentary elections – in which it was appealing primarily to a defined, and more extreme, subsection of the electorate – than it did in the presidential elections, in which its task was to construct an overall majority of voters. The chapter provides convincing evidence for the utility of conventional spatial models of voting in understanding the Russian electoral process. Davidheiser uses principal components analysis as a method of mapping the distribution of the Russian electorate in terms of its attitudes to economic reform and to issues relating to the collapse of the Soviet Union. This methodology enables her to locate the more important parties, on the basis of their election programmes, with respect to how near or far they found themselves from the average Russian voter. The analysis, indeed, confirms that the CPRF's platform was more centrist and consensual in 1995, when it was less necessary, than in 1996, when it was more critical.

Explaining this in the second part of her analysis, Davidheiser turns to interviews with Communist Party activists, conducted in the course of the election campaigns. What emerges most strongly from this is the lack of awareness of the views of ordinary Russians on the part of the communist membership. This is the case in part because the impetus for the conduct of the campaign was coming from party activists, who of course tended to be much more extreme than rank-and-file voters. It reflected, secondly, a strategic error by party activists. Basing themselves on the results of the 1995 Duma vote, the CPRF and its allies identified nationalist voters as the key group that they needed to attract in order to construct a majority. This proved a great strategic mistake, as Yeltsin's better-resourced strategists understood clearly that the secret of a second-round majority was to pick up the votes of those who had chosen the array of moderate and centrist parties in 1995, as well as persuading some non-voters to re-join the fray.[11]

Let us now return to the questions posed at the beginning of this introduction. How typical is the electoral behaviour of Russians in comparative perspective? Collectively, our authors show that it is in fact not particularly unusual. Ways of approaching the voting decision that have proved useful to analysts of many diverse parts of the world are no less valid in post-communist Russia. The context in which electoral competition occurs is, however, unusual in its combination of economic crisis and the crises of post-imperialism and post-authoritarianism. Also important is the starting-point for the Russian electoral process. The absence of historic experience of elections and electoral competition means that there is a lack of familiarity among the electorate with the new process of collective decision making, reflected in high volatility, low levels of party identification and so forth. Not enough time has passed to judge whether these phenomena are transitory or likely to be permanent features of the Russian electoral landscape. However, it is clear that the deployment of concepts and analysis from comparative politics is useful in understanding the development of the Russian political system, just as the Russian experience can challenge our conceptions of elections, parties and voters across many nations.

---

11.   Michael McFaul, *Russia's 1996 Presidential Election: The End of Polarized Politics* (Stanford, CA: Hoover Institute Press, 1997).

2. To Vote or Not to Vote: Election Turnout in Post-communist Russia

Ian McAllister and Stephen White

Election turnout is often viewed as a primary indicator of the health of a country's democratic system. Among the range of political activities that citizens may engage in, voting involves the greatest number of people for the smallest amount of time; in most cases it also poses the simplest choices for voters. Countries that exhibit consistently high levels of turnout at competitive elections are usually regarded as secure and legitimate democracies; countries that have low or fluctuating levels are seen as unhealthy and potentially unstable. Although low turnout can also reflect the availability of other avenues of political participation aside from voting,[1] it remains the core political act within a democratic society.

Under communism Russia had one of the highest levels of turnout in the world, although it never attained the 100 per cent that was reported by Albania, Mongolia and a small number of regimes in Africa.[2] The official figures included an element of direct falsification as well as other abuses, and they were in any case misleading because increasing numbers of illegal urban residents by the 1980s, nearly 8 per cent of the total, were excluded from voters' lists.[3] The results were so predictable that newspapers could prepare photographs of the successful candidates

1. Mark Franklin, 'Electoral Participation', in Lawrence LeDuc, Richard G. Niemi and Pippa Norris (eds), *Comparing Democracies: Elections and Voting in Global Perspective* (Thousand Oaks, CA: Sage, 1996).
2. Charles L. Taylor and David A. Jodice (eds), *World Handbook of Political and Social Indicators*, Vol. 1 (New Haven, CT: Yale University Press, 1983), Table 2.6.
3. Philip G. Roeder, 'Electoral Avoidance in the Soviet Union', *Soviet Studies*, Vol. 41, No. 3 (July 1989), pp. 462–83.

before the polls had opened, and the Politburo could approve the final communiqué two days in advance.[4] The electoral reform of 1988, however, introduced the principle of competition, and in the first-ever elections on this basis in March 1989 there was a turnout of 89.8 per cent, reflecting a population that (the surveys suggested) had for the first time come to realize that 'voters could choose'.[5]

In early post-communist Russia, there was more than a choice of candidate: there was a choice of parties as well. And yet the immediate result was a fall in turnout, at successive elections and at referendums, with a partial recovery in the parliamentary and presidential elections of 1995 and 1996. In December 1993, turnout fell so low that there was considerable doubt whether the new Constitution had been properly adopted; and it was lower than in other states that shared the legacy of communist rule. Who voted, in early post-communist Russia, and who abstained? What were the views of the substantial numbers of electors who stayed outside the contest, and what was the significance of their abstention? We draw on two representative national surveys in considering these questions, one conducted at the time of the December 1993 elections to the Federal Assembly, and the other in January 1996 after elections had taken place to a new State Duma (see Appendix 2A).

1. TRADITIONAL EXPLANATIONS FOR ELECTION TURNOUT

Explanations for why citizens turn out to vote within a democratic society can be grouped into three categories (following Franklin, 1996[6]). Although these explanations overlap to some degree, they reflect the stages of research into electoral participation over the past three decades. The first explanation places its primary emphasis upon the socioeconomic resources that citizens possess, such as their education and income. The second explanation identifies the mobilizing

---

4. *Izvestiya*, 13 July 1992, p. 2.
5. Stephen White, 'The Soviet Elections of 1989: From Acclamation to Limited Choice', *Coexistence*, Vol. 28, No. 4 (December 1991), pp. 513–39.
6. See also Richard Rose, *Evaluating Election Turnout*, Studies in Public Policy 290 (Glasgow: University of Strathclyde, Centre for the Study of Public Policy, 1997).

activities of various groups and organizations as of particular importance, so that the more complex the group structure of the society, the greater the likelihood of turnout. Finally, recent research has identified the salience of elections to the ordinary voter as a crucial variable – what has been called instrumentalism.

The classic formulation of political participation identifies the socioeconomic resources that citizens can bring to bear in the political arena as crucial to whether or not they vote. Such resources include inherited resources, such as ethnicity and family background, as well as achieved resources such as educational attainment, income and social status.[7] According to this approach, differential access to these resources helps to mould the lifestyle, social networks and personal motivations of individuals; it shapes, indirectly, different levels of political participation and ultimately determines the ability of ordinary citizens to influence government policy. Although resources have most impact on the more complex modes of political participation, they also have an important role, it is suggested, in determining turnout.

The resource explanation gained widespread currency in the 1970s, providing clear public policy solutions for the low levels of participation found among black and other ethnic minorities in the United States. Since these groups suffer considerable socioeconomic disadvantages compared to whites, it was argued that improving their levels of participation hinged on improving their collective social position.[8] However, more recent studies have taken issue with this view, pointing out that socioeconomic status provides only a partial explanation for different levels of electoral participation. Differences in social learning have also been shown to be important, with citizens absorbing certain values from the political culture within which they are socialized and which in turn influence their political behaviour.[9] A second problem is the inability of differential socioeconomic resources to account for the widespread variations that are found in electoral turnout across democratic societies.[10]

7. Sidney Verba and Norman H. Nie, *Participation in America: Political Democracy and Social Equality* (New York: Harper & Row, 1972).

8. Sidney Verba, Norman H. Nie and Jae-On Kim, *Participation and Political Equality* (Cambridge: Cambridge University Press, 1978).

9. Paul M. Sniderman, *Personality and Democratic Politics* (Berkeley: University of California Press, 1975).

10. Franklin, op. cit.

An alternative formulation to account for electoral participation emerged in the 1970s in the form of mobilization. This approach argued that it was the ability of political parties, interest groups and the mass media to stimulate the political awareness that must be central to explanations of turnout.[11] In plural societies with complex group membership and a highly developed mass media, turnout was held to depend on these groups' politicizing citizens, directly or through the mass media.

This explanation fitted in with the dominant role of the electronic media in reporting elections, and the displacement of political parties as the major focus of media interest by political leaders. Once limited to presidential systems, this is a phenomenon now widely encountered in parliamentary systems as well.[12]

There is again some empirical evidence to support the mobilization explanation. In Italy, for instance, Putnam has demonstrated that political participation, of which election turnout is one component, is partly dependent on the social capital that has accumulated over many centuries.[13] Regions that are organizationally complex and which have overlapping membership among their citizens display high levels of participation, political trust and obedience, while regions whose public affairs are organized in a more hierarchical way exhibit *incivisme*. Powell's 1982 cross-national study of citizen involvement in the 1960s and 1970s suggested that party–group links are also important in promoting turnout.[14] However, his study was conducted before the decline in religiosity, and Powell himself suggested that turnout should be expected to decline as religiosity weakened.[15] A more recent European study failed to detect any significant relationship between party–group linkage and election turnout.[16]

11. Sidney Verba, Kay Schlozman and Henry Brady, *Voice and Equality: Civic Voluntarism in American Politics* (Cambridge, MA: Harvard University Press, 1995).

12. Ian McAllister, 'Leaders', in Lawrence DeDuc, Richard G. Niemi and Pippa Norris (eds), *Comparing Democracies: Elections and Voting in Global Perspective* (Thousand Oaks, CA: Sage, 1996).

13. Robert D. Putnam, *Making Democracy Work: Civic Traditions in Modern Italy* (Princeton, NJ: Princeton University Press, 1993).

14. G. Bingham Powell, *Contemporary Democracies: Participation, Stability and Violence* (Cambridge, MA: Harvard University Press, 1982).

15. Ibid., p.118.

16. Cees van der Eijk, Mark Franklin et al., *Choosing Europe? The European Electorate and National Politics in the Face of the Union* (Ann Arbor, MI: University of

The third approach to explaining turnout suggests that instrumentalism and the belief on the part of citizens that their vote will make a difference may play an important role. There has already been considerable research indicating that certain institutional arrangements provide incentives for citizens to vote. Studies in the United States have focused on such factors as enrolment procedures and residential requirements, but there is evidence that broader institutional factors related to the nature of competition are also involved. For example, turnout is usually higher in systems that have a two-party as opposed to a multiparty system, a unicameral legislature, and a proportional electoral system.[17] In these circumstances, citizens may see greater salience in elections and believe that their vote may have a greater impact than might otherwise be the case. Franklin's cross-national study of 29 democratic countries suggests that instrumentalism can make a major contribution to explaining contemporary variations in turnout.[18]

2. ELECTION TURNOUT IN POST-COMMUNIST RUSSIA

Russia entered the post-communist era with a parliament that had been elected in 1990, and a president who had also been elected under Soviet rule in the summer of 1991. The result was a deadlock between the two institutions, both of which could claim a mandate from the Russian electorate and both of which saw themselves as central to the post-communist order. The deadlock was resolved in late 1993 when President Yeltsin's decree number 1400 of 21 September, an acknowledged departure from the Constitution, dissolved the parliament and called for elections to an entirely new state body, the Federal Assembly. The parliament, under its chairman Ruslan Khasbulatov, resisted what it regarded as an improper challenge to its authority until 4 October, when it was seized after an artillery bombardment and

Michigan Press, 1996).

17. Robert Jackman, 'Political Institutions and Voter Turnout in the Industrial Democracies', *American Political Science Review*, Vol. 81, No. 2 (June 1987), pp. 405–23; Robert Jackman and Ross A. Miller, 'Voter Turnout in the Industrial Democracies During the 1980s', *Comparative Political Studies*, Vol. 27, No. 4 (January 1995), pp. 467–92.

18. Franklin, op. cit.

Khasbulatov himself was arrested. The election that followed took place under rather unusual circumstances, with several newspapers banned along with a number of parties that might otherwise have put forward candidates.

The election was also unusual in that it introduced the principle of proportional representation, untried since the elections to the Constituent Assembly in 1917. There were 450 deputies altogether in the lower house, the State Duma: 225 elected by single-member constituencies with the result determined by a simple majority, and another 225 that were to be allocated proportionally among the parties or movements that secured at least 5 per cent of the vote in a Russia-wide ballot. Levels of turnout had already been falling since the first competitive elections of 1989, and there was considerable apprehension that the turnout might fall even further and that the validity of the result might itself be in doubt. The old law had required a turnout of 50 per cent for the results to be valid; the regulations that governed the elections of December 1993 reduced this to 25 per cent, although the requirement was still 50 per cent for the referendum (*golosovanie*) on the new draft Constitution.

In the event, an official turnout of 54.8 per cent was reported, of which 1.7 per cent were spoiled ballots; even so, four of the 225 single-member seats had to be left vacant because the turnout had fallen below the legal minimum, and there were large votes 'against all the candidates' (in some constituencies up to 17 per cent).[19] Other estimates suggested that between 38 and 43 per cent might have voted, well short of the legal requirement;[20] and there were many individual reports of falsification, including large numbers of deceased 'voters' at a house in Moscow that had once belonged to Nikolai Gogol, the author of the satirical novel *Dead Souls*.[21] The size of the electorate had also fallen, making it easier to achieve the turnout that the authorities required. The electorate had been 107.3 million at the time of the April 1993 referendum; by December, however, it was being reported as 105.2 million, a fall for which there was no obvious explanation. Where, asked a Moscow journalist, had all the voters gone?[22]

19. *Segodnya*, 21 December 1993, p. 2.
20. *Konstitutsionnyi vestnik*, 1994, No. 17, p. 32.
21. Boris Kagarlitsky, *Restoration in Russia* (London: Verso, 1995).
22. *Moskovskii komsomolets*, 11 January 1994, p. 1.

Even if the official results were to be taken at face value, there had still been a dramatic fall in turnout since the late Soviet years (see Table 2.1). Although it recovered somewhat in December 1995, when a new

Table 2.1   Election turnout in Russian elections, 1984–96

Date	Type of election	Turnout (per cent)
March 1984	USSR Supreme Soviet	99.9
March 1989	USSR Congress of People's Deputies	74.7
March 1991	USSR Referendum	75.1
June 1991	RSFSR Presidency	74.7
April 1993	Referendum	64.2[a]
December 1993	Referendum/Federal Assembly	54.8
December 1995	State Duma	64.4
June 1996	Presidency (first round)	69.7
July 1996	Presidency (second round)	68.8

Note: [a] Average of the four questions asked in the referendum.

Source: Stephen White, Richard Rose and Ian McAllister, *How Russia Votes* (Chatham NJ: Chatham House, 1997).

Duma was elected for a normal four-year term, the average level of turnout at the two elections was still no more than 60 per cent, close to the bottom of the league table of turnout in comparable OECD countries, and ahead only of the United States, Switzerland and Poland (see Table 2.2). At least two of these, moreover, were special cases. In the United States, electoral laws that involve complicated registration procedures, literacy tests and poll taxes have been identified as a major disincentive to turnout,[23] while in Switzerland, the lack of competition at the executive level – and the widespread use of other means by which voters can express their views, such as local and national referendums – reduces the incentive to participate.

23. G. Bingham Powell, 'American Voter Turnout in Comparative Perspective', *American Political Science Review*, Vol. 80, No. 1 (March 1986), pp. 17–44; Jackman, op. cit.

Table 2.2   Voting turnout in 24 OECD countries and Russia

Country and rank	(N cases)	Per cent	Country and rank	(N cases)	Per cent
1. Austria	(9)	92	13. Portugal	(9)	79
2. Italy	(9)	90	14. Finland	(10)	78
3. Luxembourg	(7)	89	15. Canada	(11)	76
4. Iceland	(10)	88	16. France	(9)	76
5. New Zealand	(12)	87	17. United Kingdom	(9)	75
6. Denmark	(14)	86	18. Ireland	(11)	74
7. Germany	(9)	86	19. Spain	(6)	73
8. Sweden	(14)	86	20. Japan	(12)	71
9. Greece	(10)	86	21. Hungary	(2)	66
10. Czech Republic	(2)	85	22. Russia	(2)	60
11. Netherlands	(7)	83	23. United States	(9)	54
12. Norway	(9)	81	24. Switzerland	(8)	54
			25. Poland	(2)	51

Note: Estimates are for lower house elections and exclude Australia, Belgium, Mexico and Turkey which have compulsory voting and Korea which does not meet the criteria for a representative democracy. The Russian estimate is the average turnout in the December 1993 and December 1995 Duma elections.

Sources: Franklin (1996: Table 8.1); White et al. (1997).

3.   TESTING THE THREE EXPLANATIONS

The three explanations for election turnout all make different predictions about who will or will not vote. Resource explanations suggest that socioeconomic characteristics (such as age) and attainments (such as education) play the largest part in determining whether or not a citizen will decide to vote. The mobilization explanation suggests that the activities of groups within the society, such as political parties and the mass media, will promote political awareness and in this way encourage electoral participation. Finally, the instrumental explanation suggests that those who vote are likely to have a greater sense of efficacy – and more likely to think their vote will matter – than those who choose to abstain.

To test the three explanations, we examine voting intention in the December 1993 Duma elections. Surveys, clearly, are not a particularly effective means of measuring turnout – particularly when they measure turnout in terms of future intention rather than past act – since they overestimate the proportions of voters, often by 10 per cent or more.[24] The 1993 survey was no exception to this. While the actual turnout in the election was 54.8 per cent, definite abstainers in the survey numbered just 20 per cent, followed by those who were undecided, who made up a further 14 per cent,[25] which gives a turnout of 66 per cent. However, if we add to these two groups some 4 per cent of the respondents who said that they opposed all the parties in the election, and on that basis might reasonably be considered potential abstainers, the turnout estimated by the survey declines to 62 per cent, which is a comparatively modest overestimate of 7 per cent.

The measurement of election turnout by a question about voting intention, moreover, allows us to make an important conceptual distinction among intending non-voters. Since those who said they would not vote in the forthcoming Duma election were making a definite commitment, unhindered by whatever circumstances might promote or inhibit their propensity to vote on polling day, they may be termed *principled abstainers*: as we define them, these were electors who had taken a firm decision not to vote based on their evaluation of the political system itself as well as of the candidates and parties. To this group of principled abstainers can be added the much smaller group who said they were opposed to all the choices on offer. By contrast, those who said they did not know for whom to vote may be defined as *uncommitted abstainers*: while not in a position to make a decision, they were less likely to be opposed to the system on principle and more likely just to be unsure about their own choices.

To estimate the effect of socioeconomic resources in predicting election turnout, logistic regression techniques are used since the dependent variable is dichotomous. Overall, the results show that socioeconomic resources account for just 3 per cent of the total variance in election turnout, a comparatively modest contribution, although all but one of the seven variables included in the model are statistically

24. Kevin Swaddle and Anthony Heath, 'Official and Reported Turnout in the British General election of 1987', *British Journal of Political Science*, Vol. 19, No. 4 (October 1989), pp. 537–51.
25. The non-voting and 'don't know' options were not read out to the respondent. The question related to party support in the Duma election, and was asked both shortly before and shortly after polling day.

Table 2.3   Resources and election turnout, 1993 Duma elections[a]

	Mean	Est	(SE)
Gender (male)	0.43	0.32*	(0.09)
Age (years)	45.20	0.01*	(0.00)
Rural resident	0.26	0.41*	(0.11)
Education			
Technical	0.31	0.16	(0.11)
Higher	0.22	0.37*	(0.13)
Labour force	0.62	0.43*	(0.10)
Consumer goods (N)	1.30	0.13*	(0.04)
Constant		0.91	
Pseudo *R*-squared		0.03	
(*N*)		(2,136)	

Notes

* Statistically significant at $p < 0.01$, two-tailed.

[a] Logistic regression results showing parameter estimates (est) and standard errors (SE) predicting election turnout in the December 1993 Duma elections.

Source: 1996 Russia and Eastern Europe Survey.

significant (Table 2.3). The two strongest effects are for labour force participation and age. Those who were engaged in the active labour force were significantly more likely to vote, net of other circumstances, while those who are younger were more likely to abstain. Among the other effects, rural residents were more likely to vote than their urban counterparts, a finding that has been noted in other inquiries.[26] As an indicator of wealth, the number of consumer goods that a person reported possessing was a strong positive predictor of voting. Education also tended to increase turnout, but only in the form of a university education: there was no effect for technical education when compared with those who lacked any post-secondary education.

The impact of age deserves separate and more detailed consideration. A consistent finding in studies of turnout is that it is the young

26. See, for example, Matthew Wyman, Bill Miller, Stephen White and Paul Heywood, 'The Russian Elections of December 1993', *Electoral Studies*, Vol. 13, No. 3 (September 1994), pp. 254–71.

who are more likely to abstain than the old, an effect that is normally attributed to their lower levels of partisanship, their lack of established social networks, and their relatively high levels of geographical and residential mobility.[27] However, graphing the probability of turnout among different age groups shows that it is both the old and the young who register the lowest levels of turnout, while it is those in their thirties and forties who register the highest levels (Figure 2.1, top graph). This contrasts with the established Western democracies, where abstention tends to be concentrated among those who have just become eligible to vote and turnout increases in a linear fashion with age.[28]

Why does age produce these two peaks in abstention, among the young and the old, respectively? The answer may be that it is not age as such that is causing the effect, but generation. Theories of socialization posit that political experiences in adolescence and early adulthood have a major impact on later political behaviour. There is also extensive evidence that the experiences of particular generations within the post-communist societies have shaped political attitudes.[29] One explanation might be that the young are confused by the new democratic system, in much the same way as the young in the established democracies tend to be non-voters: in other words, that they are uncommitted abstainers. Furthermore, we might expect that the old, who have lived under communism the longest and are more dependent than others on social benefits, would be the most attached to the previous system with its comprehensive welfare provision and accordingly the most likely to be principled abstainers.

When we test this hypothesis by graphing the two types of abstainers against age and generation, we find that the opposite is the case (Figure 2.1, bottom graph). Rather than principled abstainers

27. An additional difficulty in systems such as the United States is initial voter registration.
28. In the 1992 British general election, non-voting was 25 per cent among those aged 18–24, 12 per cent among those aged 25–34 and 35–44, 9 per cent among those aged 45–54, 12 per cent among those aged 55–64, and 9 per cent among those aged 65 and over (estimates from the 1992 British Election Survey cross-section).
29. See, for instance, Ada Finifter and Ellen Mickiewiz, 'Refining the Political System of the USSR: Mass Support for Political Change', *American Political Science Review*, Vol. 86, No. 4 (December 1992), pp. 857–74; Arthur H. Miller, Vicki L. Hesli and William S. Reisinger, 'Reassessing Mass Support for Political and Economic Change in the Former USSR', *American Political Science Review*, Vol. 88, No. 2 (June 1994), pp. 399–411.

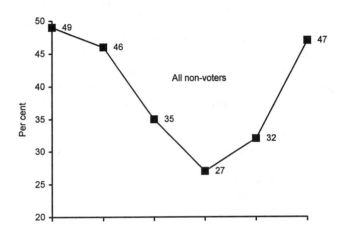

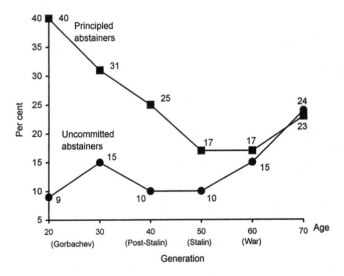

Source: 1993 Russia and Eastern Europe survey.

Figure 2.1 Abstention by age and generation, 1993 Duma elections

being older citizens who were socialized under communism, principled abstainers are actually the youngest group of citizens. Among those aged in their twenties, principled abstainers outnumber uncommitted abstainers by more than four to one; among those aged in their seventies and over, the two groups are almost equal in size. The results indicate that those who have taken a definite decision not to vote are actually the youngest citizens; the old are as likely to be uncommitted as they are to be definite about their abstention. We return to this finding later in the chapter.

The second explanation for election turnout is the activity of organizations in stimulating citizens' political awareness. It is argued that the plethora of groups and associations within civil society can promote turnout both directly and indirectly. The most direct method is by political parties themselves mobilizing the vote, although in many societies this function has been passed to the electronic media through their role as agenda-setters.[30] In Russia, the large number of parties contesting the 1993 elections and their often haphazard organization suggests that party effects on turnout are likely to be weak. But equally, the sharp fall that has taken place in newspaper circulations since the end of the Soviet period – although not in television viewing – suggests that media impact may also be limited. Among the non-political organizations that might promote turnout by highlighting public policy alternatives, the Church is perhaps the most significant: certainly, for much of the twentieth century the responsibility for political mobilization in many countries has rested with organized religion.

These predictions can be tested by examining the impact of various party and non-party factors on the likelihood of voting in the 1993 Duma elections, while taking into account socioeconomic resources. Table 2.4 shows that the explanatory power of the overall model rises to 12 per cent, but only two of the five factors included in the model are statistically significant: party support, and discussing politics with others. Being religious has no influence on turnout, nor does organizational membership or following politics in the mass media. Among all of these effects, party support is by far the most significant, although it applied to a relatively small proportion of the electorate. Just 26 per cent said they supported a particular party; but of those who said

30. Holli A. Semetko, 'The Media', in DeDuc, Niemi and Norris (eds), *Comparing Democracies*.

Table 2.4   Mobilization and election turnout, 1993 Duma elections[a]

	Mean	Est	(SE)
Party supporter	0.26	1.70*	(0.14)
Religious	0.58	0.09	(0.10)
Discusses politics often	0.31	0.60*	(0.12)
Organization member (N)	0.63	0.11	(0.08)
Follows mass media (N)	1.10	0.11	(0.06)
Constant		1.10	
Pseudo *R*-squared		0.12	
(*N*)		(2,136)	

Notes

* Statistically significant at $p < 0.01$, two-tailed.

[a] Logistic regression results showing parameter estimates (est) and standard errors (SE) predicting election turnout in the December 1993 Duma elections. Estimates control for, but do not show, resources, as defined in Table 2.3. The *R*-squared figure is for the total model.

Source: 1996 Russia and Eastern Europe Survey.

they did so, their loyalty provided a major incentive to cast their vote.

The third and final explanation identifies instrumentalism as the main reason for election turnout. If voters – it is suggested – consider the election relevant and believe that by casting a vote in concert with others they can influence the outcome, then they will do so. Traditionally, a sense of political effectiveness has been one of the major factors underpinning electoral participation, and in the United States the decline in turnout mirrors closely the decline in political efficacy across the electorate.[31] Table 2.5 measures instrumentalism in terms of five different variables: the extent to which the respondent felt that the political parties represented citizens' interests and that elections offered clear choices; the effectiveness of using groups or letter writing

31. Paul R. Abramson, *Political Attitudes in America: Formation and Change* (San Francisco: W.H. Freeman 1983); Ruy A. Teixeira, *The Disappearing American Voter* (Washington, DC: Brookings, 1992); R. Teixeira, *Why Americans Don't Vote: Turnout Decline in the United States, 1960–84* (New York: Greenwood, 1987); Warren E. Miller, and J. Merrill Shanks, *The New American Voter* (Cambridge, MA: Harvard University Press, 1996).

Table 2.5 Instrumentalism and election turnout, 1993 Duma elections[a]

	Mean	Est	(SE)
Parties represent interests	0.43	0.46*	(0.10)
Elections offer clear choice	0.54	0.70*	(0.10)
Change law by:			
Working through groups	0.10	0.39	(0.19)
Writing to politicians	0.14	0.24	(0.15)
Government affects economy	0.39	0.08	(0.10)
Constant		0.93	
Pseudo *R*-squared		0.15	
(*N*)		(2,136)	

Notes

* statistically significant at $p < 0.01$, two-tailed.

[a] Logistic regression results showing parameter estimates (est) and standard errors (SE) predicting election turnout in the December 1993 Duma elections. Estimates control for, but do not show, resources and mobilization, as defined in Tables 2.3 and 2.4. The *R*-squared figure is for the total model.

Source: 1993 Russia and Eastern Europe Survey.

to politicians to change an unjust law; and whether or not the respondent considered that the government could influence the economy.

These five variables increase the variance explained in turnout to 15 per cent, 3 per cent above what is predicted by resources and mobilization combined. However, only two of the five effects are statistically significant, and both relate to efficacy: the belief that parties represent the interests of citizens, and that elections offer citizens a clear choice. In each case, a respondent who held these views was significantly more likely to vote than a person who did not hold them, independent of other circumstances. By contrast, how respondents felt about different methods of changing an unjust law, or their assessment of the government's effectiveness in managing the economy, made no significant difference to the likelihood of voting.

All three explanations therefore play some role in explaining turnout, and the pattern that emerges is not dissimilar to the one that we encounter in established democracies. What is different, at least in early post-communist Russia, is the commitment of the young not to vote – what we have termed principled abstention. In more established democracies the young are less definite in their views, as a consequence of their lack of party commitment or other social networks. A second difference is the strength of party support as a factor that contributes to turnout, although the association loses something of its force when we take into account the limited extent of party identification within the electorate as a whole.

4. COMMUNISTS, TURNOUT AND DEMOCRACY

The transition to democracy in Russia has created many stresses and strains, but for no group more so, perhaps, than for former communists – those who were party members, and also those who lacked a formal affiliation but still believed in communist ideals. From the 1917 Revolution until the late 1980s the Communist Party remained the central political institution in the Soviet Union, organizing political life and behaviour and, for those within the *nomenklatura* system, regulating and supervising career paths.[32] By the late 1980s, party membership had peaked at about 10 per cent of the adult population, and about a third of those with a college degree.[33] Since the admissions procedure for party membership was both lengthy and exhaustive, once a person became a full member they were likely to be well indoctrinated;[34] and once a member, it was considered that 'the greatest sin was to be passive'.[35]

Studies of the socioeconomic background of former communists and of their attitudes towards the post-Soviet system have come to several conclusions. For a start, party members, particularly those who were in the *nomenklatura* or close to it, have for the most part retained their

32. John P. Willerton, *Patronage and Politics in the USSR* (Cambridge: Cambridge University Press, 1992).
33. *Izvestiya TsK KPSS*, 1989, No. 2, p. 138.
34. Ronald J. Hill and Peter Frank, *The Soviet Communist Party*, 3rd edn (Boston, MA, and London: Allen & Unwin, 1986).
35. Ronald J. Hill, 'The Communist Party and After', in Stephen White, Alex Pravda and Zvi Gitelman (eds), *Development in Soviet and Post-Soviet Politics* (Basingstoke: Macmillan, 1992), p. 78.

economic privileges and networks within the new system.[36] In terms of political beliefs, on the other hand, former communists tend to differ less than we might expect in comparison with their non-party counterparts. The major difference that emerges is between those who still consider themselves to be party members or who retain a commitment to communist ideals, and former members.[37] These committed communists display political beliefs that are quite different from those of the rest of the electorate.

To what extent does previous Communist Party membership and a belief in the ideals of communism influence electoral participation? Table 2.6 uses two questions about belief in communism and one

Table 2.6 Attitudes towards communism and electoral participation[a]

	(Column) per cent	(Per cent)		
		Principled abstainers	Uncommitted abstainers	Voters
Current believer, member	(4)	10	20	70
Past believer, member	(7)	20	7	73
Never a believer, member	(5)	18	16	65
Current believer, never a member	(12)	20	15	66
Past believer, never a member	(28)	25	12	63
Never a believer, never a member	(44)	28	15	58
(N)	(2,120)	(Chi-sq = 33.6, df = 10, $p < 0.000$)		

Note: [a] See text and appendix for definition of dependent variable.

Source: 1996 Russia Survey.

question on party membership to discriminate between principled abstainers, uncommitted abstainers, and voters. The largest group within the electorate reported that they had never believed in communist

36. Ian McAllister and Stephen White, 'The Legacy of the Nomenklatura', *Coexistence*, Vol. 32, No. 3 (September 1995), pp. 217–39; Ian McAllister, Stephen White and Richard Rose, 'Communists, Privilege, and Postcommunism in Russia', *International Politics*, Vol. 34, No. 1 (March 1997), pp. 79–95.
37. Stephen White and Ian McAllister, 'The CPSU and its Members: Between Communism and Postcommunism', *British Journal of Political Science*, Vol. 26, No. 1 (January 1996), pp. 105–22.

ideals and never been a party member, but 28 per cent also said that they did believe in communism in the past although they had never joined the party. The smallest group, 4 per cent, consists of those who remain communist believers and were party members at some time in the past. By contrast, a surprisingly large number – given the indoctrination and effort required to gain full membership – say that while they were party members, they never believed in communist ideals; indeed, this group accounts for one in three of all those who reported party membership.

The results in Table 2.6 show that communist belief and party membership do exert a major influence on electoral participation, but not in the way that might have been expected. While uncommitted abstainers are distributed across the various groups (although they make up one in five of communist believers and party members), principled abstainers are significantly more numerous among those with least communist belief and attachment. Almost one in three of those who have no belief and who were never party members are principled abstainers, nearly three times the proportion found among current believers and members. Equally, electoral participation ranges from 70 per cent among this group to 58 per cent among the former group. Attitudes to the previous communist regime thus have an important impact on electoral participation in the new Russia, the effect of which is to raise the proportion who take part in the democratic process and (if they abstain) to lower the proportion that do so on grounds of political principle.

As we found in the previous section, principled abstainers are again a highly distinctive group in terms of their political beliefs and behaviour. Although they have made a definite commitment to abstain in the election, they were (and are) also less committed to communism. If they are not wedded to communism, then why are they not more committed to the new democratic system? In other words, why is their abstention so definitive? In the context of post-communist Russia there are four possibilities that might help to explain this finding. The first, which we have already discounted, is that it is committed communists who are the principled abstainers. Rather, if anything, it is uncommitted abstainers who are the communists.

The second possible explanation of principled abstention is that the economic stress caused to individuals and households by the transition to a market economy has generated disaffection from the political system. The impact of the transition has been to force Russians to participate even more fully in the informal economy, involving the exchange of goods and services, the use of networks and favours, and the growing of food in order to maintain a reasonable standard of living. Some nine out of every ten Russians participate in the social economy to some degree.[38] Since the government is inextricably linked to the introduction of the market economy and to the problems it has engendered, those suffering most economic stress may be the least supportive of democratic institutions and therefore the least likely to participate in them.

The other two possible explanations concern citizens' views of the democratic system. Political efficacy, the feeling that an individual can influence the political process, is usually considered to be at the core of the democratic system, and is strongly linked to political participation. In turn, a sense of personal effectiveness is linked to the accountability that comes from regular, competitive elections between small groups of competing elites – what has evolved into responsible party government in the established democracies. Since this has yet to emerge in Russia, we might hypothesize that the relatively low levels of political efficacy that result from a lack of accountability in government are in turn associated with principled abstention. The final possibility also relates to the absence of a tradition of regular, competitive elections. Under communism, the state and the government were one and the same. It may be that principled abstentionists have not made the distinction between state and government, and that their abstention is accordingly a statement of opposition to the government rather than to the system as a whole.

These three hypotheses are tested in Table 2.7 using three groups of variables that correspond to the possible explanations. The results provide no support for the hypothesis that economic stress motivates either form of abstention: neither of the two measures of family economic conditions comes close to statistical significance. Moreover, there is little effect from the two measures of political efficacy that we have employed – whether respondents thought they would be treated fairly by officials, and whether they thought politics too difficult to understand. There are more consistent effects across the two groups of non-voters for the direction and strength of their views about the political

38. Richard Rose, *Getting by Without Government: Everyday Life in Stressful Society* (Glasgow: University of Strathclyde, Centre for the Study of Public Policy, 1994).

Table 2.7   Economic stress, political efficacy, system support and non-voting[a]

	Mean	Principled abstainers		Uncommitted abstainers	
		Est	(SE)	Est	(SE)
Economic stress					
Current income is not enough	0.54	−0.06	(0.18)	−0.11	(0.24)
Family income worse than before	0.71	−0.04	(0.19)	0.13	(0.27)
Political efficacy					
Treated fairly by official	0.14	0.33	(0.22)	−0.25	(0.33)
Politics too complicated to understand	0.70	0.15	(0.19)	−0.02	(0.25)
System support					
Idea of democracy	0.51	0.26	(0.18)	0.67*	(0.24)
The government	0.29	−0.62*	(0.27)	−0.53	(0.36)
Government policies	0.24	−0.49	(0.28)	−0.50	(0.38)
Idea of market economy	0.38	0.05	(0.19)	−0.37	(0.27)
Constant		0.85		−1.10	
Pseudo *R*-squared		0.48		0.16	
(*N*)		(1,844)		(1,620)	

Notes:

* Statistically significant at $p < 0.01$, two-tailed.

[a] Logistic regression results showing parameter estimates (est) and standard errors (SE) predicting two types of non-voters in the December 1993 Duma elections. Estimates control for, but do not show, resources, mobilization and instrumentalism, as defined in Tables 2.3, 2.4 and 2.5. The *R*-squared figure is for the total model. Mean figures are for all respondents.

Source: 1993 Russia and Eastern Europe Survey.

system. Thus, principled abstainers are significantly more likely than voters to oppose the government, a pattern which is not replicated among uncommitted abstainers. Similarly, while uncommitted abstainers are more likely than voters to support the ideas of democracy and of the market economy, there is no similar effect for principled abstainers.

These findings suggest that what motivates principled abstainers is not economic stress caused by the transition to a market economy, but the belief that elections do not make politicians accountable and also their opposition to the government. In this, principled abstainers appear not to have developed the distinction between government and the state, and translate their opposition to the government into opposition to the state itself. But as the results show, they are neither more nor less likely than others to approve or disapprove of democracy as such. Uncommitted abstainers differ from their principled counterparts in strongly approving of democracy but not of the market economy; although their own economic circumstances do not motivate their abstention, the belief that the market economy is inappropriate for Russia does provide a basis for their position.

5. TURNOUT, PARTIES AND RESPONSIBLE GOVERNMENT

The previous sections have suggested that electoral participation has a number of important correlates in post-communist Russia. Of the various factors included as predictors of electoral participation in Tables 2.3 to 2.5, the most important overall is party support. If citizens think of themselves as supporters of one of the parties, then that loyalty provides a significant incentive to vote. Support for a party as a factor in turnout is more important in Russia than in the established democracies because of the relative paucity of those who say that they are party supporters: in December 1993, this was just 26 per cent of all respondents. The proportion of party supporters, however, has been increasing, up to 47 per cent in our January 1996 survey. At least part of the increase in turnout between the 1993 and 1995 Duma elections can be attributed to the greater mobilizing potential of the parties in such circumstances; we might also predict that as party support begins to reach the levels found in the established democracies, turnout will increase proportionately.

Against this optimistic prediction, however, stands the fact that voters consider there are too many parties operating in Russia. In the 1993 and 1996 surveys, respondents were asked what type of party system they considered most appropriate for Russia. The results show that, in both surveys, most of the respondents favoured a party system with fewer parties than existed at the time they were interviewed: between 13 and 17 per cent more voters took this view in each survey

Table 2.8   Attitudes towards the party system[a]

	1993		1996	
	Non-voters	Voters	Non-voters	Voters
One-party system	13	14	31	30
Multiparty system, as it is now	14	21	5	6
Multiparty system, fewer parties	39	52	37	54
No parties at all	16	7	13	5
Don't know	18	6	14	6
Total	100	100	100	100
(*N*)	(818)	(1,323)	(416)	(1,165)

Note: [a] The question was: 'Which of these would be best for Russia today?'.

Sources: 1993 Russia and Eastern Europe Survey; 1996 Russia Survey.

than non-voters (see Table 2.8). The major change between the two surveys is the increase in support for a return to the one-party system: in 1993, between 13 and 14 per cent of the respondents took this position; by 1996 these proportions had more than doubled, largely at the expense of those who favoured the status quo. Indeed, in 1996 just one in 20 of those interviewed opted for the multiparty system existing at the time of the interview. The continuing existence (and unpopularity) of a complex and fragmented party system may therefore weaken some of the positive effects of increased party loyalties on electoral participation.

What are the political consequences of changing levels of turnout in Russia in such circumstances? There is evidence that differential turnout in the established democracies has a series of implications for party support, as particular groups of individuals move in and out of the electoral system. Differential levels of turnout in Britain, for example, can change support for the Conservative and Labour parties by several percentage points, with higher turnout advantaging Labour, lower turnout the Conservatives.[39] Making such calculations in the context of

39. Ian McAllister and Anthony Mughan, 'Differential Turnout and Party Advantage in British General Elections, 1964–1983', *Electoral Studies*, Vol. 5, No. 2 (August 1986), pp. 143–52.

the Russian party system presents several problems. The first is that turnout has fluctuated considerably since the introduction of democratic elections: between the two Duma elections by almost ten percentage points, and by more than that in the 1996 presidential election. A second difficulty is that the party system also is in flux, so that there are few parties with secure and readily identifiable social bases. It would be premature to attempt to assess the effect of turnout on party support of this insubstantial kind.

While it is too early to link differential turnout to changes in the electoral fortunes of the parties, it is possible to trace the implications of turnout for the way in which citizens view the system of responsible government which in turn is at the core of democratic politics. In the 1993 and 1996 surveys, respondents were asked how much they thought having regular elections made politicians accountable. Overall, opinion did not change significantly between the two surveys. In 1993, 12 per cent thought regular elections would have 'very much' effect and a further 29 per cent said it would have 'some' effect; in 1996 the comparable figures were 10 and 32 per cent, respectively (the largest group – 36 per cent in both surveys – took the view that regular elections would have no effect at all). On the other hand, in both surveys, a belief in regular elections as a means of enforcing accountability on politicians is strongly linked to the probability of voting. Figure 2.2 shows that in each survey, voters are much more numerous among those who see elections as an important tool for responsible government compared with those who do not. In 1993, for example, of those who thought that regular elections had 'very much effect', 78 per cent reported voting or intending to vote, compared with just 49 per cent of voters among those who thought elections had no effect. In the 1996 survey, the more important distinction is between those who see no effect for elections, and those who believe they have some consequences.

There is accordingly a reciprocal link between voting, elections and party support. The higher the level of party support, the higher the level of voting. But voters, at the same time, are dissatisfied with the existing party system, and favour a smaller number of parties or even a reversion to the single but undeniably effective party system of the communist period. A more coherent party system, if it were to develop, would accordingly have a positive effect on turnout. The same is true of the electoral mechanism itself. So long as ordinary Russians see

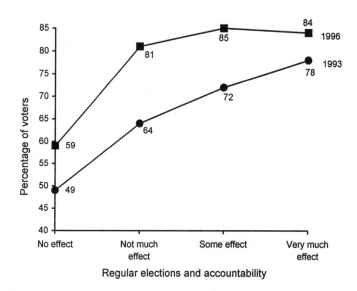

Note: The question was: 'How much do you think having regular elections makes politicians do what ordinary people want?'.

Sources: 1993 Russia and Eastern Europe Survey; 1996 Russia Survey.

Figure 2.2 Regular elections, accountability and electoral participation

no clear association between their vote in the polling station, the composition of the Duma and the conduct of national government, they have little incentive to take part in elections. But there are higher turnouts in presidential elections, where the link between voting and the conduct of national government is much clearer (the same is true in other countries with presidential systems, such as the United States). And there might be higher turnouts in Duma elections if the Duma itself developed a greater degree of control over the composition and conduct of government, as several of its leading officials have sought to achieve. 'To vote or not to vote', in Russia as in other countries, reflects a variety of factors: not just the social and attitudinal composition of the mass electorate, but also the political system in which they are invited to engage.

APPENDIX 2A

The 1993 Russia and Eastern Europe Survey was conducted in the Russian Federation between 25 November 1993 and 13 January 1994 by ROMIR (Russian Public Opinion and Market Research) for William L. Miller, Stephen White and Paul Heywood of the University of Glasgow. In total, 2,141 interviews were carried out, each of which averaged about an hour. The survey was based on a clustered multi-stage random sample intended to be representative of the population aged 18 and over, and incorporating 128 different sampling points. A full report including the results for the Czech Republic, Hungary, Slovakia and Ukraine is available in William L. Miller, Stephen White and Paul Heywood, *Values and Political Change in Postcommunist Europe* (London: Macmillan, 1998).

The 1996 Russia survey was conducted between 12 January and 7 February 1996, also by ROMIR; 1,581 respondents were interviewed at 156 different sampling points.

Both surveys were funded by the UK Economic and Social Research Council under grants R233538 and R221888, respectively.

3. Regional Patterns of Voter Turnout in Russian Elections, 1993–96

Ralph S. Clem and Peter R. Craumer[1]

Voter turnout is one of the most important – if not *the* most important – aspects of political activity on the part of individuals in democracies. Given that, an intriguing question connected with voter turnout is: why do turnout rates vary so considerably from country to country? There is a rich literature on the subject in political science, replete with theory and extensive testing of empirical evidence, both of which are brought to bear on widespread cross-national disparities in electoral participation. Interestingly, however, comparatively little attention has been given to *regional* differences in electoral participation, even though these spatial patterns often manifest quite large variations which, given geographically uneven political affinities, may affect the outcome of national political contests.

Our purpose in this chapter is to test a set of propositions on the regional dimension of voter turnout developed from the theoretical and comparative literature in the context of the post-Soviet Russian elections and referendums. In doing so, we hope to shed some light on the Russian case specifically, and perhaps to use the Russian example to inform theory. As will be made clear below, the current Russian political scene is very much a work-in-progress, and therefore requires a cautious approach in so far as the application of concepts deriving from the mature democracies of Europe, the United States, Canada, Japan and other countries is concerned. Nevertheless, the opportunity to

1. The authors wish to acknowledge funding support from the National Council for Soviet and East European Research, which is not responsible, however, for the contents or findings of this chapter. We are also grateful to Andrei Berezkin for his advice and Judith Rasoletti for her assistance.

40

explore from a comparative perspective the momentous political changes under way in Russia, nascent though they may be, is not only timely but also potentially rewarding intellectually.

1. NATIONAL DIFFERENCES IN VOTER TURNOUT

In the broadest and perhaps over-simplified terms, the central divide on the issue of cross-national differences in voter turnout is between those who see *political culture* as the most important determinant of turnout (and other forms of efficacy), and those who maintain that *political institutions* shape the extent to which people participate in electoral (and other) politics. Thus, on the one hand, '[the] political cultural approach [argues] that (1) people's responses to their situations are shaped by subjective orientations, which vary cross-culturally ... *and* (2) these variations in subjective orientations reflect differences in one's socialization experience'.[2] On the other hand, 'political institutions shape the distribution of incentives for political actors, whether they are candidates for office or simply citizens contemplating whether to vote'.[3]

Operationalizing the concepts of political culture and institutions and linking these to differences in voter turnout is problematic, but we can summarize the main arguments as follows. Political cultural norms develop through a lengthy, inter-generational process, and condition people's reactions to 'external situations', including changes in political systems and the opportunities for participation that these offer, or do not offer.[4] Thus, for example, in the transition from authoritarian to democratic government, electoral participation would be attenuated by the 'lessons' learned under the earlier regime. Norms involving one's satisfaction with life, with the willingness to discuss politics, and with levels of trust in others would be key elements of efficacy.

In the study of the role of political institutions in determining levels of voter turnout, such factors as nationally competitive districts,

2. Ronald Inglehart, *Culture Shift in Advanced Industrial Society* (Princeton, NJ: Princeton University Press, 1990), p. 19 (emphasis in original).
3. Robert W. Jackman, 'Political Institutions and Voter Turnout in the Industrial Democracies', *American Political Science Review*, Vol. 81, No. 2 (1987), p. 407.
4. Inglehart, p. 4.

electoral disproportionality, multipartism, unicameralism and compulsory voting laws are commonly seen as having the potential to affect electoral behaviour.[5] In nationally competitive elections, it is argued, 'parties have the incentive to mobilize everywhere, [whereas] with single-member districts, some areas may be written off as hopeless'.[6] Likewise, 'the degree of proportionality in the translation of votes into seats' will encourage adherents of minor parties to vote or discourage them from doing so.[7] The proliferation of political parties has also been shown to have a depressing effect on turnout, even though proponents of proportional representation (PR) electoral systems, which are widely thought to encourage party formation, often view PR as a vehicle for mobilizing the electorate.[8] Finally, the existence of compulsory voting laws obviously results in higher turnout, and unicameral legislatures allow the electorate to have a more direct influence on politics (rather than have a situation of bicameral gridlock which would render the legislative process ineffectual and thus unappealing to voters).[9]

5. See Andre Blais and R.K. Carty, 'Does Proportional Representation Foster Voter Turnout?', *European Journal of Political Research*, Vol. 18 (1990), pp. 167–81; Jackman, op. cit.; Robert W. Jackman and Ross A. Miller, 'Voter Turnout in the Industrial Democracies During the 1980s', *Comparative Political Studies*, Vol. 27, No. 4 (1995), pp. 467–92; and G. Bingham Powell, Jr, 'American Voter Turnout in Comparative Perspective', *American Political Science Review*, Vol. 80, No. 1 (1986), pp. 17–43.

6. Powell, op. cit., p. 21. Nationally competitive elections to legislatures based on proportional representation typically generate higher voter turnout than those that involve single-member, plurality-winner districts. Moreover, turnout increases with district magnitude (that is, the number of members elected).

7. Jackman and Miller, op. cit., p. 470. Blais and Carty, op. cit., p. 177, found that in a larger set of elections than those studied by Jackman (1987), 'the extent of disproportionality does not appear to have any significant impact'. This difference is due mainly to the time periods involved; when Blais and Carty considered only post-Second World War elections, as did Jackman, they found a statistically significant relationship between disproportionality and turnout.

8. Jackman, op. cit., p. 408; Blais and Carty, op. cit., p. 178. For a discussion of the effects of proportional representation on party formation, see Arend Lijphart, 'The Political Consequences of Electoral Laws, 1945–85', *American Political Science Review*, Vol. 84, No. 2 (1990), pp. 481–96.

9. Franklin referred to '*instrumental motivation* largely determined by the context in which elections are held ... the salience of elections, the use of compulsory voting, a highly proportional electoral system, postal voting, and weekend polling provide the most plausible explanations of cross-national differences in voting turnout':

2. THE PROBLEM OF SPATIAL VARIATIONS IN VOTER TURNOUT

Significant regional variations in voter turnout are typical of most countries. In the case of the 1992 American presidential election, for example, voter turnout among the states ranged from a high of 72 per cent (Maine) to a low of 42 per cent (Hawaii); this spread of 30 percentage points is greater than that found in most studies of voter turnout among democratic countries.[10] In the 1994 federal elections in Germany, turnout ranged from 70.6 per cent in Saxony-Anhalt to 83.5 per cent in the Saarland, almost a 13-percentage-point difference.[11] The 1997 general election in Britain produced an even greater range in turnout among the 659 parliamentary constituencies, from a low of 50 per cent in Hackney North and Stoke Newington to a high of 88 per cent turnout in Stevenage.[12] Yet virtually all the 'classic' works on voter turnout totally ignore, or give only passing attention to, sub-national patterns of electoral participation.

Regardless of whether emphasis is placed on the political culture or the political institutions approach to explaining differences in electoral participation, there are major problems in accounting for sub-national variations conceptually. The principal difficulty in explaining inter-regional dissimilarities in turnout is that both the concepts and the operational factors discussed in the existing literature are almost exclusively *national* or *individual* in scope. A strong case can be made that national-level factors carry much greater weight than individual characteristics in explaining cross-national voter turnout patterns; in this

Mark N. Franklin, 'Electoral Participation', in Lawrence LeDuc, Richard G. Niemi and Pippa Norris (eds), *Comparing Democracies: Elections and Voting in Global Perspective* (Thousand Oaks, CA: Sage, 1996), pp. 216–35 (emphasis in original).

10. Fred M. Shelley, J. Clark Archer, Fiona M. Davidson and Stanley D. Brunn, *Political Geography of the United States* (New York: Guilford Press, 1996), p. 119. Excluding the cases of Switzerland and the United States, which they consider atypical, Jackman and Miller (op. cit., p. 485) found that voter turnout, averaged over multiple elections in the period 1981–90, ranged from a low of 69 per cent (Canada) to a high of 93 per cent (Italy, which has a compulsory voting law).

11. American Institute for Contemporary German Studies, Johns Hopkins University, 'Election Year 1994 Reports, Federal Election (Bundestagswahl)', 1996.

12. The Parliamentary Channel, 'Results of the General Election held on 1 May 1997', www.parlchan.co.uk/election, 1997.

regard, Franklin points out that 'the most striking message is that turnout varies much more from country to country than it does between different types of individuals'.[13] Likewise, Blais and Carty maintain that '[the] available evidence gives little indication that socio-economic variables substantially alter aggregate results'.[14] That being the case, how do we account for regional differences? That is, if political culture and political institutions vary principally *between* rather than *within* countries, then nationally-specific norms, institutions, or both together, cannot explain marked regional disparities in electoral participation. Specifically, if from the institutional perspective the role of unicameralism, multipartism and electoral disproportionality affect voter participation, it is hard to see how such national factors would contribute much to understanding sub-national variations in the rate at which people vote, since such influences would be national in scope. At the sub-national level, it may be the case that variations in social structure and regional economic conditions have a more pronounced effect on turnout than analysts of cross-national differences appreciate.

Political geographers, however, have challenged the view that regions are simply summations of individual traits: rather, regions assume a particular character deriving from the influences of place. Unfortunately, a shortfall remains in the theoretical framework of place as an intermediary between the national and individual levels. Initially, theories of modernization provided the theoretical basis for electoral geography, but the failure of the expected national homogenization to materialize called this notion increasingly into question.[15] Theories of 'uneven development' have also been adduced to explain spatial aspects of political behaviour, with socioeconomic inequalities engendered by the effects of world economic forces on individual regions translating into changes in the composition and outlook of the electorate.[16] More recently, political geographers have increasingly taken into account theories of political behaviour from political science and political sociology, especially those based on social cleavages or rational choice theory. The principal difficulty in this approach has been that regional variations in voting behaviour cannot be explained

13. Franklin, op. cit., pp. 217–18.
14. Blais and Carty, op. cit., p. 172.
15. John A. Agnew, *Place and Politics: The Geographical Mediation of State and Society* (Boston: Allen & Unwin, 1987), pp. 16–17.
16. Ibid.

completely, or even close to completely, by reference to national-level forces. As Reynolds and Knight suggest, scholars have been reluctant to discount the importance of the social cleavage model, which assumes that by disaggregating regional populations along class or social composition lines, and then applying the national alignments of party affiliation or other manifestations of political behaviour to these groupings, an explanation of how the regions voted will be reached.[17]

For many geographers, it has become an increasingly more attractive idea that place provides a context in which both structural and utility models operate, but under the influence of local forces that might shape political (and other) behaviour.[18] The problem to date has been a lack of specification of the local or contextual influences, be they socialization, variations in political culture, degree of political mobilization, or something else. For example, O'Loughlin and his colleagues tested several propositions drawn from neighbouring disciplines in their analysis of the German election of 1930, and found mixed support for national cross-cutting generalizations based on class, alienation, 'political confessionalism', economic self-interest, and a 'catch all' category.[19] They concluded that 'insights into the complex voting decision are obtained by the union of spatial and socio-economic data in mixed spatial-structural regression models', whereas in stating that 'German local circumstances mediated voting behaviour' they suggested that these 'local circumstances [may be] obscure to the analyst'.[20] Furthermore, electoral geographers have concentrated on regional patterns of party preference as the primary subject of research; voter turnout has largely been overlooked.[21]

17. David R. Reynolds and David B. Knight, 'Political Geography', in Gary L. Gaile and Cort J. Willmott (eds), *Geography in America* (Columbus, OH: Merrill, 1989), pp. 582–618.
18. Agnew, op. cit., pp. 4–6.
19. John O'Loughlin, Colin Flint and Luc Anselin, 'The Geography of the Nazi Vote: Context, Confession, and Class in the Reichstag Election of 1930', *Annals of the Association of American Geographers*, Vol. 84, No. 3 (1994), pp. 351–80.
20. Ibid., pp. 372–3.
21. One exception is the work by O'Loughlin and colleagues (ibid.), which related changes in turnout to increases in the vote for the Nazi Party in the German election of 1930; among other things, this study disaggregated the relationship between turnout and party preference by region, and found significantly different impacts on electoral outcomes.

The importance of place as a mediating context for various social structural features, or as the conduit through which macroeconomic forces shape the individual in the rational choice mode, or as the venue for local cultural influences, has become ever more clear as additional cases are tested empirically. Often seen in the past as an inconvenient residual or unexplained digression from national trends, considerations of place must now be included in any analysis of sub-national electoral results.

It is also the case that the increasing sophistication, both technical and conceptual, of electoral geography models has assuaged concerns of the ecological fallacy.[22] In fact, a place-based approach using aggregate data (rather than individual data obtained from surveys) allows one to avoid the shortcomings of a strict compositional approach derived from national cleavages. Furthermore, the use of aggregate data on the regional scale compensates for a lack of survey data, especially in those cases – such as Russia – where rigorous survey-taking is only now coming into its own.

The challenge, therefore, is to identify in the literature on electoral participation the social-demographic traits, norms or institutions that might manifest themselves differently among regions and which might be adduced to explain spatial patterns of turnout. Here we shall propose such factors as seem reasonable conceptually and which we can operationalize empirically; at the outset, we wish to make it clear that this is exploratory work, and that certainly much remains to be done before we can even hazard meaningful conclusions about the underlying causes of geographical variations in voting rates.

3.　TRENDS IN RUSSIAN VOTER TURNOUT

The totality of the Russian political process since 1989 suggests that an electoral geography of that country has emerged, with some regions identified as supportive of the economic liberalization policies of the government, and other regions clearly opposed to reform. These regional patterns of political affinity have been remarkably stable from

---

22.　R.J. Johnston, C.J. Pattie and L.C. Johnston, 'The Role of Ecological Analysis in Electoral Geography: The Changing Pattern of Labour Voting in Great Britain 1983–1987', *Geografiska Annaler*, Vol. 70B, No. 3 (1988), pp. 307–24.

the first electoral event in post-Soviet Russia – the national referendum on the efficacy of the Yeltsin government in April 1993 – right through to the elections to the new Duma and simultaneous constitutional plebiscite in December 1993, the elections to the second Duma in December 1995, and the presidential elections in June–July 1996.[23] Support for Yeltsin and the reform parties has been strongest in the North and Northwest, the city and *oblast* (province) of Moscow, the Urals, Siberia, and the Far East, whereas areas along the western and southern margins of the country have tended to vote for nationalist parties or parties of the left.[24] The emergence of regional power bases for different political viewpoints is to be expected in a country as large and diverse as Russia, and to some extent this regionalization of politics may be viewed as normal.

Voter turnout in the four national electoral events in Russia since early 1993 has also varied over both time and space, often dramatically.[25] National turnout levels experienced a significant decline between the April 1993 referendum (64.5 per cent) and the December 1993 parliamentary election and constitutional plebiscite (54.8 per cent), but then recovered (to 64.8 per cent) for the December 1995 Duma vote and rose again (to 68.9 per cent) for the presidential race of July 1996.[26] These global changes are understandable in the light of the

---

23. Ralph S. Clem and Peter R. Craumer, 'The Geography of the April 25 (1993) Russian Referendum', *Post-Soviet Geography*, Vol. 34, No. 8 (1993), pp. 481–96; 'The Politics of Russia's Regions: A Geographical Analysis of the Russian Election and Constitutional Plebiscite of December 1993', *Post-Soviet Geography*, Vol. 36, No. 2 (1995), pp. 67–86; 'The Geography of the Russian 1995 Parliamentary Election: Continuity, Change, and Correlates', *Post-Soviet Geography*, Vol. 36, No. 10 (1995), pp. 587–616; 'Roadmap to Victory: Boris Yeltsin and the Russian Presidential Elections of 1996', *Post-Soviet Geography and Economics*, Vol. 37, No. 6 (1996), pp. 335–54.
24. Ibid.; Darrell Slider, Vladimir Gimpel'son and Sergei Chugrov, 'Political Tendencies in Russia's Regions: Evidence from the 1993 Parliamentary Elections', *Slavic Review*, Vol. 53, No. 3 (1994), pp. 711–32.
25. Russian electoral law enfranchises all citizens 18 years of age and older, except for those declared incompetent by a court and those in prison. Voter registration lists are compiled by local heads of administration, are updated twice a year, and are provided to polling station election committees. In this study, we use 'ballots in box' as the measure of participation. There is some wastage between ballots issued and ballots in box, and some ballots are invalidated for various reasons.
26. Actually, declines in voter turnout manifested themselves beginning in the contested elections during the Soviet period. Turnout was 78.8 per cent for the March

external political and social turmoil that preceded or accompanied each event. Thus, the rancorous exchanges between President Yeltsin and the Congress of People's Deputies through 1992 and into 1993 no doubt alienated many voters from the political process; even so, about two-thirds of those eligible voted in the referendum of 25 April 1993, and in only one of the 87 units of Russia which participated did turnout fall below 50 per cent. The violent and abrupt end of the Congress of People's Deputies in October 1993 and the suddenness with which the new Duma was elected that December certainly contributed further to voter absenteeism: it was clearly unrealistic to expect that new parties could form and mount campaigns at such short notice, or that candidates in the single-member district races would conduct meaningful, issue-orientated or ideologically-based races. What became clear was that parties with a structural base, notably the Communist Party of the Russian Federation (CPRF), which had inherited a grassroots organization from its Soviet-era predecessor, would do comparatively well. The higher turnout in the December 1995 Duma election can be attributed to the generally more stable political situation in Russia and the longer lead-time for parties to coalesce and to participate in the pre-election campaign. In the event, over 11 million more voters went to the polls in the 1995 election than in the 1993 Duma election. Finally, the much-publicized and energetic campaign for the Russian presidency in June and July 1996 generated a record high turnout for the post-Soviet period.

A comparison of national turnout levels in the post-Soviet Russian elections and referendums with those both in the established and transitional democracies places Russia close to the bottom of the list.[27] However, the inclusion of only the two most recent electoral events in Russia, with turnouts in the mid-to-high 60 per cent range, would raise it to within a few percentage points of Japan, Spain, Ireland and the 1997 British parliamentary election (71.3 per cent turnout), and ahead of Hungary and Poland. It is difficult to explain Russian national turnout by reference to the factors discussed in the more general literature on voter participation because Russia's electoral system is a hybrid

1990 voting for the Russian Federation Congress of People's Deputies and 74.7 per cent for the Russian Federation presidential election of June 1991.

27. Franklin, op. cit., p. 218.

of the institutional types which are usually employed to explain cross-national differences. Thus, although half of the Russian Duma is elected through PR in a national district, which ordinarily increases voter turnout, the other half comes from single-member districts, a fact that typically depresses turnout. Moreover, the 5 per cent threshold required to obtain Duma seats through the party list (PR) vote probably discourages voting for minor parties and thereby reduces turnout. The proliferation of parties in the Russian Duma elections (13 in 1993 and 43 in 1995) would likewise be expected to lower voting participation rates in general, but turnout actually went up between the two Duma elections, even though the latter featured considerably more parties. On the other hand, direct elections for a powerful executive, such as the 1996 presidential races, would be likely to have the effect observed: higher turnout due to the salience of the event. Again, to what extent these institutional factors operate regionally is much more difficult to conceptualize, but clearly, given the spatial patterns discussed below, powerful influences are at work to shape the electoral landscape, not only in terms of party affiliation and attitudes, but also as regards voter turnout.

4. REGIONAL PATTERNS OF VOTER TURNOUT

Our main purpose here is to describe and explain the geographical dimension to voter turnout in the post-Soviet Russian elections, patterns that have remained generally stable over time, but with changes important to the overall result. Since the first post-Soviet electoral event in Russia (the April 1993 referendum), it has been clear that certain regions typically manifest higher turnout and others lower turnout. As the results of the 1993 referendum show, areas along the western border, across the Central *Chernozem* (black earth) region, the North Caucasus, the Volga, and eastwards along the southern tier of units in the Urals, Western Siberia and Eastern Siberia were typically higher turnout areas, whereas units to the Northwest and North had lower turnout rates (see Figure 3.1). Among the 86 of the 87 units of Russia which participated fully in the April 1993 referendum, the highest turnout was in Ryazan' *oblast* (78.8 per cent) and the lowest in the Khanty-Mansy Autonomous Okrug (54.3 per cent), for a percentage

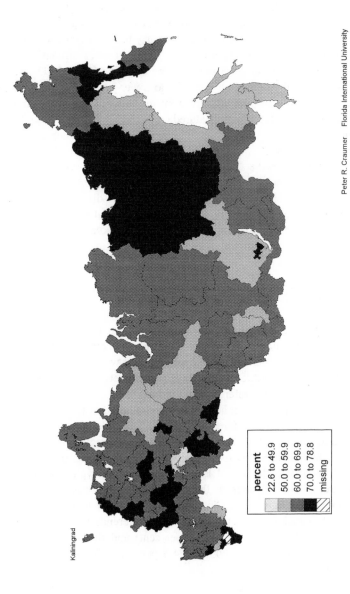

Figure 3.1   April 1993 Russian referendum turnout

point spread of 24.5 (see Table 3.1).[28] Within the lower turnout in the December 1993 Duma election and constitutional plebiscite, the same regional pattern emerged as with that manifested in April (see Figure 3.2): generally higher turnout along the western and southern margins of the country, generally lower turnout across the Northwest and North (the correlation coefficient for turnout in April and that in December 1993 was .813). In keeping with the lower national turnout, the mean for regional turnout levels declined, and the standard deviation increased owing to a greater range among units; the highest turnout among the 87 units participating fully was in the Karachai-Cherkess Republic (70.3 per cent) and the lowest, again, in the Khanty-Mansy Autonomous Okrug (39.7 per cent): the range in the turnout thus

Table 3.1   Regional voter turnout, Russian elections, April 1993–
July 1996*

	Range (% points)	Minimum (%)	Maximum (%)	Mean	Standard Deviation
April 1993[†]	24.5	54.3	78.8	66.2	5.439
December 1993[‡]	30.6	39.7	70.3	56.6	6.403
December 1995	22.4	53.1	75.5	65.0	4.675
June 1996	19.4	59.6	79.0	69.8	3.913
July 1996	26.8	56.6	83.4	68.6	4.806

Notes

* Turnout measured by ballots in box as a percentage of eligible voters.

† $N = 86$ (excludes Tatarstan, Chechnya, and Aga-Buryat AO).

‡ $N = 87$ (excludes Tatarstan and Chechnya). Turnout is for constitutional plebiscite.

Sources: April 1993 – Central Electoral Commission on the All-Russian Referendum, Moscow, May 1993; December 1993 – *Rossiiskaya gazeta*, 28 December 1993, pp. 3–6; December 1995 – *Rossiiskaya gazeta*, 24 January 1996, p. 2; June 1996 – *Rossiiskaya gazeta*, 26 June 1996, p. 1; July 1996 – *Rossiiskaya gazeta*, 16 July 1996, pp. 5–6.

28.   The Chechen Republic did not participate in the referendum. Returns from the Agin-Buryat Autonomous Okrug were received late and thus not included in the official results. The referendum was essentially boycotted in Tatarstan, where a low turnout (22.6 per cent) invalidated the results.

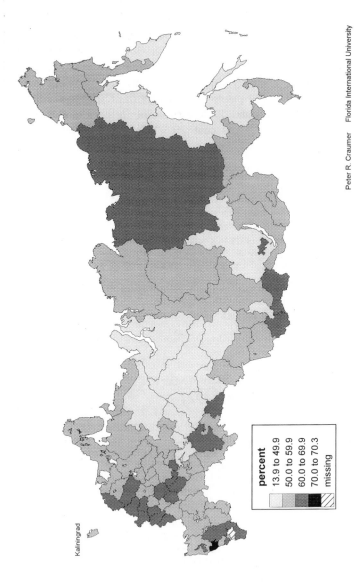

Kal_ningrad

percent
13.9 to 49.9
50.0 to 59.9
60.0 to 69.9
70.0 to 70.3
missing

Peter R. Craumer   Florida International University

Figure 3.2 December 1993 Russian plebiscite turnout

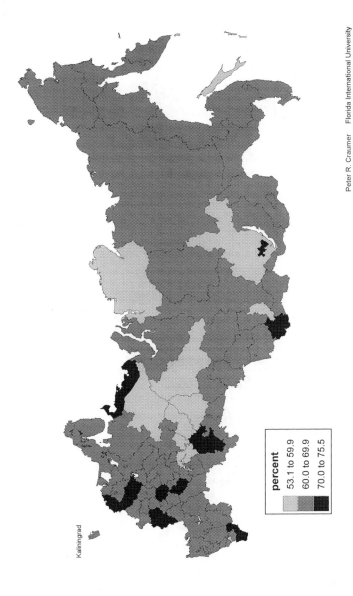

Figure 3.3   December 1995 Russian Duma election turnout

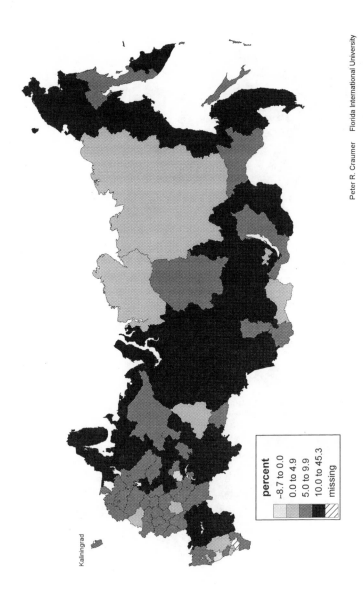

Kaliningrad

percent
- −8.7 to 0.0
- 0.0 to 4.9
- 5.0 to 9.9
- 10.0 to 45.3
- missing

Peter R. Craumer   Florida International University

Figure 3.4   Percentage point change in voter turnout, December 1993 to December 1995

increased to 30.6 percentage points (Table 3.1).[29] Disproportionately large declines in regional turnout occurred in the North, the Urals, West Siberia, and East Siberia (compare Figures 3.1 and 3.2), with especially notable decreases in the city of Moscow (down 12 percentage points) and Sverdlovsk *oblast* (down 18 points).

The rebound in voter turnout in the Duma election of December 1995 is evident also in the regional figures (Table 3.1). The mean among the 89 units participating rose to 65 per cent, and the range decreased to 22.4 percentage points, with an accompanying narrowing of the standard deviation; a high of 75.5 per cent in Belgorod *oblast* and a low of 53.1 per cent in Sverdlovsk *oblast* bounded the range. Again, one finds the by-now familiar spatial pattern of turnout, with a generally south–north divide (Figure 3.3). However, a lower correlation between regional turnout in December 1993 and that for December 1995 (0.674) suggests that this pattern changed more during this inter-election period than between April and December 1993. In fact, most of the change in turnout is accounted for by larger than average increases in the Northwest, Urals, North Caucasus, West Siberia, East Siberia, and the Far East (see Figure 3.4).

Regional patterns of electoral participation for the presidential election of June–July 1996 again appear very similar to those seen in previous contests (see Figure 3.5). For the first round on 16 June, the mean turnout among regions was up from that of December 1995, and the range and standard deviation declined still further from the previous election (Table 3.1). Among the 89 units of Russia, the highest turnout was in Bashkortostan (79.0 per cent) and the lowest in Murmansk *oblast* (59.6 per cent). The correlation coefficient for regional turnout in June 1996 compared with December 1995 is 0.758, illustrating again the general stability of the spatial patterns. Residuals from the regression revealed that much of the change over this period is accounted for by increases in turnout in the Urals, Volga and North Caucasus regions (Figure 3.6). In the run-off election between Yeltsin and Zyuganov on 3 July, national turnout declined by almost a percentage point, with an accompanying effect on mean turnout among regions (Table 3.1). Likewise, the range and standard deviation increased, indicating greater

29. The Chechen Republic did not participate in the December elections, and once again a boycott of the election in Tatarstan produced a very low turnout (13.9 per cent) which invalidated the result.

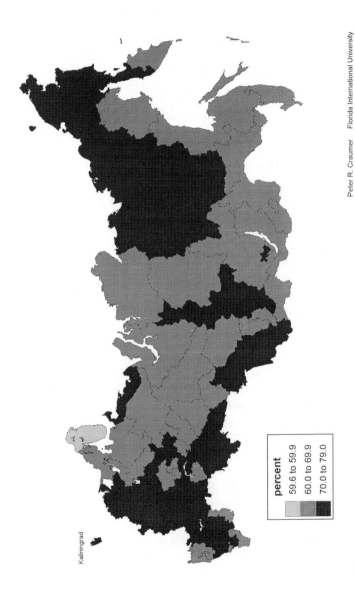

Kalingrad

percent
59.6 to 59.9
60.0 to 69.9
70.0 to 79.0

Peter R. Craumer   Florida International University

Figure 3.5   June 1996 Russian presidential election turnout

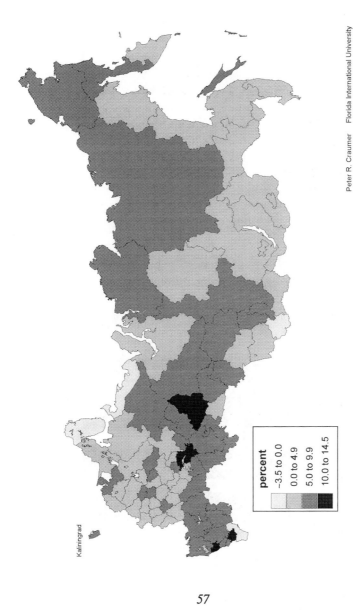

57

Peter R. Craumer   Florida International University

Figure 3.6 Percentage point change in voter turnout, December 1995–June 1996

Kaliningrad

percent

-3.5 to 0.0
0.0 to 4.9
5.0 to 9.9
10.0 to 14.5

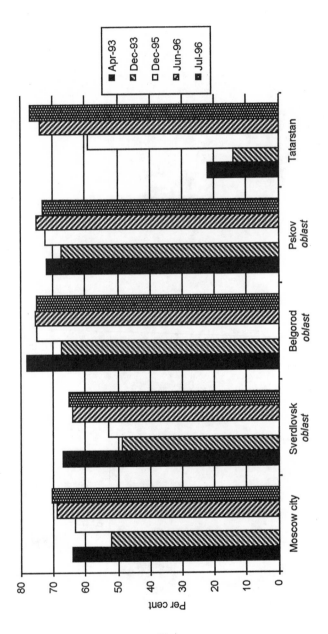

Figure 3.7 Turnout by region, 1993–1996

Per cent

Apr-93
Dec-93
Dec-95
Jun-96
Jul-96

Moscow city　Sverdlovsk *oblast*　Belgorod *oblast*　Pskov *oblast*　Tatarstan

dispersion at the regional level. Highest turnout on 3 July 1996 was in the Ingush Republic (83.4 per cent) and lowest was, again, in Murmansk *oblast* (56.5 per cent).

We selected five units representing different parts of the political spectrum to illustrate how turnout levels and changes therein vary from region to region across Russia. The city of Moscow and Sverdlovsk *oblast* are units in which the reform-orientated parties have done well; Belgorod *oblast*, in the Central Chernozem region, has voted overwhelmingly for the left (the CPRF and the Agrarian Party, for the most part); Pskov *oblast* has been a bastion of the right-wing or nationalist parties; and Tatarstan is of interest because of its very different electoral participation rates. As is clear from Figure 3.7, turnout levels have been consistently higher in Belgorod and Pskov *oblasts*, but increases from the low point of December 1993 to December 1995 and June–July 1996 were much greater in Moscow and Sverdlovsk *oblast*. Tatarstan, which effectively boycotted the two elections of 1993 and had a relatively low turnout in December 1995, surged to very high rates in the 1996 races. Clearly, very different factors must be at work in these regions to produce such differences in voting behaviour.

5. CORRELATES OF REGIONAL VOTER TURNOUT

In the literature on voter participation at the national level, there is some support for the idea that turnout is higher in cases where party organization is sufficiently strong to mobilize voters. As Powell put it, 'We would expect dense, penetrative, nationally-oriented party organizations to be most effective in getting voters to the polls in national elections'.[30] From this we would propose that in those regions of Russia where well-organized parties are strongest, voter turnout will be relatively higher. In the Russian case, this would lead us to expect relatively higher turnout in regions where the vote is predominantly for the CPRF or other parties of the left, thanks to their superior organizations.

In our previously published work on the Russian elections, we investigated the statistical relationships between voter turnout and

30. Powell, *op. cit.*, p. 22.

various aspects of political preference. In the April 1993 referendum, we found that turnout correlated negatively and significantly (at the 0.01 level) with support for Yeltsin, but the coefficients (–0.391 and –0.406 on Questions 1 and 2 regarding support for Yeltsin and for his economic policies) were not especially strong.[31] In analysing the December 1993 Duma elections and the simultaneous constitutional plebiscite, we determined that voter turnout among regions correlated positively and significantly with the percentage of the national party list vote going to the Agrarian–CPRF alliance (0.596), negatively and significantly with the vote for reform parties (–0.573), and negatively and significantly with the percentage of voters approving the new Constitution (–0.723).[32] In the December 1995 Duma elections, the correlation coefficient between turnout and the left vote was 0.532 and between turnout and the vote for reform parties –0.461 (both significant at the 0.01 level), which suggests that the strength of the linkage between party preferences and turnout among regions deteriorated somewhat between 1993 and 1995. In interpreting that change, it was evident that turnout increased at more than the national rate in some regions associated with reform voting.[33]

In the presidential elections of June and July 1996, the statistical relationship between turnout and candidate preference was considerably weaker than in the Duma contests. Specifically, the correlation between the percentage of the vote for Yeltsin and turnout in round one was –0.283 and in round two –0.203, neither of which is significant at the 0.01 level; the relationship between the percentage of the vote for Zyuganov and turnout was 0.410 and 0.253, respectively (the first is significant and the second not). Thus, although the signs are in the expected direction (higher turnout in left-voting regions and lower in reformist or pro-Yeltsin territory), the magnitude of the coefficients suggests that regional loyalties evident in previous elections weakened considerably in this type of election, that Yeltsin made strong inroads in previously left-voting regions, especially between the two rounds, and that turnout rose in pro-Yeltsin regions and declined in some CPRF strongholds.

31. Clem and Craumer, 'The Geography of the April 25 (1993) Russian Referendum', p. 487.
32. Clem and Craumer, 'The Politics of Russia's Regions', p. 83
33. Clem and Craumer, 'The Geography of the Russian 1995 Parliamentary Election'.

6. EFFECTIVE NUMBER OF PARTIES AND TURNOUT

In a previous work, we investigated the relationship between voting for party groupings among the regions, using what political scientists refer to as the 'effective number of parties'.[34] In multiparty elections, such measures as the 'N coefficient' are used to describe the extent to which voters disperse or concentrate their votes among ballot choices.[35] Observed values for N across numerous elections world-wide range from 1.8 to 10.3, with the lower value indicating just under two effective parties and the upper value representing about ten effective parties.[36] Elections in which many parties garner relatively large shares of the vote will result in a higher N value, whereas two- or three-party systems produce lower N values.

The Russian Duma election of December 1993 resulted in a highly fractionalized N coefficient of 7.58.[37] The December 1995 Duma election, with 43 parties on the national party list ballot, yielded an N value of 10.7 for Russia as a whole, placing it near the very top of the range of observed national elections in terms of the degree of fractionalization.

As with all aspects of Russian electoral politics, there are huge differences among the regions in terms of the degree of concentration of voting for parties. For example, in the 1995 Duma elections, among the 89 units of Russia the N coefficient varied from 3.4 to 16.4 effective parties, suggesting that in some regions the voters concentrated on a few parties, and in others dispersed their votes widely among many choices.[38] Furthermore, in our previous study we found that the N coefficient was highly and significantly correlated (-0.736) with voting for political parties of the left; that is, those regions with lower N values

34. Ralph S. Clem and Peter R. Craumer, 'The Regional Dimension', in Laura Belin and Robert W. Orttung (eds), *The Russian Parliamentary Elections of 1995: The Battle for the Duma* (Armonk, NY: M.E. Sharpe, 1997), pp. 137–59.

35. Rein Taagepera and Matthew S. Shugart, *Seats and Votes: The Effects and Determinants of Electoral Systems* (New Haven, CT: Yale University Press, 1989), pp. 77–85.

36. Ibid., pp. 81–3.

37. Robert G. Moser, 'The Impact of the Electoral System on Post-Communist Party Development: The Case of the 1993 Russian Parliamentary Elections', *Electoral Studies*, Vol. 14, No. 4 (1995), pp. 377–98.

38. Clem and Craumer, 'The Regional Dimension'.

are usually the ones in which the left, and especially the CPRF, did well, indicating that the concentration of votes tended to benefit the left more than the reform or rightist parties.[39] On the other hand, units in which the reform parties were a plurality (mainly in the North, North-west, and Centre regions) had relatively high N values, indicating greater dispersal of votes among parties.[40] The statistical relationship between the N coefficient itself and voter turnout for the December 1995 Duma election was –0.417 (significant at the 0.01 level).

Another view of the degree of concentration of voting by party is obtained by looking at the magnitude of the pluralities achieved by the winning parties in the 225 electoral districts in the December 1995 Duma contest. It is again evident that the CPRF in particular has a more compact electorate, winning their districts by a higher average plurality (26.4 per cent) than Yabloko (16.5 per cent), Our Home is Russia (22.0 per cent) or the Liberal Democratic Party of Russia (17.2 per cent). It is instructive that the participation of so many parties allows for a party to win a district plurality on a comparatively low share of the vote. In fact, of the individual parties, only the CPRF won a *majority* of votes in any electoral district in 1995. Among party blocs, the left gained a majority in 22 of the 225 electoral districts and the reform parties in 26 (23 of them in the cities of Moscow and St. Petersburg). The right bloc of parties won a majority in none of the 225 electoral districts in 1995.

7. SOCIAL STRUCTURE AND VOTER TURNOUT

In cross-national studies of electoral participation, several social structural variables have been found to have an effect on voter turnout; again, the preponderance of opinion relegates these influences to secondary importance compared with institutional factors. For our purposes, however, sub-national or regional differences in social structure may have some explanatory value as far as spatial patterns of turnout are concerned. In previous studies we analysed the relationship

39. Ibid.
40. Taking the analysis down to the level of 225 electoral districts and focusing on individual parties yields even more convincing evidence of the relationship between concentration of voting and preference for the left parties; the correlation coefficient between N and the percentage of the vote for the CPRF was –0.801.

between the social structure (demographic composition) of regions and voting behaviour as manifested by party and candidate preference in the Duma and presidential contests and voting on the referendum of April 1993 and the constitutional plebiscite of December 1993.[41] Generally, we found that social structural variables such as the level of urbanization, educational attainment, age and occupation related to voting results across Russia's 89 constituent territorial units. Separately, we investigated these same relationships among 300 *raions* from a sample of ten *oblasts*, and found that on a larger geographical scale the statistical relationships found at the *oblast* and republic level intensify.[42] In this section we test for the effects of regional variations in age, education, occupation, and urban or rural residence on turnout for the four national political events in the post-Soviet period (see Table 3.2).

Table 3.2   Bivariate correlation coefficients, voter turnout and selected socioeconomic variables, by region, Russian elections, April 1993–June 1996[a]

Older Population		Industrial Workers	
April 1993	0.384 *	April 1993	-0.055
December 1993	0.442 *	December 1993	-0.123
December 1995	0.318 *	December 1995	-0.179
June 1996	0.399 *	June 1996	-0.028
Education		White-collar Workers	
April 1993	-0.249	April 1993	-0.212
December 1993	-0.434 *	December 1993	-0.365 *
December 1995	-0.384 *	December 1995	-0.218
June 1996	-0.427 *	June 1996	-0.288 *
Agricultural Workers		Level of Urbanization	
April 1993	0.420 *	April 1993	-0.389 *
December 1993	0.676 *	December 1993	-0.542 *
December 1995	0.549 *	December 1995	-0.423 *
June 1996	0.425 *	June 1996	-0.344 *

Note: [a] $N = 86$ for April 1993, 87 for December 1993, 89 for December 1995 and June 1996. Coefficients with an asterisk (*) are significant at the 0.01 level.

41. Clem and Craumer, 'The Geography of the April 25 (1993) Russian Referendum'; 'The Geography of the Russian 1995 Parliamentary Election'; 'Roadmap to Victory: Boris Yel'tsin and the Russian Presidential Elections of 1996'.
42. Ralph S. Clem and Peter R. Craumer, 'A Rayon Level Analysis of the Russian Parliamentary Election and Constitutional Plebiscite of December 1993', *Post-Soviet Geography,* Vol. 36, No. 8 (1995), pp. 459–75.

Age

Age is one of the social or demographic variables mentioned most often in cross-national turnout studies.[43] Generally, the rate of voting increases with age, although not always in a linear fashion. In this study, we calculate the percentage of those older than working age (55 and older for women and 60 and older for men) in each region of Russia and compare that with voter turnout rates. The results (Table 3.2) suggest that age relates positively and significantly to turnout across the regions in all Russian elections, with the strongest coefficient in the December 1993 Duma election and plebiscite.

Education

Educational attainment at the individual level is also associated with turnout.[44] Typically, higher levels of education relate to higher turnout rates; however, this relationship is much more pronounced in the United States than in Europe.[45] To test the relationship between educational attainment and turnout among Russia's regions, we calculated the proportion of the population of working age with higher, incomplete higher, and specialized secondary education for each unit and compared those values with turnout. In the Russian case, higher levels of educational attainment correlate negatively with turnout (Table 3.2), which is to say that units with more highly educated populations have lower voter turnout, and vice versa.

Occupation

In his cross-national study of 1986, Powell examined the relationship between white-collar employment and turnout, and found essentially no correlation between the two. He acknowledges, however, that in many cases 'to know a voter's occupation or religion enables us to predict his or her voting preference to a very great degree'.[46] To investigate links between occupations and electoral participation in post-Soviet Russia,

---

43. Franklin, op. cit., p. 220; Powell, op. cit., pp. 20–30.
44. Franklin, op. cit., p. 224.
45. Powell, op. cit., p. 29.
46. Ibid., p. 22.

we related the occupational composition of units to their respective turnout rates (Table 3.2). Units with a relatively higher proportion of agricultural workers exhibited higher turnout, often strongly so, but little or no relationship was evident for either industrial workers or those in white-collar occupations.

Residence

Differences in voting behaviour along the urban–rural continuum have been noted in earlier studies of Russian elections. For example, Hough found voter turnout to be especially low in the large industrial cities and higher in smaller cities and towns and in rural areas.[47] In our previous article on voting patterns at the *raion* level among ten sample *oblasts* for the December 1993 Duma election, we likewise saw pronounced differences in turnout by size of urban population, with predominantly rural *raions* manifesting high turnout (over 70 per cent on the average) and large cities characterized by much lower turnout (about 50 per cent).[48]

Here we test the level of urbanization among the units of Russia against voter turnout, and find a fairly strong association between the two in the predicted direction (higher levels of urbanization associated with lower turnout rates). The relationship, which was statistically significant at the 0.01 level in all years, was particularly strong in the two Duma elections and less so in the April 1993 referendum and the 1996 presidential election (Table 3.2).

Voter Turnout and Economic Conditions

One of the most interesting aspects of voter turnout is the manner in which it relates – or does not relate – to economic conditions. As Radcliff put it, 'The most striking aspect of the literature [on the economy and turnout] may be its inconsistency'.[49] Do people go to the polls

47. Jerry F. Hough, 'The Russian Election of 1993: Public Attitudes Toward Economic Reform and Democratization', *Post-Soviet Affairs*, Vol. 10, No. 1 (1994), pp. 1–37.

48. Clem and Craumer, 'A Rayon Level Analysis'.

49. Benjamin Radcliff, 'The Welfare State, Turnout, and the Economy: A Comparative Analysis', *American Political Science Review*, Vol. 86, No. 2 (1992), p. 444.

in order to vote out governments which they believe to be responsible for economic hardship, or do they withdraw from the electoral process, perhaps alienated and preoccupied with managing their own affairs? Radcliff argued that 'the electoral importance of the economy varies both spatially and temporally due to contextual conditions that vary from place to place and time to time'.[50] In general, he found that deteriorating macroeconomic conditions – translated into trends in income – led to lower turnout in developing countries, mainly because they lack social insurance programmes which might cushion families and individuals against the hardships occasioned by recession. Such programmes in developed countries mitigate these circumstances, and consequently little decline in turnout results during difficult times.

Colton, in his survey-based study of the effects of economics on voting in the December 1995 Duma election, noted that 'Economic malaise had no effect on the penchant to vote or abstain, as economic pessimists came to the polls in almost identical numbers to optimists'.[51] We are interested in determining whether there are any relationships between the state of the economy and the propensity to vote among the regions of Russia; in other words, to determine whether regional differences in economic conditions have any effect on voter turnout. To investigate this relationship, we examined several variables representative of the economic situation in the regions and compared them with voter turnout.

In general, we found very little correlation between macroeconomic conditions at the regional level and voter turnout. Such measures as change in industrial production, change in agricultural production, change in the volume of retail sales, change in the consumer price index and the extent of housing privatization had no significant relationship with turnout. On the other hand, some measures of individual economic well-being did correlate with turnout. Wages, especially, had a negative association with turnout (–0.470 in December 1993 and –0.417 in December 1995, both significant at the 0.01 level), suggesting that areas with relatively lower wages had higher voter participation. However, unemployment had no discernible effect on turnout.

8. CONCLUSIONS

Regional differences in voter turnout in Russia are linked to both institutional and socioeconomic factors. In the regions, affinity for parties with strong organizational or grassroots structure (such as the CPRF) raises turnout. Age, occupation, education and levels of urbanization also relate to the degree of electoral participation. Economic conditions in the regions have less effect, although variation in wages is important as a determinant of turnout across the country. Because the social structural and economic variables are not independent of one another, what emerges from this set of factors is a complex relationship that requires further study employing multivariate analysis. Meanwhile, we can say with some confidence that regions in which the population is characterized by relatively higher levels of urbanization, education, white-collar employment and higher earnings and by a younger age distribution will typically manifest lower voter participation. By contrast, areas that are more rural and agricultural, with older and less-educated populations and lower wages, will show higher voter turnout.

In this study we have not attempted to adduce other, more idiosyncratic, influences on voter participation, especially those relating to regional elites or local issues, although we recognize that in some cases these are very important. Thus, in some cases, especially in the non-Russian republics (for example, Tatarstan and Bashkortostan), the local political leadership has effectively suppressed – or, alternatively, maximized – turnout, depending on the benefits accruing from doing either. Likewise, the national leadership has courted or scorned regional governors, some of whom (for example, Eduard Rossel of Sverdlovsk *oblast*) have been able to sway events within their constituencies. Finally, the presence on the ballot of highly popular politicians with specific regional bases ('favourite sons', such as Aman Tuleyev in Kemerovo *oblast* or Aleksandr Lebed in Tula *oblast*) no doubt increases turnout on given occasions.

Whatever the causal factors behind regional variations in voter turnout in post-Soviet Russia, these patterns have remained highly consistent over time, and can be expected to do so in future political contests. Typical of the electoral geography of large countries in general, the political landscape of Russia deserves further study as democratization in that country continues to evolve.

4. The Emerging Structure of Partisan Divisions in Russian Politics

Stephen Whitefield and Geoffrey Evans[1]

1. INTRODUCTION

The Logic of Cleavage Formation in Post-communist Societies

Parties or contenders for political office may in certain circumstances become the institutions through which citizens express their demands on government. These demands, and therefore party choices, may be differentiated along lines of opinion and ideology or on the basis of citizens' varied social locations and identities. At the same time, the nature of the institutions for which parties compete – presidential or parliamentary – and the parties and presidential contenders available to be chosen may have an effect on the character of differentiation itself.[2] Our aim, therefore, is to see how Russians are differentiated in their electoral preferences, how this may have changed over time, and whether preference differentiation varies systematically with the nature of the office competed or with the parties and candidates available.

1. Responsibility for this chapter is held equally by the two authors. The research reported here was commissioned as part of the British Economic and Social Research Council's East–West Programme: Grant no.Y309253025, 'Emerging Forms of Political Representation and Participation in Eastern Europe', and by the INTAS Project, 'Ethnicity, Nationality and Citizenship in the Former Soviet Union', funded by the European Union.
2. It is also recognized that the electoral rules under which voters express their electoral preferences may make a difference to the preferences themselves, or to the way in which they are differentiated. We do not consider this issue here, however, because these rules are constant over the three years of our study.

This chapter extends our comparative analysis of these social and ideological bases of partisanship in Eastern Europe, and of their relationship to political institutions, to a consideration of Russian democracy as it has developed from 1993 to 1996.[3] We are also interested in determining the extent to which conclusions drawn from comparative analyses of single surveys in a wide range of new post-communist democracies are consistent with the development of Russian cleavages over time. We can summarize the implications of our previous comparative research into cleavage formation as follows.[4]

1. Contrary to many theories that held that there were no ideological bases to partisanship or divisions of a unidimensional character,[5] we have predicted and demonstrated the existence of multiple potential sources of ideological division shaped by the character of inheritances and challenges facing a given society. These include the extent and

---

3. See Stephen Whitefield and Geoffrey Evans, 'From the Top Down or the Bottom Up? Explaining the Structure of Ideological Cleavages in Post-communist Societies' (manuscript submitted for publication, 1997; an earlier version was presented at the 90th annual APSA meeting, New York, September 1994); and Geoffrey Evans and Stephen Whitefield, 'The Social Bases of Political Competition in Eastern Europe' (manuscript submitted for publication, 1997; an earlier version was presented at the 91st annual APSA meeting, Chicago, September 1995).

4. Geoffrey Evans and Stephen Whitefield, 'Identifying the Bases of Party Competition in Eastern Europe', *British Journal of Political Science*, Vol. 23, No. 4 (1993), pp. 521–48; Geoffrey Evans and Stephen Whitefield, 'Social and Ideological Cleavage Formation in Post-Communist Hungary', *Europe–Asia Studies*, Vol. 47, No. 7 (1995), pp. 1177–1204; Evans and Whitefield, 'The Social Bases of Political Competition in Eastern Europe'; Geoffrey Evans and Stephen Whitefield, 'The Parting of the Ways? The Structuring of Ideological Cleavages in the Czech and Slovak Republics', *Political Studies*, Vol. 46, No. 1 (1998),; Whitefield and Evans 'From the Top Down or the Bottom Up?'; Stephen Whitefield and Geoffrey Evans, 'Electoral Politics in Eastern Europe: Social and Ideological Influences on Partisanship in Post-Communist Societies', in John Higley, Jan Pakulski and Włodzimierz Wesolowski (eds), *Postcommunist Elites and Democracy in Eastern Europe* (Basingstoke: Macmillan, 1998).

5. For example, Herbert Kitschelt, 'The Formation of Party Systems in East Central Europe', *Politics and Society*, Vol. 20, No. 1 (1992), pp. 7–50; John Gray, 'From Post-communism to Civil Society: The Re-emergence of History and the Decline of the Western Model', *Social Philosophy and Policy*, Vol. 10 (1993), pp. 26–50; Arista Maria Cirtautas, 'In Pursuit of the Democratic Interest: The Institutionalization of Parties and Interests in Eastern Europe', in Christopher G.A. Bryant and Edmund Mokrzycki (eds), *The New Great Transformation* (London: Routledge, 1994).

character of market transition; the extent and character of the political transition; issues of value and lifestyle; problems of ethnic relations; and issues of state – the criteria for citizenship, and relations to old empires and integration with the West. The nature of ideological divisions in any given country will depend on the presence or absence of these factors. Thus, issues of political liberalization matter most in countries where the political transition is weakest; issues of ethnic rights are important where substantial ethnic minorities exist, especially when this occurs in new states with uncertainty over criteria for the determination of citizenship; political divisions over economic issues emerge where there is diversity of market-related interests; and issues of value and lifestyle emerge where these are politicized by the Church. In some countries, therefore, multiple ideological divisions are to be expected; and because there exist independent sources of ideological structuring among the electorate – in other words, various distinct reasons for division – the ideological space defining the competition for votes is expected to be multidimensional, entailing cross-cutting divisions. In other countries, however, the sources of ideological division are less varied and here not only is one sort of potential division dominant, but this division may well entail a broad association among issues that in other settings are independent of one another. Thus, where values and lifestyle are politicized by the Church, they may have only a weak relationship to the economy or other issue dimensions. On the other hand, where the Church has little political impact, questions of values and lifestyle either may play a weak role or may be associated strongly with other issues, especially those concerning the economy.

2. The logic of our arguments with respect to ideological divisions also informs the expectations we had for potential social divisions. Again, contrary to many commentators who saw in Eastern Europe a social wasteland in which voters had been deprived of their social identities,[6] or others who saw in Eastern Europe a prevalence of 'primordial' social interests,[7] we have argued that there is the potential

---

6.   Stanislaw Ossowski, *Class Structure in the Social Consciousness* (New York: Free Press, 1963); Walter D. Connor, *Socialism's Dilemmas* (New York: Columbia University Press, 1988); Wlodzimierz Wesolowski, *Classes, Strata and Power* (London: Routledge & Kegan Paul, 1977; first published Warsaw 1966; translated into English with a foreword by George Kolankiewicz).

7.   George Schöpflin, 'The Road From Post-communism', in Stephen Whitefield (ed.), *The New Institutional Architecture of Eastern Europe* (Basingstoke:

for multiple sources of social division, based on long-standing differences of religion, ethnic identity and language; on economic sector and residence, especially those between town and country; on the differentiated effects of communism – between the winners and losers in that system, or between those dependent on the socialist state sector and the new private sector; and on effects resulting directly from the experience of the development of the new market economies of the post-communist period, relating to class and employment, income and so forth; or to the differential effect of marketization on some groups – such as women, the unemployed, pensioners and so on. The relationship between ideological divisions and social differences was not expected to be necessarily one to one.[8] Some ideological divisions – over ethnic rights or values – were likely to be based on social differences; others – over the market, for example – might be located in a number of different divisions: class, gender, sector and the like. Conversely, social divisions might be evident in bases of support for parties or candidates – between town and country or between men and women – that need not be manifested as ideological divisions but result simply from voters' expressive identities. Thus, even in circumstances where ideological divisions underlying partisanship are limited, there may exist multiple social divisions as voters choose parties that express their particular group identities.

3. Informing the question of *what* divides the electorates of post-communist societies, is the question of *how* such divisions might emerge. On this point, we have again taken issue with three types of explanation. First, a number of commentators have emphasized the importance of 'civil society' or of 'secondary associations' in shaping political cleavages.[9] Given the relative absence of civil society in

Macmillan, 1993); Gray, 'From Post-communism to Civil Society'; Kenneth Jowitt, *New World Disorder: The Leninist Extinction* (London: University of California Press, 1992).

8. See also Richard Rose, 'Comparability in Electoral Studies', in Richard Rose (ed.), *Electoral Behaviour: A Comparative Handbook* (New York: Free Press, 1974), pp. 3–28.

9. For example, Juan Linz and Alfred Stepan, *Problems of Democratic Transition and Consolidation: Southern Europe, South America and Post-Communist Europe* (Baltimore, MD, and London: Johns Hopkins University Press, 1996); Gerardo L Munck, 'Democratic Transitions in Comparative Perspective', *Comparative Politics*, Vol. 26, No. 3 (1994), pp. 355–75; Michael Bernhard, 'Civil Society and Democratic Transition in East Central Europe', *Political Science Quarterly*,

Eastern Europe, this would imply either that there are no bases to social division or – and these are the second and third explanations – that elite norms and party strategies,[10] or institutional arrangements (such as whether a country is primarily presidential or parliamentary), are decisive in shaping such divisions.[11] Against these views we have argued that the absence of civil society should not preclude the possibility of the existence of sufficient informal social organization and experience in relation to the challenges and inheritances described above to allow for the emergence of the identified ideological and social divisions. It is not necessary, in other words, to have a developed civil society for groups to have distinctive experiences, identities and patterns of informal association on which divisions in partisanship can be built. For these reasons, too, we conclude that there is little theory or evidence to suggest that elite norms or institutional differences can account for differences in the shape of ideological and social divisions. Indeed, given the differences in the character of elites and the nature of institutions, countries with similar legacies and challenges share remarkably similar bases to partisanship. Thus we have adopted a broadly 'sociocentric' approach to the formation and character of divisions in Eastern Europe.

There are, moreover, good theoretical reasons deriving from considerations of both the supply and demand side of politics for such an

Vol. 108, No. 3 (1993), pp. 307–26; Pradeep Chhibber and Mariano Torcal, 'Elite Strategy, Social Cleavages, and Party Systems in a New Democracy: Spain', *Comparative Political Studies*, Vol. 30 (1997), pp. 27–54; Giovanni Sartori, 'From the Sociology of Politics to Political Sociology', in Seymour Martin Lipset (ed.), *Politics and the Social Sciences* (Oxford: Oxford University Press, 1969), pp. 65–100.

10. See Chhibber and Torcal, 'Elite Strategy, Social Cleavages, and Party Systems in a New Democracy'; George Schöpflin, 'The Road From Post-communism'; John Ishiyama, 'Communist Parties in Transition: Structures, Leaders, and Processes of Democratization in Eastern Europe', *Comparative Politics*, Vol. 27 (1995), pp. 147–66; and John Ishiyama, 'Red Phoenix? The Communist Party in Post-Soviet Russian Politics', *Party Politics*, Vol. 2, No. 2 (1996), pp. 147–75.

11. More generally, see Maurice Duverger, *Political Parties: Their Origin and Activity in Modern States* (London: Methuen, 1954); Arend Lijphart (ed.), *Parliamentary versus Presidential Government* (Oxford: Oxford University Press, 1992); Matthew S. Shugart and John M. Carey, *Presidents and Assemblies: Constitutional Design and Electoral Dynamics* (Cambridge: Cambridge University Press, 1992); Giovanni Sartori, *Comparative Constitutional Engineering: An Enquiry into Structures, Incentives and Outcomes* (Basingstoke: Macmillan, 1994).

explanation of divisions in these societies. On the supply side, there has been no shortage of contending parties and candidates and, faced with such a plethora of choices, successful parties are more likely to be those that seek as far as possible to match their programmes and social appeal to relatively known characteristics of the population. On the demand side, two points must be made. First, voters in Eastern Europe appear to be far more sophisticated even in the early stages of democratization than some commentators have assumed. The voters were expected to find electoral choices so confusing that they would be mobilized to support parties on the basis of the supposedly low information cost basis of either charismatic or clientelistic appeals:[12] instead, they appear to have developed meaningful ideological orientations that parties, in the supply circumstances just described, are well advised to take seriously if they wish to succeed electorally. Second, in what is none the less a confusing environment in which voters are faced with a broad choice of parties and candidates, they will find it easiest to choose those that send them the clearest social and ideological signals. Contrary to many suppositions, therefore, elites and institutions may actually have less room to shape divisions in Eastern Europe than in more consolidated democracies, where established party organizations and long-term partisan affiliations can serve to accentuate top-down influences.

The Russian Case

We now consider how these general propositions and conclusions may be applied to the specific case of Russia, and how arguments about the structure and content of partisan divisions may change as democratic competition is iterated over time. For the first of these interests we need to examine how the factors we have identified as shaping ideological divisions generally explain divisions in Russia, and the relationship between ideological and social divisions in that country. For the second, we need to assess how ideological and social divisions develop over time. A further set of considerations derives from the role of institutions and elites in structuring cleavages. Is Russia distinctive in

12. For a defence of this view of charisma and clientelism, see Herbert Kitschelt, 'Formation of Party Cleavages in Post-Communist Democracies', *Party Politics*, Vol. 1 (1995), pp. 447–72.

the ability of elites to determine and shape divisions and does their influence grow or diminish? And are these institutions and elites more likely to shape divisions as they become more entrenched and as the logic of electoral competition narrows the field of plausible parties and candidates?

Within the framework we have described above, Russia is likely to occupy a distinctive position because of the nature of the challenges and legacies that it faces.[13] In comparison with a number of other countries in Eastern Europe, for example, Russian politics contains relatively few distinctive independent bases for ideological divisions. This is not to say, however, that it is an exception to the more general underlying mechanisms and dynamics relating to the formation of partisan divisions.

First, although it is home to a great many ethnic minorities and has an ethnic federal structure that may inflame ethnic conflicts, Russians are such a significant majority of the population that the general issue of ethnic rights – which in states such as Estonia, Lithuania and Latvia provides the principal source of division – is unlikely to become dominant. If ethnic issues do constitute a basis for ideological division, they are much more likely to be associated with particular issues and conflicts – such as Chechnya – than to form a generalized problem of citizenship.

Second, Russia lacks the distinctive independent source of politicization of values and issues of lifestyle that is found in Catholic countries where the Church and its doctrine have a direct political intervention. Orthodoxy in Russia has always lacked the prescriptive component of Catholicism and has tended to associate itself politically with support for the state rather than with views on particular categories of issues. Thus, disputes over values and lifestyle choices are likely to be much less salient and independent of other issues than they have been in predominantly Catholic countries such as Poland, Slovakia and Hungary.

Third, the relative lack of ethnic and value-orientated bases of cleavage leaves economic issues as the likely main and dominant ones

13. See Stephen Whitefield and Geoffrey Evans, 'The Russian Election of December 1993', *Post-Soviet Affairs*, Vol. 10 (1994), pp. 38–60; and Stephen Whitefield and Geoffrey Evans, 'Support for Democracy and Political Opposition in Russia, 1993–95', *Post-Soviet Affairs,* Vol. 12 (1996), pp. 218–42.

dividing the electorate. In so far as these first two sources of division become politicized, therefore, it may be in association with economic issues. As has been argued and demonstrated in other settings,[14] economic differences are the most important ones in the politics of a nation *only in the absence* of sources of ethnic, linguistic and religious difference, and Russia appears to fit this description. In these circumstances, the politicization of ethnicity and value orientations, should it occur at all, is likely to be in conjunction with economic issues. Thus economic liberals in the Russian context may also be liberals on ethnic and value questions as well, forming a single and unidimensional ideological divide counterposing economic, social and ethnic liberals with more authoritarian opponents on each of these questions.

Fourth, while Russia shares with other countries in the region challenges at the state level – especially with respect to its relations with the West – these issues may be felt more intensely than in other places. It also has distinctive state-level problems which concern adjustment to a post-imperial status, with dramatic shifts in its borders and international standing; and, consequent upon its former metropolitan position, it faces the issue of what to do about the millions of Russians living in the newly independent states (NIS). Our research in other countries in the region indicates that issues of nationalism are seldom of marked significance as a source of ideological cleavage, and that questions of relations with the West are essentially attached to the question of marketization and the economy and do not function as an independent source of ideological division. However, it is quite possible that the distinctive position of Russia in the Soviet Union should have politicized issues of Western involvement, nationalism, empire, and Russians in the NIS to a noticeable degree and in ways that cut across other ideological divides.

Next we consider the potential for change in ideological divisions over time. Three years, of course, is not in the normal course of events the kind of period in which dramatic changes in the issue divisions underlying partisanship are likely to occur. However, in new democracies where electorates at first have little knowledge of parties' and

14. Arend Lijphart, 'Religious vs. Linguistic vs. Class Voting: The "Crucial Experiment" of Comparing Belgium, Canada, South Africa, and Switzerland', *American Political Science Review*, Vol. 73 (1979), pp. 442–58; Richard Rose and Derek W. Urwin 'Persistence and Change in Western Party Systems since 1945', *Political Studies*, Vol. 18 (1970), pp. 287–319.

candidates' positions, ideological divisions may be particularly prone to quick transformation, while, as political transformation has advanced, some of the issues of great relevance in 1993 may have become less important by 1996: Russians may have become inured to the collapse of the old Soviet Union; relations towards Russians in the NIS may have become more stable and predictable and thus less salient at both the grassroots and state levels; and the war in Chechnya may have declined somewhat as a source of division as movement towards ending the conflict – if not settling the issue constitutionally – occurred. Were the first of these conditions to be true, then we might expect volatility in the nature of ideological divisions; if the second set of claims are correct, then we should expect, if anything, even greater unidimensionality of division as the economy comes to be the only source of ideological differentiation. Finally, the presence of continuity over time would attest to the continuing character of concerns among the electorate, despite considerable elite turmoil and great social transformation.

What, then, are our expectations regarding social divisions to partisanship in Russia and their development over the period 1993–96? We have mentioned already the relative absence of ethnic and religious divisions in Russia. Moreover, despite evident disparities in income and wealth, social differentiation along Western class lines – defined by a complex position of occupation within a market structure – is likely to be undeveloped, though almost certainly growing alongside the market itself. Other economic differences (which might also be reflected in differences in value-orientations) can therefore be expected to be of greater salience: between old and young, educated and uneducated, men and women, budget and non-budget sectors. In addition, there remain enormous differences in the capacity to adapt to change – and in the infrastructure and resources that would allow change – between town and country, between peasants and those integrated into the urban economy. Thus, if Russian ideological divisions are unidimensional, there are multiple possible sources of social division that might be tapped by parties or candidates.

The final issue from the general comparative framework that needs to be considered in the Russian context concerns the impact of institutions and elites on the shape and development of divisions. Our comparative investigations have led to the conclusion that this impact is weaker than many commentators have predicted. There are a number of ways of investigating whether this claim is valid for Russia over time.

First, competition for different institutions – president and parliament – under different electoral rules might be expected to produce distinct types of division. Thus, party competition might be more orientated towards programmes and social constituencies and thus might maximize the number and type of ideological and social divisions, while presidencies are more personalized and charismatic in character. Differences between presidential and party competition might also be enhanced by the fact that President Yeltsin has chosen not to form his own party and thus the particular sources of ideological support on which he draws may remain only latent in party-based elections.

Second, the impact of elites on the nature of divisions in Russia might be evident because of the considerable volatility of elite candidates and parties seeking votes. If elites are even more likely to have had an impact in Russia than elsewhere in Eastern Europe, then we should expect important differences in the character of social and ideological divisions depending on the particular candidates or parties competing for votes; and, as pointed out above, there has been considerable volatility in the parties and presidential candidates contending for office in Russia over the four years we are analysing. If, on the other hand, there is little variation in the nature of divisions, between institutions or over time, then we may conclude against the elitist and institutional approaches. Of course, different conclusions may be reached depending on whether social or ideological divisions are considered.

The rest of this chapter investigates the accuracy of these competing claims and hypotheses using data we have collected from national random samples of the Russian population in 1993, 1995 and 1996 (see Appendix 4A1). Section 2 discusses the nature of the surveys, our measures of the vote and of voting intention, and how we operationalize the ideological and social divisions discussed above. It also discusses the statistical approach that allows us to estimate the number, character and strength of ideological and social divisions. Section 3 presents our results in summary form and relates them to the questions raised in the introduction. The conclusion considers the broader implications of our findings for democratic development in Russia.

2. MODELLING THE STRUCTURE OF SOCIAL AND IDEOLOGICAL CLEAVAGES

To talk about the structure of social and ideological cleavages underlying partisanship in Russia, as elsewhere, is to ask, first, about the dimensionality or cross-cutting character of the social characteristics or ideological commitments shaping partisanship; second, about the nature of the dimensions themselves and the most salient factors shaping them; third, about the relative strength of one dimension compared with another; and, finally, about the positions of particular party or presidential supporters on any given dimension. We noted above the contending hypotheses about the forms of politically relevant social characteristics and ideological commitments in post-communist societies in general and Russia in particular. The aim of this section of the study is to see how these hypotheses may be tested empirically.

Measures

The first stage of our analysis was to operationalize the electoral choices around which relevant bases of differentiation among voters may be formed (for information on the surveys, see Appendix 4A1). Our aim was to give emerging political divisions a chance to be expressed at the time the surveys were conducted, rather than in earlier phases of transition, when they may have been less well-formed. Partisanship is thus measured in 1993 and 1995 by asking respondents for whom they would vote – both president and party – if there were an election in their country.[15] This prospective measure is also preferred in these cases to using respondents' vote in previous elections because it avoids recall biases[16] resulting from the fact that elections had taken place some time before the surveys were conducted. The 1996 survey, however, was conducted immediately following the presidential elections, when the choice of candidate was still fresh in the minds of

15. In 1993 the proportion of respondents able to make a choice of party was too small to allow an informative analysis.
16. Hilde T. Himmelweit, Marianne Jaeger and Janet Stockdale, 'Memory for Past Vote: Implications of a Study of Bias in Recall', *British Journal of Political Science*, Vol. 8 (1978), pp. 365–76.

the public and correspondingly few people had an opinion on their future presidential preferences. For this reason, reported vote for presidential candidates was used as the dependent variable, although party choice was still modelled using voting intention.

The analysis uses only those respondents who indicate support for the main parties and presidential candidates. Those who support minor parties, are undecided or prefer not to vote have been excluded. The distribution of respondents within each of these categories is given in Table 4.1. The variables used to predict voting intention are intended to represent the social characteristics and ideological commitments most relevant to explaining political preferences. Social factors include social class, education, age, gender, religious denomination, church attendance, ethnicity, language use, region of residence, urban or rural residence, employment status, employment sector, whether in receipt of a state pension, home ownership, share ownership and household income. Mass attitudes towards the social, economic and political issues that are likely to be salient to partisanship are measured using batteries of questions taken from the surveys. Two different models are run to reflect the potentially distinct character of ideological cleavages in Russia. The first model distinguishes the following types of issues: support for the market; attitudes towards Western involvement in economic and political developments in a given country; social and political liberalism, which relates to the willingness to support individuals' rights to adopt distinct lifestyles and values and the rights of the individual to secure political rights against the authorities or the community; and, finally, issues involving tolerance of ethnic rights, opposition to prejudice against Jews or Gypsies, and opposition to nationalism. The second model includes these ideological dimensions plus others – measured only in 1995 and 1996 – for attitudes towards: the former Soviet state; law and order; the position of Russians in the NIS; the position of people from the Caucasus in Russian society; and support for the Chechen war. Where the questionnaire allowed, these possible sources of division were operationalized in the form of multiple-item scales: economic liberalism, Western involvement, social and political liberalism, ethnic rights, nationalism, Soviet state, law and order, and Russians abroad. Separate items were used to assess the importance anti-Semitic and anti-Gypsy attitudes, and for attitudes towards people from the Caucasus and the Chechen war. Detailed

Table 4.1   Distribution of supporters of parties and presidential candidates, 1993, 1995 and 1996

Year	Parties			Presidential candidates		
	Party	Number of supporters	%	Name	Number of supporters	%
1993		–		Yeltsin	510	25.5
				Rutskoi	268	13.2
				Zhirinovskii	72	3.5
				Shakhrai	85	4.2
				Others	167	8.2
				Don't know	363	17.9
				Won't vote	538	26.5
1995	Agrarian	55	2.7	Yeltsin	140	7.0
	Democratic Choice	128	6.4	Yavlinskii	261	13.0
	PRES*	40	2.0	Zhirinovskii	105	5.2
	Yabloko	234	11.7	Chernomyrdin	91	4.5
	Democratic Party	34	1.7	Zyuganov	125	6.2
	Communist Party	163	8.1	Gaidar	94	4.7
	LDPR*	85	4.2	Other	142	7.1
	Women of Russia	127	6.3	Don't know	634	31.7
	Other	112	5.6	Won't vote	409	20.4
	Don't know	514	25.7			
	Won't vote	510	25.5			
1996	Women of Russia	27	1.3	*First Round*		
	Our Home is Russia	192	9.5	Yeltsin	558	27.1
	Yabloko	158	7.9	Zhirinovskii	69	3.4
	Democratic Choice	41	2.0	Zyuganov	484	24.1
	Communist Party	370	18.4	Lebed	291	14.5
	CRC*	71	3.5	Yavlinskii	168	8.3
	LDPR*	59	2.9	Other	39	1.9
	Others	94	4.7	Don't know	40	2.0
	Don't know	720	35.8	Against all	24	1.2
	Won't vote	270	13.4	Didn't vote	339	16.8
				Second Round		
				Yeltsin	926	46.0
				Zyuganov	545	27.1
				Against all	150	7.5
				Unsure	36	1.8
				Didn't vote	355	17.6

Note: *PRES = Party of Russian Unity and Concord; LDPR = Liberal Democratic Party of Russia; CRC = Congress of Russian Communities.

information on the coding of the independent variables and question wordings is given in Appendix 4A2.

Statistical analysis

The relations between social characteristics and voting preferences are modelled using discriminant analysis.[17] Discriminant analysis enables us to examine the multivariate effects of a set of interval level predictors on a nominal dependent variable. There is no need to order the parties or to simplify the data by dichotomizing the dependent variable.

The technique estimates one or more linear weighted combinations ('functions') of the discriminating variables (the various sociodemographic characteristics) which maximize the difference between the grouping variable (preference for parties or presidential candidates). The functions are orthogonal to each other and are derived by maximising the ratio of between-to-within group variance for the first function and then likewise for each consecutive orthogonal function, rather as occurs in a principal components analysis. The maximum number of functions is the number of categories in the dependent variable minus one, or the number of independent variables, whichever is the smaller.

For example, if there is one dimension of social division, then a weighted combination of social characteristics should form one significant and substantively meaningful discriminant function. If, however, there are multiple cleavages which need to be taken into account to represent adequately the structure of the political system, then other functions will also be significant (and meaningful). The analysis thus informs us of (i) how many distinct dimensions of support there are for parties or for presidential candidates; (ii) which social characteristics are most relevant for differentiating between parties or between presidential candidates; (iii) the strength of each significant dimension of division (measured by the canonical correlation); and (iv) the mean position of supporters of each party and candidate on any given division.

Discriminant analysis produces several informative coefficients. The *standardized function coefficients* and *structure coefficients* indicate the

---

17. For a general overview, see William R. Klecka, *Discriminant Analysis* (Beverly Hills, CA: Sage, 1980).

contribution of the independent variables (that is, social characteristics or dimensions of ideology) to any given dimension of electoral choice – the largest coefficients define the nature of the social cleavage. The standardized function coefficients are comparable to the beta coefficients in an OLS regression (in the case of a dichotomous dependent variable they are formally equivalent). The structure coefficients measure the zero-order correlation between each of the ideological scales or social characteristics and the discriminant function, thus allowing an assessment of the contribution of any variable before its correlation with other variables in the model is taken into account. Although we do not in this analysis report these sets of coefficients, we use information from both of them to identify the substantive content of a function. In general, only variables with coefficients of 0.40 or above are used to define functions.[18]

Two measures of the strength of association between the discriminant functions and voting intention are also useful: the *canonical correlation* measures the extent of association between each function and voting intention; *Wilks's Lambda* provides a measure of the overall strength of association between all the functions produced in an analysis and voting intention. Here we confine ourselves to presenting only the canonical correlations for each of the significant functions derived from the analysis. These coefficients provide information on the magnitude of the association between the independent variables and voting intention.[19]

In summary, discriminant analysis models the complex relations

18. Detailed information on the results of the discriminant analyses which form the basis of the summaries presented here is available from the authors on request.

19. Readers should note that as both canonical correlations and Wilks' Lambda are derived from the variance explained in the independent variables by the dependent variable rather than vice versa, it is possible that strong associations can be obtained for respondent characteristics which nevertheless affect intention to vote for only one or two parties. Ethnicity, for example, might be very strongly related to support for a minority 'ethnic' party, but does little to explain voting preferences for parties whose appeal is directed only towards a majority ethnic group. Fortunately, in the analyses presented here such potential difficulties have not arisen. A useful analysis of the caution which needs to be exercised when interpreting the substantive implications of the summary statistics obtained with discriminant analysis is presented in Mark R. Daniels and R. Darcy, 'Notes on the Use and Interpretation of Discriminant Analysis', *American Journal of Political Science*, Vol. 27 (1983), pp. 359–81.

between partisan choice and social and ideological divisions parsimoniously and so permits the general structure of the political system to be observed. In this way it is preferable to more fashionable techniques, such as multinomial logistic regression,[20] which compare one party or presidential candidate against all others. Although, unlike logistic regression, discriminant analysis assumes multivariate normality,[21] it is better suited to reducing the complexity of multiple party comparisons so as to reveal the main summary dimensions of political cleavage.

3. RESULTS AND DISCUSSION

Ideological Divisions

Let us recapitulate our expectations of the character and development of ideological division in Russia. In contrast to other countries in Eastern Europe, and resulting from the relative absence of independent sources of ideological structuring, politics in Russia was predicted to be strongly unidimensional, with associations between economic liberalism and issues of value and lifestyle, weak sources of division over generalized questions of ethnic liberalism but with particular ethnic issues relating to Chechnya, and evidence of considerable division resulting from the special challenge facing Russia as a post-imperial power.

Evidence for the accuracy of these findings is presented in summary form in Table 4.2, which shows the number and nature of the divisions for president and party vote for over the three surveys, the strength of each division, and, for two of the years, models containing measures of further issue divisions that may be relevant to the Russian context.

The ideological divisions can be tracked over all three surveys for the presidential models that include only the more restricted range of indicators. No clear trends are evident. The number of cleavages moves

20. See John Aldrich and Forrest Nelson, *Linear, Probability, Logit and Probit Models* (Beverley Hills, CA: Sage, 1984).
21. Fortunately, discriminant analysis is considered to be reasonably robust to deviations from normality: see Peter A. Lachenbruch, *Discriminant Analysis* (New York: Hafner, 1975).

Table 4.2 *The ideological bases of partisanship in Russia, 1993, 1995 and 1996*

	Parties		Presidents	
	Model 1	Model 2	Model 1	Model 2
1993	–	–	1. Economic liberalism: **0.45**	–
1995	1. Economic liberalism, West: **0.50** 2. Social and political liberalism, Ethnic liberalism: **0.22**	1. Soviet Union, Social and political liberalism, Economic liberalism, West: **0.53** 2. Chechnya, Economic liberalism, Ethnic liberalism: **0.26** 3. Nationalism, Pro/anti-Caucasian: **0.23**	1. Economic liberalism, West: **0.47** 2. Social and political liberalism, Ethnic liberalism: **0.26**	1. Soviet Union, West, Social and political liberalism, Economic liberalism: **0.47** 2. Ethnic liberalism, Economic liberalism, Pro/anti-Caucasian: **0.26** 3. West, Chechnya, Social and political liberalism: **0.19**
1996	*First round* 1. Social and political liberalism, Economic liberalism: **0.58** 2. West, Nationalism, Economic liberalism: **0.17**	*First round* 1. Soviet Union, Economic liberalism, Social and political liberalism, West: **0.18** 2. West, Chechnya: **0.18**	*First round* 1. Economic liberalism, West, Social and political liberalism, nationalism: **0.44** *Second round* 1. Economic liberalism, West, Social and political liberalism, nationalism: **0.46**	*First round* 1. Economic liberalism, West, Social and political liberalism, Soviet Union: **0.49** *Second round* 1. Soviet Union, Economic liberalism, Social and political liberalism, Nationalism: **0.52**

Note: Canonical correlations of discriminant functions are shown in **bold**; Variables listed in order of magnitude on discriminant functions.

from a unidimensional structure in 1993 to two dimensions in 1995 and then back to unidimensionality again in 1996. The character of the principal dimension remains orientated towards disputes over economic liberalization in all three waves. Other potential influences, such as Western involvement, are closely associated with those concerning the economy. While issues of social and political liberalism and ethnic liberalism do constitute a separate basis for voters' choice among potential candidates in 1995, the dimension is weak (as shown by the canonical correlation of only 0.26). This evidence, therefore, tends to support our view of Russia as harbouring – in comparative terms – relatively restricted sources of electoral structure, a picture that remains true over time.

The ideological bases of partisanship do appear to become more complex when further challenges and legacies that may be relevant to the Russian context are taken into account. In Model 2 the number of significant ideological divisions increases, to three in 1995 and two in 1996. Economic issues are now joined in importance by the question of the Soviet Union – people's identification with it and estimation of the value of its dissolution. Given the strength of the Soviet issue, it is also difficult to believe that this would not also have been a central component to electoral choice in 1993. It is important to note, however, that there is a strong association between attitudes towards the Soviet Union and those towards the economy and towards social and political liberalism. Indeed, there is little difference in the character of the main dimensions between the two models. Although the war in Chechnya provides an issue that adds (weakly) to ideological dimensionality in the period in which it was salient, the implications of the expanded analysis do not depart significantly from those of the more limited set of scales shown in Model 1, in which Russia appears to be largely structured along a single line of ideological cleavage composed of various forms of liberalism and antipathy to the communist Soviet state.

Social Divisions

If our expectations for the structure of ideological divisions were that they would be relatively stable and unidimensional, those for social divisions were much more dynamic. Certainly, it is again true that there are fewer sources of social division – religion, ethnicity – in Russia than in other transition states, such as Poland and Estonia, and that this is likely to limit the dimensionality and certainly the sharpness of divisions associated with these forms of social differentiation. Moreover, market differences were at least initially relatively undeveloped in Russia. However, the fact that social differences need have no counterparts in ideological divisions allows for considerable diversity and development in the social bases of politics even in the context of a predominantly stable and unidimensional ideological framework.

The analysis of the social bases of partisanship offers some support for this view (see Table 4.3). There is little evidence that in 1993

Table 4.3   The social bases of partisanship in Russia, 1993, 1995 and 1996

Year	Parties	Presidents
1993	–	1. Income, Age/pensions, Urban/rural: **0.27**
1995	1. Gender: **0.42**	1. Age/pensions: **0.34**
	2. Age/pensions: **0.35**	2. Age, Class: **0.29**
	3. Urban/rural, Ethnicity: **0.27**	3. Ethnicity, Moscow/ St. Petersburg: **0.24**
		First round
1996	1. Age/pensions: **0.48**	1. Class, Pensions: **0.36**
	2. Class: **0.32**	2. Age: **0.22**
	3. Ethnicity, Gender: **0.25**	3. Moscow/St. Petersburg, Pensions, Gender, Rural/ urban: **0.18**
	4. Moscow/St. Petersburg: **0.20**	4. Church attendance: **0.15**
		Second round
		1. Income, Age/pensions, Education, Privatization: **0.35**

Notes: Canonical correlations of discriminant functions are shown in **bold**; variables are listed in order of magnitude on the discriminant functions.

unidimensional ideological divisions reflected the presence of highly politicized social divisions. The analysis shows that there is also only one significant social division; moreover, as shown by the canonical correlation of just 0.27, the magnitude of the division is relatively weak. However, such division as is evident is based on essentially economic criteria: between those on high rather than low incomes and older voters on pensions, and between urban and rural respondents. These essentially class-based divisions, orientated towards economic resources and sector, were expected to be present, if weakly, and to grow.

By 1995, however, we see increasing strength, as shown by the higher canonical correlations, and diversity of social structural differences of various sorts. These remain fixed principally in the economy, although this relates now not only to class differences, to urban versus rural residence, and to the metropolitan centres of Moscow and St. Petersburg where reform has been most advanced, but also particularly to divisions between those reliant on state budgets and the rest of society. Thus, especially clear is a political division that revolves around age and pensions (parties, dimension 2 in 1995, dimension 1 in 1996: presidents, dimension 1 and 2 in 1995, dimension 1 and 2 in 1996). Older voters and pensioners are now more clearly distinct from others, and constitute the sharpest source of division. These sorts of growing divisions are precisely what we expect in a society undergoing rapid marketization, and experiencing severe state budget problems.

At the same time, and in line with our predictions and the evidence of ideological division, non-economic alternative bases to social differentiation in Russia are quite weak, although they are present. Ethnic differences are there (parties and presidents, dimension 3 in 1995; parties, dimension 3 in 1996) but on minor dimensions with weak canonical correlations. Religious denomination barely figures at all as a basis of party support, seen only on the minor fourth dimension for presidents in 1996. The strongest social factor not already discussed is gender (parties, dimension 1 in 1995, dimension 3 in 1996; presidents, dimension 3 in 1996), which is directly related to the presence of support among women for 'Women of Russia' and antipathy among women for both Vladimir Zhirinovsii and Aleksandr Lebed – the latter relationship appearing, however, on a very minor dimension.

The evidence, then, suggests that partisan division in Russia is not subject to multiple distinct types of social division but – as was the case ideologically – is mainly structured by economic differences. Social division, however, is more developed and complex than ideological division as economic change results in various social groups having clearer associations between their interests and their choice of party or president. Moreover, as with gender, some social divisions are largely expressive rather than representing distinct ideological preferences; women may want parties to represent their interests, especially their economic ones, but from the evidence presented here they do not have a distinct position on general economic strategy which might be adapted to realize this. Thus, although in general women are slightly more likely to support interventionist policies than are men,[22] there is nothing particularly distinctive about the ideological preferences of women who support 'Women of Russia'.

Institutional and Elite Impact on Divisions

The final question addressed by our data concerns the impact of institutions and elites on the shape of social and ideological divisions. In addressing these questions we are concerned to infer from the nature and development of ideological and social divisions answers concerning how they came about and changed. Institutional differences might be felt in a number of ways. In the absence of 'civil society' or developed secondary associations – and there is little doubt that such organization is weak in Russia – the nature of divisions and their development might be especially prone to elite or institutional shaping. First, differences in the nature of divisions might be evident between party and presidential competition: the former might be more programmatic, the latter more personalized, in which case we should expect to see significant differences in the strength of social and ideological divisions. Moreover, because party competition may be more programmatic, it may tap differences in the population that presidential competition ignores. Or, conversely, because Yeltsin contends for presidential office but does not have a party, presidential divisions may be structured by additional elements associated with his appeal. Second, because there has been a considerable turnover in the parties and candidates available to and chosen by voters – and thus considerable change in the nature of elites

---

22. Geoffrey Evans, 'The Social Bases of Mass Support for Political and Economic Liberalization in Eastern Europe', *Centre for European Studies Discussion Paper no. 39* (Oxford: Nuffield College, 1995).

themselves – differences may be expected in the divisions that underlie support for these various parties and candidates. If differences of these two kinds do not appear, however, it would provide support for our alternative 'sociocentric' explanation of the formation and development of divisions. If elites and institutions do not make a clear difference, and if the possibility of a 'civil society' explanation does not exist (because civil society itself does not exist in any developed form), the best remaining explanation for divisions and their development relates to informal social responses to the kinds of challenges faced by Russia to which elites themselves must react if they are to be electorally successful, and to which the institutional structure itself may be more or less well adapted.

The evidence in our analysis and from the discussion in the previous sections does not seem to offer great support to either of the institutional theories of the formation of divisions. This is not to say that differences in the social and ideological divisions underlying party and presidential competition are not present with respect to both the relative strength and the content of any given sort of division. First, when Model 1 is considered, in 1996 party competition does appear to tap into one more dimension of ideological differentiation than presidential competition does, although this difference is not evident in 1995. Second, there are signs that parties have tapped into social differences that presidential candidates did not, at least in such a clear way: the most obvious case is that of gender in 1995, reflecting, as noted above, the presence of 'Women of Russia' as a choice for voters. Third, there is some indication that the strength (as measured by the canonical correlations) of the dimensions that are comparable between the two types of electoral competition is higher for parties than for presidents, which might suggest that competition among presidential candidates fosters more personalized and less programmatic relationships between voters and their partisan choices.

This evidence, however, is not especially compelling. To take each point in turn. The difference in the number of ideological divisions in 1996 disappears when we consider Model 2 rather than Model 1. The extra significant dimension detected in the analysis of parties is in any case very weak. By 1996 there is also no real difference in the strength of gender as a division between parties and presidents. Moreover, it can be argued that the emergence of this division in 1995 is not institutional in character; the presence of a 'women's' candidate for president might well have had the same effect and, certainly, the absence of such a candidate can be only marginally explained by institutional incentives. Finally, the appearance of differences in the relative strength of the canonical correlations in the 1996 survey may be an effect of the timing of the surveys relative to elections. In 1996 we are modelling vote rather than intended vote and thus include a large number of people who otherwise – as in their choice of party in 1996 or president in 1995 – would not have been able to express a preference. The inclusion of larger numbers of very probably less-well-informed respondents is likely to depress the canonical correlations precisely because these people are less certain about their partisan preferences. In 1995, the only year in which direct comparability between presidential and party preferences is possible, differences in the canonical correlations for both ideological and social divisions are trivial. While not wishing to dismiss entirely the evidence for the importance of institutional factors in shaping divisions, these appear to be much weaker than institutionalists might expect. Most important, in our view, is the extent of similarity between the social and ideological bases of such competition.

The same point may be made about the effects of elites on the nature of divisions. Clearly, there is one sense in which elite actions do make a difference: had they not waged war on Chechnya, the issue would never have arisen. A similar point might be made – though less cogently – for the divisive effects of the collapse of the Soviet Union for which elites must take a great share of the responsibility. However, there is little evidence that elites are able to determine the character of divisions themselves. Parties and presidential contenders have come and gone but the nature of the ideological divisions underlying partisanship has not fluctuated with them. Rather, they appear to be determined and shaped by the kinds of legacies and challenges that we outlined at the beginning of the chapter; elites – at least with respect to the electorate – appear constrained to position themselves within divisions that they must treat as relatively given. Even where there is evidence of pronounced and systematic change in the basis of partisanship – such as has been observed with respect to social cleavages – these changes are most plausibly seen as responses to evolving social circumstances in the context of a relatively stable structure of ideological divisions. Although partisan divisions in Russia are different from those found in many other post-communist societies, therefore, the explanation for their shape and development remains the same.

4. CONCLUSIONS

The final question that we address concerns the relationship between the structure of divisions (and their explanation) and the development of democracy in Russia. Two issues are relevant here. First, as a number of commentators have argued, certain partisan divisions are more conducive to the efficient functioning of democracy than are others.[23] How suitable for democratic functioning are Russia's divisions? Second, in so far as divisions can be ameliorated, the nature of institutions is highly important.[24] How adapted are Russia's institutions to its divisions?

Clearly, addressing these questions comprehensively goes far beyond the scope of this study. Here, we can consider only one factor – the structure of social and ideological divisions – in isolation and speculate about its impact. But our evidence does, at least *prima facie*, suggest a far more positive picture in some respects than commentators on Russia are prone to adopt.

First, there are divisions of various kinds, and these are developing. Parties and presidents thus have a structure to which to orientate themselves and this may promote stability in their behaviour rather than seeking constantly to succeed by manipulating public opinion. Indeed, our evidence suggests that elites have not proved able to dictate the nature of partisan divisions and, in consequence, may need to attend to these divisions in order to obtain electoral success. Conversely, the public appears to have more meaningful policy preferences and ideological stances than has often been thought and so its members have some basis at least on which to choose their representatives and to judge their performance. Indeed, the clearly developed links between respondents' attitudes and their party preferences revealed here and in previous work,[25] and which occurred in the absence of a developed civil society, is suggestive of an unexpected level of political

23. Kitschelt, 'Formation of Party Cleavages'; Lijphart, 'Religious vs. Linguistic vs. Class Voting'.
24. Richard Gunther and Anthony Mughan, 'Political Institutions and Cleavage Management', in R. Kent Weaver and Bert A. Rockman (eds), *Do Institutions Matter? Government Capabilities in the United States and Abroad* (Washington, DC: Brookings, 1993), pp. 272–301.
25. Whitefield and Evans, 'From the Top Down or the Bottom Up?'.

sophistication on their part in what must presumably have been a very confusing political context.

Second, the content of Russia's ideological divisions may be conducive – and increasingly so – to a stable democratic framework. The greatest fear for democracy has been expressed when ideological divisions are orientated towards ethnic, linguistic, or religious divisions.[26] These are notably weak in Russia. Most optimism arises from divisions that are principally economic in character and this sort of division is clearly the most dominant in Russia. Certainly, there is evidence that questions concerning the state are of some importance, and, in policy terms, they have been the source of great political conflict within the country. There are signs, however, that the Chechen issue is moving to resolution and, in so far as nostalgia for the Soviet Union is strongly associated with the economy, there is no clear reason at the mass level for Russia not to build democracy on the basis of its principal ideological division.

Third, social divisions are becoming increasingly located in differences of economic interests.[27] To a greater extent than before, support for parties and presidential candidates has a social basis and this is generally held to temper political competition and to stabilize elite behaviour in office. Moreover, the nature of these social bases is not generally or principally expressive or identity based but founded on instrumental, and thus more negotiable, differences that may be more amenable to institutionally directed compromise. This is not to say that elites are sufficiently constrained in their actions by the electorate; nor that institutions are adapted to achieving compromise or adequately representing the population or giving them a sense of efficacy. Institutions may not determine divisions, but this does not mean that they are appropriate for them. This question, however, cannot be addressed here. For the moment, it is important to say only that the political divisions of Russia are in themselves no clear impediment to democratic consolidation.

26. Lijphart, 'Religious vs. Linguistic vs. Class Voting'.
27. Indeed, Russia corresponds closely to the ideal type of structure initially proposed by Herbert Kitschelt as a representation of the pattern of cleavage structure in Central and Eastern Europe more generally: Kitschelt, 'The Formation of Party Systems'.

APPENDIX 4A1: THE SURVEYS

Response rates were generally high. Non-response biases appear to be predictably like those in the West. Compared with census data, non-respondents tend to be older and to have lower levels of education. Non-response resulted mainly from non-contacts and refusals. Table 4A1.1 summarizes the main characteristics of the surveys.

The questionnaires contained approximately 300 items. They were originally pilot tested on 50–100 respondents prior to being finalized for use in the main survey. Back-translation of the items took several months of iterative adjustment. It was facilitated by the presence of fluent Russian speakers in the British team and by academic translators, and the helpful contribution of Russian collaborators, who also provided additional information regarding the political salience of the issues being examined.

All interviews were conducted face to face in the respondents' homes. Interviewers were generally experienced and were also given special training for some of the more difficult aspects of the interview schedule. Checks on the interviewers were carried out by local area supervisors. Quality was also checked using a follow-up study of 10 per cent of the respondents, who were selected randomly and re-interviewed a few weeks later.

The field work in 1993 was directed by Professor Vladimir Yadov, director of the Institute of Sociology of the Russian Academy of Sciences; the 1995 and 1996 surveys were directed by Professor Vladimir Andreenkov of the Centre for Comparative Social Research, Moscow.

Table 4A1.1 The surveys

Date of survey	Sampling frame	Sample design and procedure	Response rates	
Summer 1993	Adult population (18+) Lists of 'privatization vouchers'	1. 10 regions 2. 56 settlements 3. individuals sampled from lists of vouchers	names issued: non-contact: refused: achieved: Response rate:	2,420 264 126 2,030 0.84
Summer 1995	Adult population (18+) 1989 census of households (stages 1,2); electoral register (stage 3) list of households (stage 4)	1. 4 economic–geographical zones; 15 clusters; 2. 49 *raions*+2 (Moscow and St. Petersburg) sampling points; 3. 51 communities 4. Multi-stage probability sampling and random route with Kish Grid selection	names issued: non-contact: refused: achieved: Response rate	2,600 397 200 2,003 0.77
Summer 1995	Adult population (18+) Electoral lists	1. 4 economic–geographical zones; 15 clusters; 2. 49 *raions*+2 (Moscow and St. Petersburg) sampling points; 3. 51 communities 4. Multi-stage probability sampling and random route with Kish Grid selection	names issued: non-contact: refused: achieved: Response rate	2,658 389 249 2,020 0.76

APPENDIX 4A2: MEASURES OF SOCIAL AND IDEOLOGICAL DIVISIONS

(i) Social Divisions

Variables indicating demographic characteristics are measured as follows:

Age is actual age; sex (*women*) is scored male, 0; female, 1; *Pensions* refers to respondents on a state pension.

Educational qualifications are measured using three categories: none and primary qualifications; middle range and vocational; degree and higher degree.

Social class is measured using a slightly modified version of Goldthorpe's class schema,[28] in which class is operationalized by distinctions both in employment status (that is, between employers, self-employed and employees) and within the broad category of employees. The main distinguishing characteristics of employee classes are their conditions of employment, degree of occupational security and career prospects.[29] Allocation to a class position is derived from the respondent's occupation and employment status, since recent research suggests that in Eastern Europe allocation on an individual basis is likely to be the most effective strategy.[30] For individuals who are not at present working, we take their most recent job.

Household income is self-reported (missing income is also included in the models as a dummy variable).

Unemployment is scored 1 if currently unemployed, 0 if not.

Private sector employment includes respondents who own or work in private companies, workers on their own account, and respondents who work in companies in the process of privatization.

---

28. See Robert Erikson and John H. Goldthorpe, *The Constant Flux: A Study of Class Mobility in Industrial Societies* (Oxford: Clarendon Press, 1992), pp. 36–42.
29. A more detailed elaboration of Goldthorpe's class concept and its application in post-communist societies is presented in Geoffrey Evans, 'Social Class and Interest Formation in Post-communist Eastern Europe', in David Lee and Bryan Turner (eds), *Conflicts about Class* (London: Longman, 1996).
30. Gordon Marshall, Steven Roberts, Carole Burgoyne, Adam Swift and David Routh, 'Class, Gender, and the Asymmetry Hypothesis', *European Sociological Review*, Vol. 11, No. 1 (1995), pp. 1–15.

Two consumption sector variables measure *home ownership* (1, else = 0) and *share ownership* (1, else = 0).

Ethnicity includes the major self-identified groups (Tatars, Ukrainians); the reference category is Russian; residual categories of very small minorities are coded as 'other ethnicity'.

The effect of *religious denomination* is measured relative to the reference category, which is Russian Orthodox. Residual categories are coded as 'others'.

Church attendance is measured using a scale from 'more than once a week' (6) to never (1).

Rural or urban residence is measured with a 4-point scale (1 = village, through to 4 = city). Moscow or St. Petersburg residence is indicated separately by the variable *City* (1, else = 0).

(ii) Ideological Divisions

Each ideological scale was constructed using Likert-style items with five-point response formats. The selection of items for the multiple-item scales was done partly on a priori grounds, partly through an item analysis. In some cases, items that reduced overall reliability (as measured by internal consistency estimated using Cronbach's alpha) were removed from the scale. This was not done, however, with some items that helped to preserve the balance of the scales with regard to the direction of the wording of questions. These were retained even when their presence reduced the internal consistency of the scales, because the preservation of balance helps to limit the likelihood of acquiescence effects, and thus has beneficial consequences for validity.[31]

Economic liberalism is measured with a multi-item Likert scale. The scale includes four double-sided items:

---

31. For similar treatments of acquiescence effects in comparable data to that presented here, see Anthony Heath, Geoffrey Evans and Jean Martin, 'The Measurement of Core Beliefs and Values: The Development of Balanced Socialist/Laissez-faire and Libertarian/Authoritarian Scales', *British Journal of Political Science*, Vol. 24, No. 1 (1994), pp. 115–32; for an assessment of the consequences of using balanced and unbalanced scales to measure ideology, see Geoffrey Evans and Anthony Heath, 'The Measurement of Left–Right and Libertarian–Authoritarian Values: Comparing Balanced and Unbalanced Scales', *Quality and Quantity*, Vol. 29, No. 1 (1995), pp. 191–206.

Which one of these two statements comes closest to your own views (definitely the first, the first rather than the second, in between, definitely the second, the second rather than the first) ...

The government should see to it that every person has a job and a good standard of living ... or ... The government should just let each person get ahead on their own.

The government should not concern itself with how equal people's incomes are ... or ... The government should try to make differences between incomes as small as possible.

The government should take all major industries into state ownership ... or ... The government should place all major industries in private ownership.

The government should just leave it up to individual companies to decide their wages, prices and profits ... or ... The government should control wages, prices and profits.

In addition, it included the following five-point (strongly agree, agree, neither agree nor disagree, strongly disagree, disagree) scales:

Please choose one of the phrases from this card to tell me whether and to what degree you agree with each statement. In [respondent's country] ...

Private enterprise is the best way to solve the country's economic problems.

Major public services and industries ought to be in state ownership.

Large differences in income are necessary for prosperity.

Allowing business to make good profits is the best way to improve everyone's standard of living.

It is the responsibility of the government to reduce the differences in income between people with high incomes and those with low incomes.

The government should provide everyone with a guaranteed basic income.

The *social and political liberalism* scale has seven five-point agree/disagree items:

In [respondent's country] ...

People should be allowed to organize public meetings to protest against the government.

Homosexual relationships are always wrong.

People in this country should be more tolerant of those who lead unconventional lives.

Young people today don't have enough respect for traditional values.

Censorship of films and magazines is necessary to uphold moral standards.

What this country needs to resolve its economic problems is government with a strong hand.

People in [respondent's country] should be free to emigrate even if the country needs their skills.

Ethnic rights attitudes are measured using four agree/disagree items:

> Minority ethnic groups in [respondent's country] should have far more rights than they do now.
> Everyone who lives in [respondent's country] should have the right to become a citizen regardless of their ethnic origins.
> The ethnic group a person belongs to should not influence the benefits they can get from the state.
> All minority ethnic groups in this country should have to be taught in [respondent's country's language].

Attitudes towards the *Soviet Union* are measured using two agree/disagree items:

> I identify more strongly with the Soviet Union than I do with Russia.
> The dissolution of the Soviet Union was a good thing.

Attitudes towards *Russians in the NIS* are measure by four agree/disagree items:

> The borders of Russia should be expanded to include ethnic Russians in 'the near abroad'.
> Russians living in the former republics should give their allegiance to the states where they live and not to Russia.
> Russian living in the former republics are treated unfairly by the authorities of these new states.
> The Russian government should not concern itself with the rights of ethnic Russians in 'the near abroad'.

Attitudes towards *law and order* are measure by four agree/disagree items:

> The death penalty is never an appropriate sentence.
> People who break the law should be given stiffer sentences.
> It is more important to defeat crime than to strictly observe civil rights.
> The rights of people accused of crimes should be protected even if this means that sometimes the guilty go free.

Attitudes towards *people from the Caucasus* are measured using two agree/disagree items:

> The political authorities will be justified in sending people from the Caucasus back to their land.
> It is wrong to blame rising crime on people from the Caucasus.

Attitudes towards the *Chechen war* are measured using a single agree/disagree item:

> Russia is right to go to war with Chechnya.

Anti-Semitic attitudes are measured using a single agree/disagree item:

> Jews in [respondent's country] today have too much power and influence.

Anti-Gypsy attitudes are also measured using a single agree/disagree item:

> There are too many Gypsies in [respondent's country].

Nationalism is measured using two items:

> We have a lot to learn from other countries in running [respondent's country's] affairs.
> [Respondent's country] should cooperate with other countries even if it means giving up some independence.

Pro- and anti-Western attitudes are measured using two double-sided items:

> *Which one of these two statements comes closest to your own views ...*

> Western institutions have been helpful and supportive of our country ... or ... Western institutions have been interfering in our affairs and using our difficulties for their own advantage.
> Foreign ownership of enterprises is acceptable if it improves the state of our economy ... or ... It is better that we should continue to own our enterprises even if it means more hardship in the future.

In the more extensive analyses conducted in the 1995 and 1996 waves, two further agree/disagree items were added to make an augmented scale of pro- and anti-Western attitudes:

> Western influence is corrupting traditional Russian values.
> Closer links with the West will help make Russia great again.

Note: All the scales are scored so that high scores indicate liberal positions. Scores on items that are inconsistent with this direction have been reversed. 'Don't know' responses have been recoded to mid-point so as to preserve sample size in the multivariate analyses. Scales constructed with 'don't know' responses excluded produce very similar results.

5. Leader Popularity and Party Development in Post-Soviet Russia[1]

Arthur H. Miller, William M. Reisinger and Vicki L. Hesli

The extent to which political parties and party systems have developed in post-Soviet societies has become quite controversial.[2] One aspect of this controversy involves the extent to which public support for a political party reflects merely a response to the popularity and appealing personality of the party leader.

A number of scholars have argued that citizen identification with a political party in Russia is rare, but when it does occur it reflects little more than a superficial response to the popularity of individual political leaders. In speaking of the organizational superiority of the Communist Party of the Russian Federation, for example, White and his collaborators say: 'it was virtually the only party that was more than the fan club of its leader'.[3] Other scholars maintain that the present post-Soviet parties are ephemeral, impotent, personalistic and undifferentiated.[4]

1. Partial support for this research was provided by the National Science Foundation Grant No. SBR-94-11643. We thank Gwyn Erb and Thomas Klobucar for assistance with the analysis and Peggy Swails for her secretarial assistance.
2. For a review of the debate see Arthur H. Miller, Gwyn Erb, William M. Reisinger and Vicki L. Hesli, 'Emerging Party Systems in Post-Soviet Societies: Fact or Fiction', paper presented at the annual meeting of the International Society of Political Psychology, Vancouver, BC, Canada, July 1996.
3. Stephen White, Richard Rose and Ian McAllister, *How Russia Votes* (Chatham, NJ: Chatham House, 1997), p. 209.
4. See, for example, Peter Reddaway, 'Instability and Fragmentation', *Journal of Democracy*, Vol. 6, No. 2 (1994), pp.13–19; Peter Rutland, 'Has Democracy

This school of thought argues that since many of the numerous political parties competing in Duma elections (of which there were 43 in the elections of 1995) appear to have similar political programmes, the personalities of the party leaders become the basis for public identification with the parties. For example, Filippov and Shvetsova contend that

> electoral uncertainty combined with the lack of commonly recognized meaningful cleavages, in the absence of party affiliation or even general political affiliation, makes personalities of politicians the key feature that distinguishes numerous political parties with similar electoral platforms from one another. Personalities thus become the essential asset of a 'new' political party.[5]

Many of these claims regarding both the rarity of meaningful party identification among Russian citizens and the 'personality' basis of political parties are made with very little relevant empirical evidence. The purpose of this investigation is to examine these claims with survey data from early 1997 that are better designed to test directly the hypothesis that public support for political parties reflects no more than a response to the personality of the party leaders. The study proceeds by first briefly addressing the present extent of party identification in Russia. Next the question of whether or not survey respondents can be directly asked about the relative importance of party leader appeal as the basis for partisan identification is examined. Indirect methods for assessing the relationship between leader appeal and party identification are then investigated and the results compared with those obtained from more direct measures. The hypothesized effects of party leader 'personality' on partisan identification requires a fuller definition of 'personality', hence one aim of the section on indirect methods will be an examination of the correlation between public assessments of various leadership traits and the extent to which citizens identify with the particular leader's party. The hypothesis regarding political parties

Failed in Russia?', *The National Interest*, Vol. 38 (1994), pp. 3-12; Peter C. Ordeshook, 'Institutions and Incentives', *Journal of Democracy*, Vol. 6, No. 2 (1995), pp. 46-60.

5. Mikhail G. Filippov and Olga V. Shvetsova, 'Direct Presidential Elections and Party Systems in Eastern Europe', paper presented at the Annual Meeting of the American Political Science Association, San Francisco, 26 August-1 September 1996.

as no more than 'fan clubs' for a given politician assumes that the party leader's popularity completely explains public support for the party. To examine this aspect of the hypothesis requires a multivariate analysis aimed at determining whether issue or social cleavages add anything to a general explanation of party identification in Russia. The final analytical section of the study will therefore present a broader multivariate test of the hypothesis. The chapter ends with a brief conclusion drawing out the implications of the analysis for the future of party development in Russia.

1. RECENT TRENDS IN PARTISANSHIP

The rate at which partisanship is developing in post-Soviet Russia is a rather controversial topic. Some scholars, pointing to the earlier work of Lipset and Rokkan, argue that political parties and party systems take many years to solidify because party development depends on a slow process of socialization that links parties with the social cleavages existing in society.[6] Proponents of this view maintain that the existing post-Soviet political parties, other than the Communist Party, will develop very slowly given the single-party history of the Soviet Union.[7] In fact, Reddaway argues that Russia may never attain a truly representative multiparty system.[8]

Other proponents of the traditional perspective are somewhat less pessimistic, but still they argue that consolidation of emerging party systems in the post-communist states will take considerable time.[9] They believe that post-communist citizens at present lack a civic culture and are generally distrustful of and apathetic towards political parties. Rose, for example, contends that post-communist citizens lack stable positive identification with political parties. Instead, they 'divide their support

---

6. Seymour Martin Lipset and Stein Rokkan (eds), *Party Systems and Voter Alignment* (New York: Free Press, 1967).

7. See, for example, Reddaway, 'Instability and Fragmentation'; Rutland, 'Has Democracy Failed in Russia?'; and Ordeshook, 'Institutions and Incentives'.

8. Reddaway, 'Instability and Fragmentation', p. 13.

9. See, for example, Richard Rose, 'Mobilizing Demobilized Voters in Post-Communist Societies', paper presented at the Workshop on Public Opinion and Party Formation in Post-Communist and Authoritarian Democracies, Duke University, 24–25 March 1995; and White et al., *How Russia Votes*.

among an average of 15 parties'[10] and are more apt to feel strongly about parties they would not vote for compared with parties they feel represent their interests. White et al. similarly argue, with reference to the 1995 Duma election, that 'the great majority of Russian voters did not support a party in the sense of identifying with it'.[11] Likewise, Miller, White and Heywood write that 'the dominance of "the party" through 70 years of Soviet experience left voters in the former Soviet Union peculiarly allergic to the idea of committing themselves to any party'.[12]

The empirical evidence, however, strongly refutes the views expressed by the proponents of the traditional perspective on party development. Data collected as part of the University of Iowa Post-Soviet Citizen Survey (PSCS) project[13] reveal that Russians are not negative towards political parties as institutions but primarily neutral, a finding that today is typical of many democracies, including the United States.[14] For example, in the early spring of 1997, when asked to rate 'political parties' as an institution, 22 per cent gave a negative response, 62 per cent were neutral and 16 per cent gave a positive evaluation. While Russians were largely neutral towards 'political parties' in general, this did not keep them from identifying a specific party as best reflecting their interests. The Post-Soviet Citizen Surveys, in fact, show a significant growth in party identification among Russian citizens between 1992 and 1997. In the early summer of 1992, only about one-fifth of the Russian mass public indicated that there was a political party that best represented their interests. But by the spring of 1995 the percentage of partisans had increased to 52 per cent and at the beginning of 1997 party identification had risen to 61 per cent. This rapid rise in partisanship lends support to theories of endogenous partisan

10. Rose, 'Mobilizing Demobilized Voters', p. 5.
11. White et al., *How Russia Votes*, p. 229.
12. William Miller, Stephen White and Paul Heywood, 'Twenty-Five Days to Go: Measuring and Interpreting the Trends in Public Opinion During the 1993 Russian Election Campaign', *Public Opinion Quarterly*, Vol. 60 (1996), pp. 106–27.
13. The survey data used in this report are based on face-to-face interviews taken throughout Russia in February–March 1997. The sample 1,810 respondents was selected with a multi-stage probability design using the Kish method at the final stage. More information on the sample design is available from the authors.
14. Martin Wattenberg, *The Decline of American Political Parties 1952–1992* (Cambridge, MA: Harvard University Press, 1990).

identification articulated by a number of American scholars who argue that party identification can form relatively quickly in response to contemporary political events and issues or ideological polarization.[15]

Of course, we are not suggesting here that all the various parties that have been forming in Russia during the recent past have establishing enduring party organizations. In fact, very little empirical evidence on the organizational aspects of these parties exists. Rather, we are suggesting that some of the political parties are taking different policy stands, that these partisan differences are evident to the public and that the resulting identification with a party provides a meaningful framework for organizing the political world and for making choices about how to vote. If this is true, identification with particular political parties should begin to attain some degree of stability over time.[16]

Operationalizing identification with a political party in a multiparty system is not a straightforward task. As was the original intent of *The American Voter*,[17] we would want a measure that is simple to use but that captures a psychological sense of attachment or closeness to the party rather than membership of the party or a vote for it. Nevertheless, the survey question must allow the respondent to specify any one of the many parties that existed in Russia at the time of the survey. Hence, as our measure of party identification, we used a series of questions that first asked the respondents whether any one political party best represented their interests.[18] If the respondents answered 'yes', they

---

15. See, for example, Gregory B. Markus, 'The Political Environment and the Dynamics of Public Attitudes: A Panel Study', *American Journal of Political Science*, Vol. 23 (1979), pp. 338–59.

16. For previous work making this argument, see Steven M. Fish, 'Democracy Begins to Emerge', *Current History*, Vol. 94 (1995), pp. 317–21.

17. Angus Campbell, Philip D. Converse, Warren E. Miller and Donald Stokes, *The American Voter* (New York: John Wiley & Sons, 1960).

18. A follow-up question asking about the extent to which the party represented the respondents' interests was also asked in the survey, thus allowing one to construct a measure of the strength of party identification. That item, however, is not used in this chapter.

Our approach to operationalizing party identification has yielded higher levels of partisanship than has been found with other approaches. The explanation for this difference may be that our approach is simpler to understand and it may be more meaningful for the respondents. For example, the New Russian Barometer asks, 'Do you identify with any particular political party or movement?' (see White et al., *How Russia Votes*, p. 136 for an application of this question). Asking someone whether they 'identify' with a political party, however, is rather jargonistic and

were then asked a subsequent question inquiring about which particular party it was that best represented their interests. The response to this question is used throughout this chapter whenever reference is made to party identification.

The extent to which party identification had attained some degree of stability, at least in the aggregate, by early in 1997 is evident in Table 5.1. The frequency of identification with particular political parties is presented in Table 5.1 by party blocs for purposes of parsimony; however, previous work presents party identification for individual parties and demonstrates the substantive rationale for collapsing the various parties into these coalitional blocs.[19] Despite Yeltsin's re-election victory in July 1996, identification with the communist bloc increased between 1995 and 1997 (see Table 5.1). This growing support for the communists, however, appears to have come at the expense of the centrist bloc of parties more than of the pro-reform parties most closely aligned with the Yeltsin government. In short, while Table 5.1 reveals some recent gain in support for the Communist Party, it also reveals enough aggregate stability in levels of party

unclear. Surely the average citizen should not be expected to know what it means to 'identify' with a party, quite apart from difficulties of rendering such a concept into other languages. Similarly, Zimmerman and Colton asked the survey respondent whether they felt any party or political movement to be 'my party' (*moya partiya*). Such phrasing could be rather confusing for the respondent. For example, the respondent might wonder, does this phrase refer to the interviewer's party or my own party? It would have been better for the interviewer to say 'your party' (*vasha partiya*). For an application of this question, see Timothy Colton, 'Ivan Ivanovich Picks a President: Aspects of Public Choice', paper presented at the Annual Meeting of the American Association for the Advancement of Slavic Studies, Boston, MA, November 1996, pp. 13–14. By comparison our approach is very straightforward as it asks whether there is any party that best reflects the respondent's interests, and if they say 'yes' we ask which one.

Additional analysis with our party identification measure demonstrates that it does indeed reflect affective ties with the political parties. For example, the correlation between the party identification measure and a simple affective rating scale ranging from 1 = very negative to 7 = very positive for ratings of the Communist Party was –0.55 and for ratings of democratic reformers was 0.42. Similarly, the correlation between party identification and a measure asking how much the respondent had in common with the Communist Party and democratic reformers (where 1 = a great deal and 4 = nothing), was 0.52 and –0.38. These correlations validate the party identification measure as an indicator of psychological attachment similar to that found in the case of the United States.

19. Miller et al., 'Emerging Party Systems in Post-Soviet Societies'.

identification to pursue the question of whether this attachment to a party reflects only the popular appeal of the party leaders.

Table 5.1   Russian party identification by blocs (per cent)

Bloc[a]	1995	1997
Communists	30	44
Nationalists	10	9
Centrists	24	14
Pro-reform	36	33
Total	100	100
(N)	(752)	(1104)

Notes: [a] The party identification questions was: 'Is there one particular party that expresses your views better than any of the others?' If the answer was 'Yes', the respondent was asked, 'Which one?'.

Communists include:	Communist Party of the Russian Federation; Agrarian Party.
Nationalists include:	Liberal Democratic Party; Social Patriot Movement.
Centrists include:	Women of Russia; Congress of Russian Communities; Workers' Party for Self-government; Ecology Party (KEDR).
Pro-reform includes:	Russia's Democratic Choice; Our Home is Russia; Party of Russian Unity and Accord; Yabloko.

Source: The University of Iowa Post-Soviet Citizen Surveys (PSCS) for 1995 and 1997.

2. INVESTIGATING THE BASIS OF PARTISANSHIP THROUGH DIRECT MEANS

A variety of approaches can be used to investigate the hypothesis that popular support for a political party in Russia reflects the appeal of particular political leaders. One approach that is occasionally seen in survey studies utilizes a more direct assessment based on questions that ask the respondent to indicate the relative importance of various factors underlying their vote or support for a party. For example, Oates utilized such direct questions from a VTsIOM survey to argue that support for the Communist Party in the 1995 Duma election derived more from the representativeness of the party than from the allure of individual leaders.[20] As Oates says,

> it is significant that 43.1 per cent of those who claimed to have voted for the Communist Party listed the reason "the party expresses the interests of people such as myself" as the primary reason for their vote choice. Not only is this higher than the 30.4 per cent of the entire sample [who gave this reason], but it is more than twice the response rate given by voters for Our Home is Russia (18.3 per cent). Rather, Our Home is Russia voters said they were attracted by party leaders (27.5 per cent), a reason cited by relatively few voters (11.7 per cent) for the Communist Party. That suggests that the Communist Party is able to rely more on its ongoing strength as a party organization, rather than the appeal of individual leaders.[21]

For comparative purposes, the survey conducted by the University of Iowa in 1997 also contained a fairly direct question inquiring about what aspects of political parties the respondents found most appealing. After being asked whether there was a particular party that best expressed their views, the respondent was asked: 'What is the most appealing aspect of this party for you?' (the question, of course, referred to the party that they said best expressed their views). The possible responses, which had been determined from an earlier pilot study, were arrayed on a card presented to the respondent. In addition the respondent was asked whether there were any other aspects not included on the card. However, only 1 per cent offered an 'other' or alternative response for what they considered the most appealing aspect of the party. Roughly one-third of the respondents, on the other hand, indicated that they were not really sure what was the most appealing aspect of the party with which they identified.

The three most prevalent answers given by respondents were 'it reflects the interests of people like me' (36 per cent), 'the political platform and issue positions of the party' (23 per cent) and 'the party leaders' (16 per cent). As suggested by Oates (1996), the relative frequency of these responses did vary across the different parties. Those identifying with a party from the Communist Party bloc gave

20. Sarah Oates, 'The Impact of the Campaign on Vote Choice in the Russian Duma Elections of 1995', paper presented at the Annual Meeting of the American Political Science Association, San Francisco, 26 August–1 September 1996.
21. Ibid., p. 21.

much less emphasis to 'party leaders' than did supporters of parties from the nationalist or reform party blocs (see Table 5.2). Moreover, these differences hold even when the blocs are disaggregated into individual parties. For example, only 3 per cent of Agrarian Party identifiers and 5 per cent of Communist Party identifiers mentioned 'party leaders', whereas 23 per cent of Our Home is Russia and 34 per cent of Liberal Democratic Party identifiers pointed to party leaders as the most appealing aspect of the party they identify with.

Table 5.2   The most appealing aspect of the party identified with, by party bloc (per cent)

Most appealing aspect of party[a]	Party bloc			
	Communist	Nationalist	Centre	Pro-reform
It is important in this region	6.8	4.3	2.7	3.8
The party leaders	4.7	32.3	15.6	26.9
Organizational activities	4.9	1.1	12.9	7.5
Platform and issues	19.7	22.6	21.8	26.9
Its widespread support	10.2	8.6	2.7	7.5
My friends support the party	0.6	1.1	1.4	2.3
Reflects the interests of people like me	51.5	21.5	37.4	17.9
It can win seats in parliament	1.3	7.5	3.4	6.1
Other	0.4	1.1	2.0	1.2
Total	100	100	100	100

Note: [a] The survey question was 'What is the most appealing aspect of this party for you?'.

Source: 1997 PSCS.

Despite some variation from party to party, the data in Table 5.2 certainly suggest that the appeal of party leaders is less important in attracting support for political parties than are either the feeling that the party reflects the individual's best interests or the party platforms. The one exception may be the Liberal Democratic Party where one-third of the identifiers said that the party leader, Vladimir Zhirinovskii, was the most appealing aspect of the party. Nevertheless, even for Liberal

Democratic identifiers 24 per cent said the party's platform and 22 per cent mentioned that the party represents the interests of people like them as the most appealing aspect of the party. Hence, even with respect to the Liberal Democratic Party the data of the sort presented in Table 5.2 would lead to the conclusion that, while the appeal of party leaders may be an important aspect of why citizens are attracted to a party, this is not the overarching reason.

Before accepting this conclusion about the relative importance of party leaders, which contradicts the main hypothesis raised above, it would be prudent to heed the warnings of social psychologists regarding these types of questions. Research in cognitive social psychology has raised serious doubts about the assumptions underlying questions that ask respondents to explain their own behaviour or choices. For example, a great number of studies have now shown that people are unaware of many of the most important causes or explanations of their preferences.[22] Furthermore, when asked to explain their preferences, people are biased towards mentioning reasons that sound reasonable and that emphasize the most obvious characteristics of the object being discussed while overlooking more emotional reasons and factors other than the object's qualities.[23] Thus, people rationalize their pre-existing preferences.

All this social–psychological research raises doubts about the Russian survey respondents' ability to articulate accurately the real reasons for finding a particular party appealing. After all, what the question regarding the 'most appealing aspects of the party' does is ask the respondent to think about the reasons why they find a particular party appealing and then, having thought about that, to pick the most important reason out of all those possibilities. Cognitively this is a very difficult task even when the respondent is presented with an array of

22. See, for example, Richard E. Nisbett and Timothy D. Wilson, 'Telling More Than We Can Know: Verbal Reports on Mental Processes', *Psychological Review*, Vol. 84 (1977), pp. 231–59; or the recent review by Jon Krosnick and Lee R. Fabrigar, *Designing Questionnaires to Measure Attitudes: Insights From Cognitive and Social Psychology* (New York: Oxford University Press, 1997).

23. Timothy D. Wilson, Dana S. Dunn, Dolores Kraft and Douglas J. Lisle, 'Introspection, Attitude Change and Attitude-Behavior Consistency: The Disruptive Effects of Explaining Why We Feel the Way We Do', in Leonard Berkowitz (ed.), *Advances in Experimental Social Psychology*, Vol. 23 (New York: Academy Press, 1989).

possible reasons. In the end, as Noelle-Neumann suggests, respondents may be more likely to report what they have heard others saying about that party than what they themselves believe.[24] Likewise, these same concerns arise with respect to questions that ask voters to indicate what were the most important factors influencing their vote for a particular party or candidate.

3. INDIRECT MEANS OF INVESTIGATING THE BASIS OF PARTISANSHIP

Given the concerns about directly measuring what explains why Russians are attracted to particular political parties, it is important to examine the hypothesis through indirect means as well. Ideally such a test would involve measuring the relevant variables and examining the correlations among those variables. In this case what is important is to measure the extent to which the public finds a party leader appealing, and then compute the correlation between that assessment of leader popularity and identification with that leader's party. However, it was virtually impossible to find enough space in the survey questionnaire to measure all the relevant personality and issue assessments for more than a few leaders and parties. Alas, the survey contains a relatively full complement of measures only for Yeltsin, Zyuganov and Chernomyrdin. While this will limit our test of the hypothesis to a few rather than all parties, it is none the less an important test because these leaders and parties are certainly the major actors in Russian politics today.

Although Boris Yeltsin, the incumbent president of Russia, has resisted forming a political party, he could be viewed, in many respects, as the symbolic leader of all the pro-reform parties given the visible pro-democracy role he played during the final days of the Soviet Union. However, if any one reform party best reflected the Yeltsin government it would have to be Our Home is Russia (formed in 1995) because its leader, Viktor Chernomyrdin, was appointed prime minister by Yeltsin at the end of 1992. Gennadii Zyuganov is also very visible because he is the present leader of the Communist Party of the Russian

24. Elizabeth Noelle-Neumann, *The Spiral of Silence* (Chicago: University of Chicago Press, 1984).

Federation, and was that party's candidate who ran unsuccessfully against Yeltsin in the 1996 presidential election.

Leader Popularity

A number of scholars and journalistic writers have made light of Zyuganov's presumed lack of charisma and popular appeal. For example, Remnick says 'in Moscow and in the Western press, the conventional notion of Zyuganov was that he was a colorless, none too intelligent apparatchik whose sole talent was to make himself appear to be the sort of unthreatening communist that the audience in question was willing to accept'.[25] Also, White et al. refer to Zyuganov as having a 'lackluster personality'.[26] Yet, despite the fact that these observers attribute little personal appeal to Zyuganov, it is quite clear from empirical evidence that the Russian public found Zyuganov more appealing than is suggested by these political analysts. In absolute terms it is true that for the Russian public in general Zyuganov is not an overwhelmingly appealing individual. In the spring of 1997 only slightly more Russians rated him positively (36 per cent) than rated him negatively (32 per cent). Thus he was less popular than were Aleksandr Lebed (50 per cent positive, 18 per cent negative) or Moscow mayor Yuri Luzhkov (44 per cent positive, 13 per cent negative). Yet, Zyuganov was more positively evaluated than Yeltsin (22 per cent positive, 54 per cent negative – see Total sample means in Table 5.3). Also, at the time of the July presidential election, Zyuganov was only slightly less popular than Yeltsin (mean ratings of 44 and 47 respectively on a scale that had 100 as the most positive value).[27] Moreover, Zyuganov was relatively much more popular among those who identify with the Communist Party than Yeltsin was among those identified with Our Home is Russia (see Table 5.3).

The data of Table 5.3 do not directly shed any light on whether Russians vote more 'for' or 'against' a party,[28] as these data focus on party identification rather than the vote. Nevertheless, as far as party identification is concerned, it is quite clear not only that Russians are

25. David Remnick, *Resurrection: The Struggle for a New Russia* (New York: Random House, 1997).
26. White et al., *How Russia Votes*, p. 237.
27. See Colton, 'Ivan Ivanovich Picks a President'.
28. For a discussion of this see White et al., *How Russia Votes*, Ch. 11.

Table 5.3   Evaluations of political leaders by party identification

Party identified with	Zyuganov	Yeltsin	Chernomyrdin
Communist Party	6.0	2.2	3.0
Agrarian Party	4.7	2.9	3.8
Liberal Democratic Party	4.0	2.8	3.3
Social Patriotic Movement	3.9	3.1	3.2
Women of Russia	3.5	3.9	3.9
Congress of Russian Communities	3.7	2.8	3.1
Workers' Party for Self-government	3.4	3.1	3.2
Ecology Party	3.1	3.2	3.3
Yabloko	2.9	3.8	3.7
Party of Russian Unity and Accord	3.1	4.1	4.0
Russia's Democratic Choice	2.5	4.5	4.1
Our Home is Russia	2.7	5.0	5.2
Total sample	4.3	3.2	3.7

Note: The rating scale used to evaluate the leaders ranged from 1 = Very Negative, to 4 = Neutral, and 7 = Very Positive.

Source: 1997 PSCS.

attracted to the leader of the party with which they identify, but that they are less attracted to the leaders of parties with which they do not identify. For example, Communist Party identifiers are quite positive towards Zyuganov and relatively quite negative towards Yeltsin (see Table 5.3). Similarly, Our Home is Russia identifiers are relatively more positive towards Yeltsin and negative towards Zyuganov. Moreover, these relative differences in ratings are also true for the blocs of parties presented in Table 5.1. For example, reform party identifiers, taken as a group, were significantly more positive towards Yeltsin than towards Zyuganov, and the reverse was true for those identified with the communist bloc. There was also a significant difference in the popularity of the two leaders among those identified with the nationalist parties, with Zyuganov more positively evaluated than

Yeltsin (an average rating of 3.95 and 2.92, respectively). Centrist party identifiers, on the other hand, rated the two leaders nearly the same on average (3.42 for Zyuganov and 3.28 for Yeltsin).

The ratings of Chernomyrdin are also of interest as they reflect differences across party identification that are similar to those found for Yeltsin. For example, he was significantly more popular among Our Home is Russia identifiers than among those who identify with the Communist Party (see Table 5.3). Yet his overall popularity in early 1997 was higher than that found for Yeltsin, no doubt in part because Yeltsin was just recovering from his heart surgery and was just getting back into actively heading the government. But this is not the entire explanation for why the prime minister was somewhat more popular than the president. After all Chernomyrdin was only very slightly more popular than Yeltsin among Our Home is Russia identifiers (see Table 5.3). The difference in the popularity of the two leaders results more from the fact that Chernomyrdin was relatively less negatively assessed than Yeltsin among those identifying with the communist and national-ist party blocs. Given that Chernomyrdin, an old-style politician, has taken a slower approach to market reform than did Yegor Gaidar, Yeltsin's earlier prime minister, it is understandable that he would be relatively less negatively assessed than Yeltsin among supporters of the communist and nationalist party blocs.

To describe Russians as primarily opposed to or 'against' politicians, and as showing only apathy or lukewarm endorsement of political leaders and parties, would be to present an inaccurate summary of Russian attitudes towards political leaders. Clearly, various sub-populations find some political leaders more appealing than other leaders, and they are attracted to the political parties associated with the leaders towards whom they feel more favourable. In general, the popu-larity ratings of Yeltsin, Zyuganov and Chernomyrdin were all signifi-cantly correlated with party identification. The Pearson correlations between leader ratings and party identification were –0.55, 0.43 and 0.29 for ratings of Zyuganov, Yeltsin and Chernomyrdin, respectively.[29] The fact that the correlation is strongest for the popularity ratings of

29. The size of these correlations is quite similar to those found with comparable variables in the United States: for example, the 1996 correlation between party identification and ratings of Bill Clinton and Bob Dole, as determined from National Election Study data were –0.59 and 0.48, respectively.

Zyuganov clearly contradicts the outcome obtained with the direct method of investigating the basis of party identification. In short, these correlations and the data of Table 5.3 strongly suggest that party identification in Russia, particularly identification with the Communist Party, is at least partially a result of the popular appeal of the party leaders. It may very well be, therefore, that attachment to political parties in Russia does reflect no more than a shallow popularity and personalistic or charismatic appeal of the particular party leaders. Again, before accepting this conclusion as definitive it is important to delve deeper into what constitutes a leader's popularity.

Leader Traits

More than three decades ago Donald Stokes, in a classic article, argued that 'personality' characteristics, rather than issues or parties, provide the best explanation for shifts in the vote from one election to the next.[30] Yet, it was not until the 1980s that systematic theoretical and empirical research focused on the impact of candidate 'personality' on voting behaviour and party development. The dearth of earlier work in this area may reflect in part a predominant concern among social scientists with examining rational choice theories of candidate selection. Voting on the basis of personality characteristics is often viewed in the literature as 'irrational'.[31] The critics of party development in Russia mentioned above who refer to the supporters of political parties as no more than the fan club of the party leaders are, likewise, suggesting that if there is any current party attachment it must be based on superficial criteria such as the leader's style, looks or charisma.

More recent research on the public images of political leaders, however, reveals that public evaluations of political leaders are not necessarily superficial or irrational.[32] For example, this work reveals

30. Donald Stokes, 'Some Dynamic Elements of Contests for the Presidency', *American Political Science Review*, Vol. 60 (1966), pp. 19–28.

31. See, for example, Philip Converse, 'The Nature of Belief Systems in Mass Publics', in David Apter (ed.), *Ideology and Discontent* (New York: Free Press, 1964).

32. Donald Kinder, Mark Peters, Robert Abelson and Susan Fiske, 'Presidential Prototypes', *Political Behavior*, Vol. 2 (1980), pp. 315–37; Arthur H. Miller, Martin Wattenberg and Oksana Malanchuk, 'Schematic Assessments of Presidential Candidates', *American Political Science Review*, Vol. 80 (1986), pp. 521–40.

that various personality traits associated with different candidates are critical for overall public evaluations of these leaders. The particular traits that are most important to these evaluations, however, are not the individual's charisma or personal qualities, but rather traits that are relevant to assessing how the individual will perform in office, such as their perceived competence, strength of leadership, trustworthiness and compassion for others. These modern empirical findings are reminiscent of what Aristotle once said, namely that the character of a leader is composed of good sense, good will and good morals.

There is no necessary reason why such traits should not also apply to citizens' evaluations of leaders in Russia, particularly since they have been found to influence mass politics in a variety of Western parliamentary systems.[33] Moreover, Colton has demonstrated that public assessments of leaders' traits played at least some role in the outcome of the 1996 Russian presidential election.[34] Given these earlier findings, the 1997 University of Iowa Post-Soviet Citizen Survey included a battery of five trait measures focused on strength of leadership, compassion for others, trustworthiness, being a person of action not just words, and being tough on criminals. An earlier pilot study revealed that there were no other traits frequently mentioned when Russians were asked if there were any other traits that came to mind when thinking about Yeltsin and Zyuganov. The exact wording of the trait questions is presented in Appendix 5A.

The overall popularity ratings of both Yeltsin and Zyuganov were strongly correlated with the trait evaluations. The five traits explained 49 per cent and 58 per cent of the overall variance in the general popularity of Yeltsin and Zyuganov, respectively. Assessments of the extent to which Yeltsin was a strong leader had the greatest impact on the overall popularity of the president. Public judgements regarding Zyuganov's level of compassion, on the other hand, had the greatest impact on his overall popular rating.

Neither Yeltsin nor Zyuganov received particularly positive evaluations on the trait measures. In fact, roughly half of the Russians answered 'not at all' when asked to what extent Yeltsin was a 'strong

33. Steven Brown, Ronald Lambert, Barry Kay and James Curtis, 'In the Eye of the Beholder: Leader Images in Canada', *Canadian Journal of Political Science*, Vol. 21 (1988), pp. 729–55.
34. See Colton, 'Ivan Ivanovich Picks a President'.

leader', 'a person of action' or 'tough on criminals'. Also, 65 per cent said he was not caring and 34 per cent said he was not trustworthy. In general, Zyuganov was more positively assessed on the traits. Yet, significant percentages of respondents still said 'not at all' when asked whether he was caring (44 per cent), a strong leader (32 per cent), a person of action (39 per cent), tough on criminals (22 per cent) or trustworthy (18 per cent). When comparing trait assessments of Yeltsin and Zyuganov directly, however, it is quite clear that Zyuganov was far more positively evaluated relative to Yeltsin on each and every trait (see Figure 5.1). The difference in how the public judged the two leaders was particularly evident with respect to perceptions of how tough each leader would be on crime and criminals. As Figure 5.1 demonstrates, six out of ten Russians felt that Zyuganov would be tougher than Yeltsin and only roughly one in ten thought Yeltsin would be tougher than Zyuganov (the remaining 27 per cent saw no difference). In general, Figure 5.1 suggests that only six months after Yeltsin was re-elected president, it was he who had a lacklustre public image, not Zyuganov.

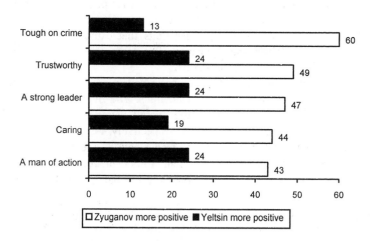

Figure 5.1 Character trait assessment of leaders

Of course, the rapid deterioration in public judgements of Yeltsin may reflect the public's response to his ill health. After all, only 10 per cent of the survey respondents disagreed with the statement that Yeltsin should resign because of his ill health. It should be recalled, however, that by the time of the survey, Yeltsin was well on his way to recovering from his heart surgery. Moreover, because of the highly skewed distribution on the responses to the health question, it was only very weakly correlated with the trait assessments for Yeltsin.

On the other hand, the trait assessments were significantly correlated with party identification. For example, those Russians identified with a communist bloc party were overwhelmingly (79 per cent) likely to perceive Zyuganov as a strong leader relative to Yeltsin, whereas pro-reform party identifiers were more likely to see Yeltsin as a stronger leader than Zyuganov (see Figure 5.2). Nationalist and centrist party identifiers, however, were relatively more positive towards Zyuganov, but not nearly to the same extent as the communist identifiers (see Figure 5.2).

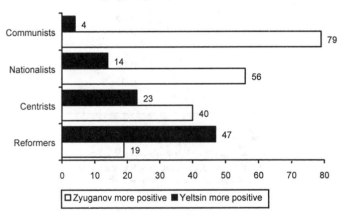

Note: Figures indicate percentage of respondents who agree with the statement that 'is a strong leader' characterizes either Zyuganov or Yeltsin.

Figure 5.2 Leadership trait assessment by party identification

To varying degrees, each of the other trait assessments was also correlated with party identification. However, because there is some overlap among the different trait assessments (the inter-item correlations ranged from 0.18 to 0.55), it is important to use multivariate analysis to sort out the relative impact of each trait dimension on party attachment. Having computed such an analysis, it is quite evident that public judgements of leader traits associated with Yeltsin and Zyuganov are strong influences on the development of party attachment in Russia. If party identification is conceptualized to reflect a running tally of political evaluations, as suggested by Fiorina, then it is clear from the regression results presented in Table 5.4 that citizen judgements regarding the relative traits of visible leaders play a significant role in determining that tally.[35] The trait measures taken as a whole explain a very significant 33 per cent of the variance in the party identification measure.[36]

Table 5.4   Predicting party identification from public assessments of leader traits

Traits	b	SE	Beta
Strong leader	0.32	0.05	0.17
Caring	0.38	0.06	0.18
Man of action	0.33	0.06	0.15
Trustworthy	0.24	0.04	0.12
Tough on crime	0.14	0.05	0.06
Adjusted R^2	0.33		

Notes: All coefficients are statistically significant at least at the level of $p < 0.001$ except for Tough on crime, which is significant at the 0.01 level.

The trait variables were measured as the difference in ratings of Zyuganov and Yeltsin on each trait as displayed in Figure 5.1. Negative values indicated that Zyuganov was relatively more positively evaluated on the trait, positive values meant that Yeltsin had a relatively better rating, and neutral indicated no difference in the trait rating of the two leaders.

The dependent variable was identification with a party bloc and was coded as follows: 1 = communist bloc, 2 = nationalist bloc, 3 = respondent not identified with a party, 4 = centrist bloc, 5 = reform bloc. For definition of party blocs, see Table 5.1.

Source: 1997 PSCS for Russia.

35. Morris Fiorina, *Retrospective Voting in American National Elections* (New Haven, CT: Yale University Press, 1981).
36. Again, the Russian regression results are very similar to those obtained with a comparable analysis of party identification in the United States. For the US case the exact same regression, using exactly comparable trait measures, for Clinton and Dole explained 40 per cent of the party identification variance.

Not all trait assessments, however, were equally important. The most significant effects on party identification occurred for judgements regarding the relative strength of leadership and compassion associated with Zyuganov and Yeltsin (see Table 5.4). The extent to which these leaders were judged to be action-orientated and trustworthy was also influential in raising support for a particular party. On the other hand, despite all the concerns about rising crime in Russia, the perception of which leader would be tougher on criminals did not seem to add much to the overall explanation for preferring one set of political parties over another.

In general, those Russians who perceived Yeltsin relative to Zyuganov as the stronger, more compassionate and action-orientated leader were much more likely to identify with a reform party. Similarly, those who evaluated Zyuganov relatively more positively with respect to these traits were more likely to identify with the Communist or Agrarian Party. And those Russians who were relatively more neutral towards both these leaders supported either a centrist or a nationalist party. The relative importance or appeal of a strong and caring leader may reflect historical Russian orientations towards authority figures who are then expected to look after the best interests of the dependent citizen in a paternalistic way.[37] On the other hand, the relative importance of the 'strong leader' and 'compassion' traits may just reflect those aspects of character most relevant to dealing with the pressing realities of the transformation process which is occurring at present in Russia. The citizens appear to be saying that they want a leader who will be strong and decisive in dealing with the changes, but yet who shows compassion towards those most adversely affected by the changes, such as those suffering hardships brought about by shifting to a market economy. After all, compassion and strength of leadership were also among the three most important traits correlated with party identification in the United States in 1996.[38] Even so, this finding surely would not lead to the interpretation that Americans prefer a paternalistic, authoritarian relationship with their political

---

37. Moshe Lewin, *The Gorbachev Phenomenon: A Historical Interpretation*, (Berkeley: University of California Press, 1988).
38. The order of relative importance for the top three traits in the US case is compassion, action and then strong leader (the standardized regression coefficients for the three traits, respectively, are 0.24, 0.17 and 0.15).

leaders. Rather, what these findings suggest is that citizens value such character traits as compassion for others and strength of leadership because these are performance-related traits that are relevant to carrying out the duties of the office — regardless of whether the office is the presidency of Russia or the United States. In short, public assessments of performance-related traits associated with political leaders appear to be a major explanation for the partisan identification rapidly emerging among post-Soviet Russian citizens.

4. CONTROLLING FOR COMPETING EXPLANATIONS

Before accepting leader traits as a major explanation of the party identification that is rapidly emerging in Russia, however, it is critical to control for potentially confounding factors and alternative explanations. After all, the associations displayed in Table 5.4 may simply be a spurious reflection of issue differences correlated with both parties and political leaders. Alternatively, underlying social cleavages may explain attitudes towards leaders and parties. Thus, a definitive statement about the direct impact of trait assessments on the development of party identification must await a multivariate test of the hypothesis, controlling for alternative explanations and possible spurious effects.

Substantively there are a number of alternative explanations that could reasonably account for the recently evident partisan attachment in Russia. These alternative explanations can be grouped into five general categories: a leftist or rightist ideology, economic considerations, democratic values, preferences for a particular type of political system, and social cleavages. Given that these alternative explanations will be treated here primarily as control variables, we present only a brief discussion of each concept. The operationalization of each plausible explanation is presented in Appendix 5A.

Leftist or Rightist Ideology

Before turning to more specific issue- and performance-related alternative explanations, it is reasonable to start with the broader ideological orientation of the political parties. A left–right continuum has long been seen as an organizing principle that individuals may use for bringing meaning to the world of politics.[39] According to this model individuals perceive the parties to be arrayed ideologically from left to right. Each individual also has a preferred left–right orientation. Individuals' own party choice subsequently results from selecting that party which they perceive as closest to their own ideological orientation.

Some scholars suggest that this model is inapplicable to post-communist countries. For example, Curry writes that 'the dilemma shared by politicians and voters is that left and right have yet to be truly meaningful in these societies'.[40] Certainly, during a period of rapid transformation in the political and economic regimes of a country the political meanings associated with left and right may shift and take on new interpretations. Yet, as Figure 5.3 vividly reveals, by early 1997 Russian citizens perceived sharp left–right differences between Yeltsin and Zyuganov.[41] Most Russians perceived Yeltsin towards the right, but not as far to the right as Zyuganov was to the left. Lebed and Zhirinovskii, on the other hand, were seen on average as only slightly to the right of centre (see Figure 5.3). These perceived differences also applied to their beliefs about where a number of political parties were located on this ideological spectrum. Moreover, a proximity index measuring the relative distance that each respondent was from Yeltsin and Zyuganov (or the CPRF and OHR parties) was significantly correlated with party identification.

Economic Considerations

Given that Russia is shifting from a command to a market economy, a number of economic factors may also influence public support for various political parties. First and foremost among those economic

39. Anthony Downs, *An Economic Theory of Democracy* (New York: Harper & Row, 1957).
40. Jane Curry, 'The Return of the Left', *Newsnet: The Newsletter of the AAASS*, Vol. 37, No. 3 (May 1997), pp. 1, 3.
41. Of course not all Russians felt comfortable with the left–right scale. Approximately one-third of the respondents failed to place themselves or the parties and leaders on the scale. This is considerably higher than the 10 per cent of survey respondents in Western Europe who usually do not provide an answer to the left–right scale, but only slightly higher than the percentage of US survey respondents who are generally unable to perform this task (about 25 per cent).

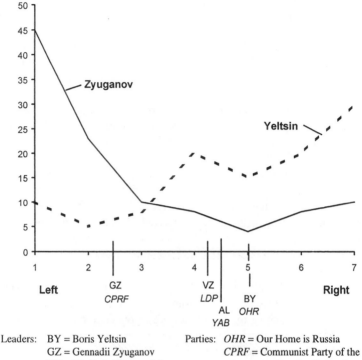

Leaders: BY = Boris Yeltsin   Parties: *OHR* = Our Home is Russia
          GZ = Gennadii Zyuganov   *CPRF* = Communist Party of the
          VZ = Vladimir Zhirinovskii   Russian Federation
          AL = Aleksandr Lebed   *YAB* = Yabloko
                                                LDP = Liberal Democratic Party

Figure 5.3 Perceptions of parties and leaders on left–right scale

factors may be how the public evaluates the past performance of the
national economy and their own individual financial situation.[42] Many
Russian citizens, particularly the elderly, have experienced severe
economic hardship under the Yeltsin government. For example, 60 per
cent of the 1997 respondents said that they and their families were

42. Kinder and Kiewiet, 'Economic Discontent and Political Behavior', pp. 495–
    527.

personally worse off than a year earlier and 75 per cent thought the national economy had deteriorated even further during the past year. Moreover, a majority of these people (56 per cent) felt that the government's economic policies were greatly responsible for their economic plight. Surely such individuals should have little incentive to identify with any of the pro-reform parties.

Under the Soviet system the government played a major role in providing for the economic well-being of Soviet citizens.[43] And, according to Inkeles and Bauer, the Soviet citizens had come to expect that their government would provide them with extensive social welfare benefits, including job security.[44] The locus of responsibility for citizen well-being has been changing, however. During the transformation period the government has been attempting to move Russian society from expecting the government to guarantee their well-being to a preference for an opportunity society in which they are responsible for their own welfare.[45] As previous research demonstrates, the locus of responsibility for well-being is an important economic issue in Russia. Virtually all Russians (97 per cent) have a preferred position on this issue. In addition, they perceive even sharper differences between Zyuganov and Yeltsin on this issue than they did in terms of left–right ideology. Zyuganov is clearly perceived as favouring a position that involves a broader government role in providing for citizen well-being, but not quite as strongly in favour of this position as is attributed to the Communist Party (see Figure 5.4). By comparison, Yeltsin, and somewhat less Our Home is Russia, are perceived as favouring individual responsibility. Yabloko, the LDP and Zhirinovskii are just somewhat to the right of centre while Lebed is perceived as somewhat left of centre on this issue (see Figure 5.4). Again it would be expected that those who are closer to Yeltsin on the locus of responsibility issue would have greater incentive to identify with a reform party while those closer to Zyuganov would be attracted to the Communist Party.

43. Ada Finifter and Ellen Mickiewicz, 'Redefining the Political System of the USSR: Mass Support for Political Change', *American Political Science Review*, Vol. 86 (1992), pp. 857–74.

44. Alex Inkeles and Raymond A. Bauer, *The Soviet Citizen: Daily Life in a Totalitarian Society* (Cambridge, MA: Harvard University Press, 1959).

45. Arthur H. Miller, William M. Reisinger and Vicki L. Hesli, 'Understanding Political Change in Post-Soviet Societies: A Further Commentary on Finifter and Mickiewicz', *American Political Science Review*, Vol. 90 (1996), pp. 153–66.

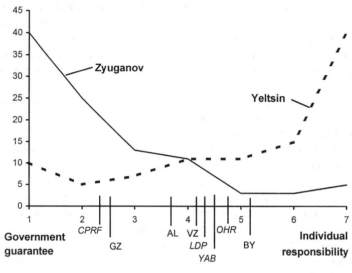

Figure 5.4 Should the government guarantee work and a standard of living? Citizens' perceptions of leaders' and parties' stances

The issue of privatization is another aspect of the current economic changes that influence party identification. Although the Yeltsin administration has pursued the privatization of industry and agriculture with varied aggressiveness over the past few years, it is clear that Yeltsin is more strongly favourable towards privatization than are Zyuganov and the Communist Party. Yet, public attitudes towards privatization do not favour Yeltsin's position. While only 27 per cent of Russians favour state ownership of small businesses, 35 per cent want the state to own farms and 75 per cent support state ownership of large industries. More importantly, when taken as a whole (by averaging across the three types of businesses), preferences for state ownership rose from 40 per cent in 1995 to 48 per cent in 1997 while support for private ownership dropped from 36 to 27 per cent.

Attitudes towards broader market norms may also influence party preferences in Russia. As Duch notes, the Soviet workplace put little emphasis on performance incentives.[46] Soviet workers could expect to retain their jobs even if their performance was only mediocre. Furthermore, the concept of a business profit was absent from the Soviet command economy. The new market economy, on the other hand, places emphasis on economic competition, a strong link between economic incentives and job performance, and also a strong motivation for earning large profits. Likewise, in a market economy workers can be dismissed from their jobs for substandard performance. Given that Yeltsin and his administration have become associated with economic reforms and a market economy we would expect that Russians who are more supportive of free-market norms would also be more likely to identify with a pro-reform party.

Similarly, public concerns about growing economic inequality may influence partisan attachment. In the former Soviet Union, the distribution of rewards was based as much on need as on merit. Despite a meritocratic incentive system, communist ideology gave strong emphasis to egalitarianism, which ensured that incomes were less highly differentiated in the former communist countries compared with Western capitalist countries.[47] Furthermore, the differences in wealth that did exist were kept as inconspicuous as possible. In the current period of change, differences in wealth have become very visible, thereby increasing public support for regulations to control differences in income. Also, a substantial proportion of Russians (42 per cent) feel that those Russians who have become wealthy in recent years have done so because they were engaged in illegal activities, not hard work. Given that the pro-reform parties have become associated with promoting equality of opportunity while the Communist Party is still more closely identified with equality of outcome, attitudes towards what is fair and equitable may also affect party identification.

46. Raymond M. Duch, 'Tolerating Economic Reform: Popular Support for Transition to a Free Market in the Former Soviet Union', *American Political Science Review*, Vol. 87 (1993), pp. 590–608.
47. Janos Kornai, *The Road to a Free Economy: Shifting From a Socialist System* (New York: Norton, 1990); James R. Kluegel, David S. Mason and Bernd Wegner, *Social Justice and Political Change* (New York: Aldine de Gruyter, 1995).

Democratic Values

Political values may potentially influence partisan identification as well. Despite relatively widespread support for democratic freedoms, the Russian public is still somewhat divided on certain democratic principles.[48] Various democratic norms, such as popular participation, the right to organize opposition to government policies, free competition among political parties, the willingness to compromise and protection for minority rights have all been associated with democratic consolidation. Many of these norms were ignored or played down under the Soviet system. A lack of public support for these democratic principles, therefore, might indicate a commitment to an earlier, more authoritarian political regime that would be more readily associated with the Communist Party than with the pro-reform parties. The extent of support for democratic principles might thus be a plausible factor influencing current party identification.

A less abstract expression of political preferences for a particular type of political system might also directly influence party attachment. A number of scholars and political pundits have argued that the 1996 Russian presidential election was a referendum on the type of political regime the Russian people preferred.[49] In early 1997, for example, 45 per cent of Russians said they preferred a Soviet-style political system, whereas only 31 per cent said they favoured either the present Russian regime or a Western-style democracy. Similarly, 38 per cent of Russians said that they still thought of themselves to a great extent as 'a Soviet person', and 35 per cent of Russians strongly disagreed with the statement that the breakup of the USSR into separate states was justified. In short, there is clearly residual support among Russians for the earlier Soviet system. Presumably those who prefer a democratic regime should be more likely to identify with pro-reform parties, while

48. James Gibson, 'A Mile Wide But an Inch Deep: The Structure of Democratic Commitments in the Former USSR', *American Journal of Political Science*, Vol. 40 (1996), pp. 396–420.

49. See, for example, Colton, 'Ivan Ivanovich Picks a President'; Warren J. Mitofsky, 'Exit Polling on the Russian Elections', *The Public Perspective*, August–September 1996, pp. 41–4; William Zimmerman, 'Foreign Policy, Political System Preference, and the Russian Presidential Election of 1996', paper presented at the Annual Meeting of the American Association for the Advancement of Slavic Studies, Boston, MA, November 1996.

those more inclined towards a Soviet-style system should have greater tendencies to identify with parties towards the communist end of the party bloc continuum.

Social Cleavages

One final set of alternative explanations arises out of the traditional social cleavage literature.[50] According to this argument, political parties develop in a fashion that reflects enduring social divisions. Evans and Whitefield find that the social bases of party attachment are instrumental in determining the speed of political party formation in newly developing democracies.[51] They argue that when parties can attract support based on appeals to specific categories of individuals, they may be able to circumvent the problems associated with the lack of a strong civil society. Their work suggests that social differences in support of various political parties in Russia, Estonia, and to a lesser extent in Ukraine, were emerging as early as 1993. By 1995 in Russia they find that gender, age, region, education and income critically differentiate among those who identify with various party blocs. In short, this research suggests that social divisions may play an important role in the current development of party identification in Russia.

Regression Results

Among all the measures indicating plausible alternative explanations for party identification, only two variables did not have a statistically significant zero-order correlation with party identification. Only gender and religious belief (that is, whether the respondent was a believer or not) lacked significant correlation with the party identification measure. When considered in a multivariate analysis, the alternative explanations certainly do add to the overall prediction of party identification, but not

---

50. See Lipset and Rokkan, *Party Systems and Voter Alignment*, for the traditional perspective on social cleavages as the basis for party formation.
51. Geoffrey Evans and Stephen Whitefield, 'Cleavage Formation in Transition Societies: Russia, Ukraine, and Estonia, 1993–1995', paper presented at the annual meeting of the American Political Science Association, San Francisco, CA, August 1996.

Table 5.5 Multivariate analysis predicting party identification in Russia

Predictors	Party bloc measure[a]			Our Home is Russia[b]		
	b	SE	Beta	*b*	SE	Beta
Traits						
Popularity rating[c]	–	–	–	0.05	0.01	0.11*
Strong leader	0.25	0.05	0.13*	–	–	–
Caring	0.23	0.06	0.10*	–	–	–
Man of action	0.20	0.06	0.09*	–	–	–
Trustworthy	0.17	0.04	0.08*	–	–	–
Tough on crime	0.13	0.05	0.06[†]	–	–	–
Ideology						
Left–right proximity	0.11	0.02	0.15*	0.17	0.04	0.20*
Economic						
Personal finances	–0.01	0.03	–0.00	0.01	0.06	0.01
National economy	–0.01	0.03	–0.00	–0.12	0.05	–0.08[†]
Locus of responsibility	0.06	0.01	0.09*	0.04	0.01	0.06[†]
State ownership	0.05	0.02	0.06[†]	0.09	0.02	0.11*
Market norms	0.02	0.01	0.03	0.06	0.02	0.10*
Distributive justice	0.01	0.01	0.02	0.02	0.03	0.04
Political values						
Democratic principles	0.01	0.01	0.03	0.01	0.02	0.03
Preferred political system	0.06	0.01	0.10*	0.09	0.01	0.16*
Social cleavages						
Age	–0.01	0.01	–0.02	–0.00	0.01	–0.01
Gender	0.08	0.05	0.03	0.05	0.11	0.02
Education	0.04	0.01	0.06[†]	0.01	0.03	0.02
Income	0.00	0.00	0.02	0.00	0.00	0.01
Urban/rural	–0.11	0.04	–0.05[†]	–0.04	0.08	–0.02
Believer	–0.10	0.06	–0.04	–0.05	0.11	–0.00
R^2	0.44			0.31		
N	1574			1320		

Notes:

*$p < 0.001$ †$p < 0.01$

[a] The party bloc dependent variable was coded 1 = communist bloc of parties, 2 = nationalist bloc, 3 = respondents not identified with any party, 4 = centrist bloc, 5 = reform bloc. For definition of the party blocs see Table 5.1.

[b] The measure of identification with Our Home is Russia (OHR) was coded 1 = all party identifiers except OHR, 2 = non-identifiers, 3 = identify with OHR.

[c] This is the affective rating for Viktor Chernomyrdin, 1 = very negative, 7 = very positive.

Source: 1997 PSCS.

all the plausible factors contributed significantly.[52] The left–right and locus of responsibility proximity measures, as well as attitudes towards privatization, the type of political system preferred, education and urban or rural residence all directly contribute to a general explanation of party identification (see Table 5.5). Furthermore, in general the explained variance for the model is much higher than it was for the model that included only the trait measures (see Table 5.4).

Yet, it is quite clear from the regression results that public assessments of Yeltsin's and Zyuganov's character traits remain the most potent explanation of party identification even after controlling for other alternative explanations.[53] A comparison of the *b* values in Tables 5.4 and 5.5 reveals that the control variables do weaken the direct effect of the trait assessments on party identification, but not to a great extent. Moreover, a similar multivariate analysis predicting party identification with Our Home is Russia provides comparable results. Unfortunately, the survey did not contain trait measures for Chernomyrdin, but the negative or positive rating of him remains significant in the equation that includes the controls.

5. CONCLUSION

On the one hand the critics of party development in Russia are correct – party identification largely reflects the popular appeal of political

52. The regression analysis presented in Table 5.5 assumes only one-way causality with party identification as the dependent variable. This assumption is based on the fact that even as recently as 1992 very few Russians identified with a political party and most political parties did not even exist prior to 1993. Of course, one might realistically argue that the Communist Party was in existence prior to this recent period and that a reciprocal relationship might exist between identification with that party and some of the predictor variables included in Table 5.5. This is a reasonable hypothesis, but testing it goes well beyond this particular report.

53. Clearly the regressions in Table 5.5 provide only for direct effects. Some of the factors explaining party identification would look stronger if both direct and indirect effects were considered. For example, social cleavages most probably influence party identification both directly and indirectly through their influence on attitudinal variables that are more proximate to the dependent variable party identification. Computing such indirect effects, however, goes beyond the purpose of this report which is to determine whether leadership traits influence party identification even after controlling for other plausible explanations.

leaders. Yet this does not mean that party attachment is irrational or based on superficial appeals. The leadership traits that the citizens evaluated reflect criteria that are relevant to the performance of tasks expected of national leaders. Whether a leader is trustworthy or compassionate may be just as important for success in the office as are his or her positions on domestic or foreign policy.

That the Russian public's partisan preferences would be so heavily influenced by leadership traits may reflect the fact that this is a newly emerging party system with little past party socialization except for the Communist Party. In the absence of a long history with a multiparty system, particularly in an age of electronic mass media, it is understandable that the running tally represented by party identification would reflect judgements regarding the character traits of political leaders. Such traits are more evident than the issue and policy positions that the leaders may attempt to pursue while in office. Moreover, earlier research suggests that judgements about character traits form an important basis from which inferences can be made regarding the types of policies and the style of leadership that a politician would pursue in office. For example, a compassionate politician is unlikely to promote policies that disregard opportunities for underprivileged individuals.

The types of leadership traits valued by Russian citizens are not superficial such as charisma, charm, or celebrity; rather, they value strength of leadership, compassion and an ability to solve problems. If the public image constructed by a politician does not match these qualities in the long run, his or her popularity may be volatile and short-lived. On the other hand, if the public assessments of the leader do reflect enduring character qualities, then those judgements may be as valid and sound a basis of party development as the perception of programmatic differences between the parties. Previous research demonstrates that these trait assessments are closely associated, in the public's perception, with judgements about the ability of the leader to perform adequately while in office.[54] Given how critical government performance is during a period of transformation from one type of regime and economic system to another, it is understandable that attachment to political parties reflects expectations of how particular

54. Arthur H. Miller and Martin Wattenberg, 'Throwing the Rascals Out: Policy and Performance Evaluations of Presidential Candidates, 1952–1980', *American Political Science Review*, Vol. 79 (1985), pp. 359–72.

leaders might perform the duties of the office. These types of judgements, however, are far more substantive than is suggested by those who argue that Russian political parties are merely fan clubs.

Of course public judgements about leader traits are not the only factors influencing party identification. It is clear that the emerging party preferences also reflect profound policy differences among the parties. Perhaps somewhat surprising is the rather weak direct effect that the social cleavage variables have on party identification. However, this is understandable in a society that is undergoing major shifts in socioeconomic status and that is lacking in the civic organizations (such as trade unions) essential to translating social cleavages into unified and represented political interests. Also, we have looked only at direct effects here. The total impact of social cleavages would be somewhat stronger if indirect effects (that is, the impact of social cleavages on the various attitudinal variables which are more directly related to party identification) were considered in addition to direct effects. But, the purpose here is not to provide a total explanation for the rise of party identification in Russia; rather, the goal is more modest. We are interested in testing for the hypothetical effect of the evaluation of leadership traits on party identification after controlling for other plausible effects.

Finally, we should note that this study deals with political parties in the electorate and only from the perspective of party identification. Before drawing conclusions about the development of political parties or party systems more generally we must look at parties as organizations as well as parties in the Duma. Moreover, critics might object that by focusing on party identification as a psychological attachment rather than a behavioural act, such as voting for a party, we confound the issue of causality. In other words, perhaps evaluations of political leaders were caused by preferences for a particular political party, rather than the reverse as we assume in our multivariate analysis. Given that the Communist Party has existed in Russia for some time, there is good reason to have concerns about reciprocal effects with respect to that party. The other parties, however, have appeared so recently that surely this cannot apply to them. Future work should certainly explore the possibility of a reciprocal relationship between affect towards the party and affect towards the party leaders. This possibility is quite ironic, however, in that the results of 'direct investigation' of the main hypothesis of this study (see Table 5.2) suggest that citizen identification with the Communist Party might reflect its programmatic orientation and organization but surely would not reflect the appeal of its leaders, particularly Zyuganov. Clearly the research approach and methods we deploy can have significant consequences for the conclusions reached. The indirect and more scientifically sound approach, however, demonstrates that leadership traits are as important for the future success of political parties in Russia as are policy and ideological preferences. Moreover, leadership appeal is important not only for the success of pro-reform or nationalist parties, but also for the future of the Communist Party. We can expect leadership appeal to be the dominant factor in the development of party identification until the political parties establish a track record that demonstrates enduring programmatic differences between them.

APPENDIX 5A

All indices were computed as a simple additive measure after ensuring that all items were coded in the same substantive direction. Variable numbers are for the 1997 study.

Candidate Appraisal

The Candidate Appraisal measures were produced by subtracting the response for each question about Zyuganov from the respective question for Yeltsin (range: –3 to +3, with neutral and missing values counted as 0).

The respondents were asked to indicate to what extent each trait fitted with their impression of the political leaders. The traits were: 'Is a strong leader'; 'Really cares about people like me'; 'Trustworthy'; 'Is a person of action, not just words'; 'Tough on crime and criminals'.

Democratic Values Index

This index was constructed by combining responses to five questions (range: 1–20, with 1 being 'Non-democratic' and 20 being 'Democratic'). The substance of the questions dealt with the role of political participation in a democracy, the right to organize opposition to government, support for a competitive party system, protection of minority rights and acceptance of compromise.

Retrospective Economic Variables

Personal
18. Would you say that you and your family (living here) are much better off, somewhat better off, about the same, somewhat worse off or much worse off economically than you were a year ago?

National
25. And as for the country in general, do you think that the condition of the economy has got much better, somewhat better, stayed the same, or got somewhat worse or much worse in comparison with the past year?

State Ownership

The state ownership indices were constructed by combining the following questions:

> Economic organizations can be owned by the government, employees of the organization, or private individuals. For each type of organization I will read, please tell me whether in your opinion, the government, the employees or private individuals should own such organizations: former *kolkhoz* and *sovkhoz* property (farms and farmland); large industry; local businesses like shops and restaurants.

Low values on the resulting index indicate a preference for state ownership of property, while high values indicate that private ownership is preferred.

Left–Right Measure

30. Self placement on a scale ranging from 1 to 7 where 1 is the far left and 7 is the far right.

Locus of Responsibility

39. Some people say the central government of the Russian Federation should guarantee everyone work and a high standard of living, others argue that every person should look after him- or herself. On this card is a scale from 1 to 7, where 1 signifies that the government guarantees everyone work and 7 that every person should look after him- or herself. You may select any number from 1–7. Which number corresponds to your views?

Market Norms

162. Some people believe that large business profits should not be allowed; others believe that business profits should be allowed to be as large as possible. Which is closest to your view?
163. Some people believe that companies should fire workers who do not work effectively enough; others think that a job should be guaranteed to everyone who at least tries to do their job regardless of how effectively they work. Which of these do you agree with?

Distributive Justice

63. I am now going to read you a number of statements. For each statement, would you please indicate whether you fully agree, partially agree, partially disagree or fully disagree. 'There should be a mechanism regulating income such that no one earns very much more than others'.

107. Next I would like to know what in your view is dangerous for our society, that is, leads towards destabilization in our country. For each item I will now mention, evaluate the degree of danger with numbers from 1 to 7, where 1 means no danger at present and 7 means the highest danger. 'The growth of economic inequality among citizens'.

161. During the past few years, some people in Russia have become wealthy. On this card are some of the reasons people give for this increasing wealth. Which *one* of the reasons listed on the card do you think is the *best* explanation for why these people have become more wealthy?

1. There are just many more opportunities for entrepreneurship;
2. They have the right connections;
3. Individual talent and creativity;
4. They are involved in illegal activities;
5. They are just very hard working people;
6. The old *nomenklatura* is acquiring for itself state property.

Preferred Political System

24. Which political system, in your opinion, would be best for Russia?

1. The Soviet system, as it was before *perestroika*;
2. The political system which exists today;
3. A Western-style democracy.

6. Ideological Divisions and Party-building Prospects in Post-Soviet Russia[1]

William M. Reisinger, Arthur H. Miller and Vicki L. Hesli

All the skill of the actors in the political world lies in the art of creating parties.

– Alexis de Tocqueville

Russia provides an opportunity to track, virtually from scratch, how a political party system develops. Numerous scholars are focusing on different aspects of the matter using diverse methods. For a complete picture eventually to emerge, though, scholars must be able to place the development of Russia's political parties in the context of Russian society. It makes sense, therefore, to complement investigations into parties' platforms, electoral strategies, membership levels and other features with investigations of the characteristics of Russia's voters and potential voters. In this chapter, we employ survey data to search for groupings of Russian citizens sufficiently similar in their outlooks that they could potentially vote as a bloc for whatever party plays to their concerns. We seek, in other words, the ways in which nascent Russian parties might engage in what Ziegler calls 'inventing the people'.[2]

We begin by demonstrating that critical issue cleavages do mirror identifiable subsets of the Russian populace. We then show that

1. We thank Frederic Fleron, Robert Grey and Matthew Wyman for helpful suggestions on revising the initial version of this chapter.
2. Harmon Ziegler, *Political Parties in Industrial Democracies* (Itasca, IL: F.E. Peacock, 1993), pp. 27–30.

Russians in these subsets show markedly different patterns of political behaviour and party support. By arraying these groupings in a two-dimensional issue space, we highlight some existing correspondence between parties and voting blocs, yet reveal many potential voting blocs not currently well targeted by Russian parties.

1. ISSUE CLUSTERING AS A SOURCE OF POTENTIAL VOTING BLOCS

By common agreement, Russia's party system has not yet 'settled down'.[3] That is, the number of parties, the issue dimensions along which parties array themselves and public identification of certain parties with certain positions continue to fluctuate. Although the settling down appears to have begun, Russian electoral politics remain in a 'shake-down' phase.

A rough mapping of the electoral environment can therefore be of

---

3. For more information on the formation of Russian political parties over the past decade, see: Joel C. Moses, 'The Challenge to Soviet Democracy from the Political Right', in Robert T. Huber and Donald R. Kelley (eds), *Perestroika-Era Politics: The New Soviet Legislature and Gorbachev's Political Reforms* (Armonk, NY: M.E. Sharpe, 1991), pp. 105-27; Michael E. Urban, 'Party Formation and Deformation on Russia's Democratic Left', in Huber and Kelley (eds), *Perestroika-Era Politics*, pp. 129-50; Geoffrey A. Hosking, Jonathan Aves and Peter J.S. Duncan, *The Road to Post-Communism: Independent Political Movements in the Soviet Union, 1985-1991* (London and New York: Pinter, 1992); Michael McFaul, 'Russia's Emerging Political Parties', *Journal of Democracy*, Vol. 3, No. 1 (January 1992), pp. 25-40; Robert W. Orttung, 'The Russian Right and the Dilemmas of Party Organization', *Soviet Studies*, Vol. 44, No. 3 (1992), pp. 445-78; Gordon M. Hahn, 'Opposition Politics in Russia', *Europe–Asia Studies*, Vol. 46, No. 2 (1994), pp. 304-35; Marcia Weigle, 'Political Participation and Party Formation in Russia, 1985-1992: Institutionalizing Democracy?', *The Russian Review*, Vol. 53, No. 2 (April 1994), pp. 240-69; Ian McAllister and Stephen White, 'Democracy, Political Parties and Party Formation in Post-communist Russia', *Party Politics*, Vol. 1, No. 1 (1995), pp. 49-72; M. Steven Fish, 'The Advent of Multipartism in Russia, 1993-95', *Post-Soviet Affairs*, Vol. 11, No. 4 (October–December 1995), pp. 340-83; Stephen White and Matthew Wyman, 'Political Parties and the Public', in David Lane (ed.), *Russia in Transition: Politics, Privatisation and Inequality* (New York: Longman, 1995), pp. 36-51, and John Löwenhardt (ed.), *Party Politics in Post-Communist Russia* (London: Cass, 1998).

value. Given what is known about the major Russian political parties from their own statements, campaign platforms, positions in the legislature and other information, at least two issue dimensions must be used when depicting relative party positions. These two issue dimensions are the economic and the national–statist. In economic debates, parties differ in their preferences concerning the extent of privatization, the role of the government in the economy, and other limits on market economics. Some parties, in other words, are strongly leftist in the Western sense, while others are more strongly rightist. Arraying parties along this dimension by itself may hide too many salient differences among parties that share an approximate position on the economic dimension, however,[4] and a clearer picture is likely to emerge by also distinguishing parties' positions in the debate over the type of state Russia should be and how it should interact with foreign countries. Figure 6.1 shows an approximation of the positions of the leading parties in the resulting two-dimensional issue space.[5]

The positioning of the political parties in Figure 6.1 is merely illustrative. The distances from one party to another on either scale are not precise. Parties were placed in certain positions on the basis of how they portray themselves and how they were portrayed in the Russian media, and also on the basis of discussions of various parties by scholars. The point of the figure is to portray the way in which the two-dimensional space provides a more useful depiction of the ground for which parties are struggling (note that parties that cleared the 5 per cent barrier in 1995 fall into three of the four quadrants). We shall use a

---

4. Bringing in the second dimension also makes less puzzling the alliance between red and brown that Fish, citing Sartori, notes as a Russian peculiarity: see Fish, 'The Advent of Multipartism in Russia', pp. 363–4. Fish notes this feature of the second dimension on p. 372.

5. For another depiction of Russia's party system in a two-dimensional configuration, see R.T. Mukhaev, *Osnovy politologii: Uchebnik dlya srednei shkoly (Fundamentals of Political Science: A Secondary School Text)* (Moscow: Novaya shkola, 1996), p. 144. Mukhaev places parties along a left–right dimension and a dimension reflecting each party's orientation towards the West or away from the West and 'back to the soil'. The placement of key parties along the two dimensions is quite similar to that in Figure 6.1. Note also the similarity between the two dimensions employed here and the two deployed for East–Central European parties in Herbert Kitschelt, 'The Formation of Party Systems in East Central Europe', *Politics and Society*, Vol. 20, No. 1 (March 1992), pp. 7–50. See Fish's comment on Kitschelt's scheme in 'The Advent of Multipartism in Russia', pp. 369–77.

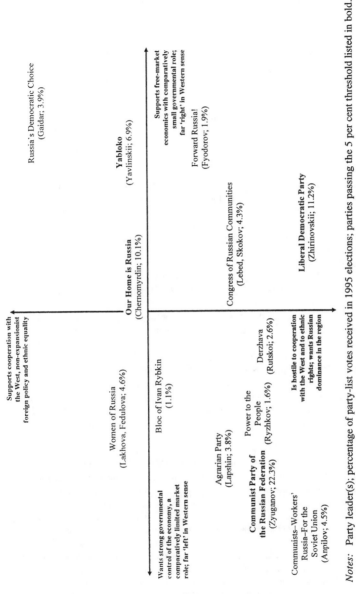

Notes: Party leader(s); percentage of party-list votes received in 1995 elections; parties passing the 5 per cent threshold listed in bold.

Figure 6.1 Major Russian political parties on two ideological dimensions

similar two-dimensional chart below to indicate where key groupings of Russian citizens are in relation to other groupings.

Our analyses will not seek to identify ideological factors associated with a citizen voting for this or that party – and therefore, perhaps, explaining party support.[6] We stand this strategy somewhat on its head by searching for the options that party organizations face in a relatively new, still changing electoral setting. As Lawson notes, 'New parties tend to form around the cleavages of the time'.[7] The most influential study of West European parties suggests that parties continue to reflect the cleavages that prevailed during the formative

6. The term 'ideology' has many meanings, and we use it differently from, for example, Stephen E. Hanson, 'Ideology and the Rise of Anti-System Parties in Post-Communist Russia', in Löwenhardt (ed.), *Party Politics*, or Evert van der Zweerde, 'Civil Society and Ideology: A Matter of Freedom', *Studies in East European Thought*, Vol. 48, No. 2–4 (September 1996), pp. 171–205. We use it as a synonym of the phrase 'issue dimension' to denote any scheme for simplifying politics by imagining that many concrete decisions and choices are interrelated in a linear fashion. The economic (horizontal) dimension in Figure 6.1, for example, is an ideological dimension in this sense because placing an individual or organization on it summarizes that person or organization's attitudes towards such concrete decisions as finalizing the privatization plan for the fourth quarter of 1997, appointing a Central Bank chairman and many others. Although a simplification, some degree of political sophistication must exist for political choices to cohere into an ideology: individuals might deal with the complexities of political life through parochialism (rejecting knowledge), by caring only about a single issue or by dichotomizing political society into 'us' and 'them' based on one or another criteria, such as ethnicity. For evidence that Russians are coming to understand politics in terms of the left–right dimension we use in Figure 6.1, see Timothy J. Colton's contribution to this volume. In addition, the dimensions in Figure 6.1 are 'ideologies' in the sense that Peter McDonough has distinguished ideologies from identities and interests. When political conflict involves religious, regional, ethnic or similar *identities*, resolution is extremely difficult. When conflict involves relatively fluid economic *interests*, the possibility of log-rolling and other forms of pay-offs makes resolution comparatively simple. Ideological conflict, though, lies between these two extremes, involving basic questions about 'property, developmental strategy, or institutional strategy'. For Russia, one would augment this list with debates over the country's basic orientation towards the external world. See Peter McDonough, 'Identities, Ideologies, and Interests: Democratization and the Culture of Mass Politics in Spain and Eastern Europe', *Journal of Politics*, Vol. 57, No. 3 (August 1995), pp. 649–76 (p. 650).
7. Kay Lawson, 'Political Parties and Party Competition', in Joel Krieger (ed.), *The Oxford Companion to Politics of the World* (New York: Oxford University Press, 1993), pp. 722–7 (p. 723).

period.[8] This fact should not suggest, however, that the matching of parties and cleavages is either simple or automatic. Much will depend on party elites' strategies.

We begin by noting that any Russian party that manages to survive and prosper will have found success in campaigning for votes among the public. To accomplish this, a party must propose '[programmes] responsive to the perceived needs and wishes of those whose support they seek'.[9] Parties must therefore deploy resources of time and money to send messages to potential voters in order to sway them to select the party from a voting list or to vote for the party's candidate. Although a party can change the emphasis it places on different themes when campaigning in different forums, credibility among its core supporters requires at least a modicum of stability in the messages sent. Hence, a successful party must put a great deal of thought into deciding its public posture. The nature of the media available for party campaigning reinforces the importance of targeting party themes. Even a campaign spot aired over a national television channel will reach different groups to different degrees, depending on the day of the week, the time of day and the nature of the surrounding programmes.

We should presume, then, that party leaderships seek information on the 'clustering' of attitude across the Russian populace. To the degree that scholars can observe such clustering through their techniques (perhaps the same as those used by party leaders, perhaps not), they will generate insight into parties' behaviour. The clustering may occur along lines of personal characteristics: gender or age, for instance. It may be along ascriptive lines such as racial, religious or ethnic identities. It may distinguish those with different places in the social and economic order, cutting across occupational categories or levels of educational attainment or rural versus urban residence. It may be regional: Russia's regions differ markedly in their mix of industries, for instance. Russia's present electoral law encourages both regional and non-regional campaigning. It provides for half the seats in the lower

8. Seymour Martin Lipset and Stein Rokkan (eds), *Party Systems and Voter Alignments* (New York: Free Press, 1967). See the discussion of the literature spawned by Lipset and Rokkan's work in Kenneth Janda, 'Comparative Political Parties: Research and Theory', in Ada W. Finifter (ed.), *Political Science: The State of the Discipline II* (Washington, DC: American Political Science Association, 1993), pp. 163–91 (pp. 169–70).

9. Lawson, 'Political Parties and Party Competition', p. 724.

house of the legislature to be elected from districts, which encourages the search for issue positions that generate regional majorities, and half to be elected on country-wide party lists, which encourages the search for issue positions that mobilize support from ascriptively defined groups.

Evidence suggests that some key components of a democratic party system are indeed emerging in Russia. Partisan attachment among the Russian public is increasing, as is the correlation between the policy views of legislators representing a party and voters who identify with the same party.[10] There is little question, though, that Russian politics has yet to generate sufficient representation (even by the often limited standards of Western democracies). One of the key rationales for party competition, in other words, is that public preferences can, over the course of several election cycles, meaningfully guide the policies that elites pursue.[11] Ziegler has noted that such public guidance of state policies will only arise when (i) competing parties offer clear policy alternatives; (ii) voters are concerned about policy; (iii) election results clarify majority preferences on these matters; (iv) elected officials are bound by the positions which they assume during the campaigns; and (v) elected officials have the institutional power to implement their commitments.[12]

Yet, even if these conditions are not fully met, party leaderships

---

10. Arthur H. Miller, Gwyn Erb, William M. Reisinger and Vicki L. Hesli, 'Emerging Party Systems in Post-Soviet Societies: Fact or Fiction', paper presented at the annual meeting of the International Society of Political Psychology, Vancouver, BC, Canada, July 1996.

11. This is only one of several possible understandings of the term representation, and the extent to which representation in this meaning exists in Western democracies remains a topic of sharp debate: see Hannah Pitkin, *The Concept of Representation* (Berkeley, CA: University of California Press, 1967), for a discussion of the term's many meanings. For studies of levels of representation in the sense we use it, see Warren E. Miller and Donald E. Stokes, 'Constituency Influence in Congress', *American Political Science Review*, Vol. 57, No. 1 (March 1963), pp. 45–56; Philip E. Converse and Roy Pierce, *Political Representation in France* (Cambridge, MA: Harvard University Press, 1986); James A. Stimson, Michael B. MacKuen and Robert S. Erikson, 'Dynamic Representation', *American Political Science Review*, Vol. 89, No. 3 (September 1995), pp. 543–65; and William M. Reisinger, Andrei Yu. Melville, Arthur H. Miller and Vicki L. Hesli, 'Mass and Elite Political Outlooks in Post-Soviet Russia: How Congruent?', *Political Research Quarterly*, Vol. 49, No. 1 (March 1996), pp. 77–101.

12. Ziegler, *Political Parties*, p. 30.

must search for potential voting blocs. They must establish an identity among, and gain loyalty from, a public many of whose members remain unaccustomed to identifying themselves with one among several competitive parties. Moreover, Russian parties do not have a base of support created by the passing down of partisanship from parent to child. With the partial exception of the Communist Party of the Russian Federation (CPRF), Russian parties are too new. To accomplish this, a party must construct an issue identity that appeals to a sizeable subset of the voters. Constructing an issue identity that resounds in the public mind entails not just matching party positions to public opinion: parties, of course, also pursue public support by such complementary strategies as redefining the terms of political debates and thereby change the lines of electoral cleavage,[13] or altering public views through advertising.[14] Ziegler's phrase 'inventing the people' conveys the interaction between public opinion and party behaviour. Thus, a successful party is one that seeks out one or more potential voting blocs and, by communicating with the members of these blocs, constructs an explicit common identity that gives those sharing it a reason to support the party.

2. ANALYSES

But which Russians will respond favourably to which messages? Analyses of survey data can shed light on this. We analyse data from a survey of 1,811 Russian citizens conducted in early 1997.[15] The

13. William H. Riker calls this 'heresthetics' in *The Art of Political Manipulation* (New Haven, CT: Yale University Press, 1986).
14. For evidence that candidates use the results of public surveys as a starting-point from which they attempt to mould a successful campaign posture, see Lawrence R. Jacobs and Robert Y. Shapiro, 'Issues, Candidate Image, and Priming: The Use of Private Polls in Kennedy's 1960 Presidential Campaign', *American Political Science Review*, Vol. 88, No. 3 (September 1994), pp. 527–40. On the process of a party 'creating demand' in the Russian electoral context, see Evelyn Davidheiser's contribution to this volume.
15. The surveys were made possible by support from the US National Science Foundation through grants: No. SES-9009698 (1990) 'Monitoring Soviet Political Change'; No. SES-9023974 (1991 and 1992) 'Monitoring Institutional Change in the Soviet Union: Comparing Legislator and Citizen Perspectives'; and No. SBR-9411643 (1995) 'Challenges to Democratization in Post-Soviet Societies: Comparing Elite and Citizen Perspectives'. Data from the surveys conducted in 1990, 1991

interviews were conducted in person, at the respondent's home, by Russians from the same district as the respondent.[16] Interviews typically lasted from three-quarters of an hour to an hour and a quarter.

In order to examine these data for cross-group 'clustering', we developed measures of an individual's outlook on the two key dimensions that distinguish Russian parties, as illustrated in Figure 6.1: (i) support for market economics and (ii) a preference for strong state power. In addition, we supplemented these two measures with measures of three additional outlooks: (iii) support for communism; (iv) perception of danger to the country; and (v) outlooks supportive of democracy. Each measure is composed of from three to eight questions that turned out to be sufficiently inter-correlated that they are highly likely to be measuring the same general outlook. (Appendix 6A provides question wordings and the method by which we constructed the index variables.) The resulting index variables have more values and a wider range of variance than any component variable, therefore they measure the underlying orientation with more accuracy.

We performed a regression for each index variable on a series of variables capturing personal, social, ascriptive and regional characteristics of the respondents. If any of these characteristics turns out to be associated with a distinct position on several of the index variables, that characteristic may demarcate a potential voting bloc. Table 6.1 shows the results of the regressions. Note that the explanatory variables used in the regression analyses shown in Table 6.1 do not include ideological or policy preference questions. If we sought the social–psychological causes of a Russian's views, we would have incorporated

and 1992 have been deposited with the Inter-University Consortium for Political and Social Research, Ann Arbor, MI, USA.

16. The sample approach used for selecting respondents was a four-stage stratified sample. At the initial stage, Russia was divided into strata reflecting the following criteria: the extent of urbanization, geographic region, the distribution of nationalities, and population density; these criteria produced eight strata. The second stage of the sample involved listing the places that fell into each stratum and selecting, with probabilities proportionate to size, a number of sampling places (PSU) from each stratum. The third stage of the sample involved enumerating all the voting districts for each of the primary sampling units. Between four and 23 voting districts were randomly selected for each primary sampling unit depending on the size of the place. The final stage of sampling involved employing the Kish procedure to select respondents. For more information on sampling, please contact the authors.

Table 6.1 Regression analyses of five attitudinal indicators

	Support for the market		Support for a strong state		Support for communism		Perception of danger		Democratic outlook	
Female	-0.117†	(-0.088)	-0.019	(-0.023)	-0.028	(-0.021)	0.506†	(0.095)	-0.068	(-0.071)
Age	-0.010†	(-0.253)	0.004†	(0.143)	0.012†	(0.275)	0.007	(0.145)	-0.003†	(-0.089)
Highest educational level[1]	0.083†	(0.165)	-0.036†	(-0.101)	-0.020	(-0.044)	-0.122	(-0.066)	0.068†	(0.192)
Rural residence	-0.107†	(-0.072)	-0.007	(-0.008)	0.095*	(0.059)	-0.246	(-0.044)	-0.013	(-0.009)
Moscow *or* St. Petersburg	0.109*	(0.065)	-0.158†	(-0.123)	-0.080	(-0.048)	-0.263	(-0.042)	0.063	(0.056)
Other city greater than 1 million	-0.101*	(-0.055)	-0.102†	(-0.098)	-0.021	(-0.013)	-0.046	(-0.000)	0.094†	(0.094)
Family income[2]	0.073†	(0.093)	0.040*	(0.060)	-0.012	(-0.013)	-0.247*	(-0.084)	0.014	(0.023)
Family finances, coming year[3]	-0.150†	(-0.237)	0.004	(0.010)	0.133†	(0.200)	0.580†	(0.228)	-0.023	(-0.048)
Blue collar	-0.090*	(-0.065)	0.028	(0.027)	0.020	(0.014)	0.356*	(0.060)	-0.087†	(-0.084)
Unemployed	0.056	(0.027)	0.041	(0.024)	0.009	(0.003)	0.749†	(0.083)	-0.065	(-0.034)
Regional economy[4]	-0.012	(-0.019)	-0.061†	(-0.124)	-0.031	(-0.043)	-0.022	(-0.001)	0.012	(0.024)
Residence in republic or autonomous region	0.099†	(0.062)	-0.140†	(-0.133)	0.001	(0.001)	-0.411*	(-0.071)	0.078†	(0.070)
Constant	0.801		0.123		-0.871		130.748		-0.026	
R²	0.27		0.10		0.17		0.10		0.09	
Total valid cases	1,345		1,345		1,345		1,309		1,344	

Notes: * = Statistically significant at or below 0.05 level.   † = Statistically significant at or below 0.01 level.

1 1 = primary only; 2 = incomplete secondary; 3 = completed secondary including professional schools or technicums; 4 = partial higher education; 5 = completed higher education.

2 Income is measures in millions of rubles per month.

3 0 = expected to be much better; 1 = better; 2 = about the same; 3 = worse; 4 = much worse.

4 0 = depressed; 1 = stagnant; 2 = sluggish; 3 = stable.

Source: Segbers and de Spiegeliere (eds), *Post-Soviet Puzzles*, Vol. II, pp. 177–200.

145

a wider range of variables than we have done. One can certainly more accurately predict an individual's ideology if one knows certain of his or her attitudes than if one knows only external features such as the individual's age, ethnicity or place of residence. So, adding attitudinal measures would also increase the proportion of the variance explained by the regression analyses. As discussed above, however, the purpose here is to investigate attitudinal clustering across personal, social, ascriptive and regional features. For political parties, successful campaigning requires it.

In Table 6.1, the figure on the left in each column is the regression coefficient. The larger it is in absolute value terms, the stronger the impact of that explanatory variable on the attitudinal index being analysed. This coefficient is measured when holding the impact of all the other explanatory variables constant, so that the possible inter-relationship of, say, age and education does not cloud the independent impact of each. The coefficient's sign indicates the direction of the impact. Because each explanatory variable is measured in different units (0 or 1 for several, such as whether the respondent is female or not; years 17–85 for age; and so forth), the regression coefficients make it difficult to interpret which of the explanatory variables makes the most difference in explaining placement along the range of the attitudinal index. The figure on the right of each column, therefore, provides a standardized regression coefficient, which simply expresses the relationship in standard deviation terms. Hence, a standardized coefficient of 0.1 indicates that a change of one standard deviation in the explanatory variable is associated with a change of one-tenth of a standard deviation in the index.

Support for Market Economics

The transition to a post-communist, more market-based economy began abruptly in early 1992, and led to great suffering for many Russians. Many others, though, have prospered in the new economic environment. Not surprisingly, sharp differences in how Russians evaluate market norms and institutions are present. Table 6.1 shows that Russian women taken as a group are significantly less supportive of the market than Russian men. (The term 'significant' has the statistical meaning that less than a 5 per cent probability exists that this finding is a result merely of the particular sample used in this survey.) The regression analysis shows other characteristics of Russian citizens that have significant relationships to support for the market. The young are substantially more supportive of the market than older Russians. Those with a higher level of educational achievement are likewise much more likely to support the market. Urban Russians, taken as a group, tend to be more supportive than Russians living in the countryside.

Because income remains an imperfect indicator of a Russian's economic resources, we employ an additional measure of the respondent's relative economic strength. That is a question asking the respondent to indicate whether he or she feels optimistic or pessimistic about his or her family's finances in the coming year. Both Russians with higher income and those who foresee a neutral or improving financial position are significantly associated with support for the market.

In addition to personal characteristics, certain aspects of the milieu in which one lives may condition one's outlooks. We employ two measures that distinguish the region (*oblast*, *krai*, republic or autonomous republic or autonomous *krai*) in which the respondent lives. The measure listed in Table 6.1 as 'regional economy' assigns numbers from zero to three to Ilya Shkabara's characterizations of each region's economy as either 'depressed', 'stagnant', 'sluggish' or 'stable'.[17] (Evidently, no region of Russian is yet 'dynamic'.) The second measure provides a partial representation of which regions have significant non-Russian populations by distinguishing those who live in a region with an autonomous status based on some large non-Russian group. These regions are either republics (formerly autonomous republics under the Soviet federal system), or autonomous regions within *oblasts*. Table 6.1 shows that Russian citizens living in such regions (many of whom are not ethnically Russian) are significantly more likely to support market norms.

The variable with the strongest impact on support for the market is age. Partly because older generations were more successfully socialized into Soviet economic norms and partly because the young have greater

17. Ilya Shkabara, 'A Survey of Russia's Regional Economies', in Klaus Segbers and Stephan de Spiegeleire (eds), *Post-Soviet Puzzles: Mapping the Political Economy of the Former Soviet Union* (Baden-Baden: Nomos, 1996), Volume II, pp. 177–200.

opportunities to adapt and prosper in the new conditions, the generation gap in Russian economic values is immense.

Preference for Strong State Power

A strong component of opposition to President Yeltsin and his policies has come from opposition to the occurrence since 1992 of what is perceived as being a dangerous and avoidable plummeting in Russia's international prestige and power, the breaking up of a sensible and legitimate union, a diminution of the status and treatment of ethnic Russians by those of other national backgrounds, and the impotence of Russia's legal system to stop crime and enforce the law. These are all aspects of state power. As many have argued, resolving issues of state power must either precede the inauguration of democratic institutions or be dealt with very early on.[18] Vladimir Zhirinovskii's Liberal Democratic Party of Russia (LDPR) has built itself around these issues, but the platform of the CPRF also has state power issues at its core. While some Russians support a cautious Russian role in global affairs, friendly economic and political ties with the United States and other Western countries, along with tolerance and equality among Russian citizens of different nationalities, many others seek a return to a strong and proud Russian state resting on symbols of ethnic Russian heritage. Table 6.1 shows that older Russians score significantly more highly on the measure of desire for strong state power, as do those with lower education levels. Russians living in regions with poor economic performance are significantly more orientated towards strong state power. Russians in large cities are significantly less orientated towards strong state power. Finally, those living in autonomous regions are significantly less supportive of strong state power. (It should be borne in mind that many of those calling for a return to a strong and proud state have in mind a unified state that would take away from these regions' rights that they have negotiated since the end of the USSR.)

18. A well-known example is Dankwart A. Rustow, 'Transitions to Democracy: Toward a Dynamic Model', *Comparative Politics*, Vol. 2, No. 3 (April 1970), pp. 337–63.

Support for Communism

In many respects, support for communism is a mirror image of support for the market. Older Russians are significantly more disposed to support communism than are younger generations. The better-educated show less support for communism, as do urban dwellers compared with their rural counterparts. Those who foresee a worsening of their financial situation in the coming year are significantly more likely to support communism than are other Russians. As with support for the market, the most salient influence comes from the individual's age.

Perceptions of Danger to the Country

Although not an ideological dimension as such, one's perception of 'normality' versus crisis conditions could certainly motivate one's support for or opposition to political figures and parties. Almost all Russians in 1997 rate the danger facing the country due to economic problems and crime as high: on a scale from zero to 18, most Russians scored above 12. Nevertheless, important variation remains in different Russians' degree of perception of danger. Thus, women are significantly more likely to perceive danger than are men. Those who are better off economically are significantly *less* likely to perceive the country to be in sharp danger. Those employed in blue-collar occupations see a higher level of danger than others, and the unemployed are likely to provide a much higher estimate of the danger facing the country. Although the questions that we employ ask about the danger to the country, it is clear that they are tapping the impact of economic problems and crime on the respondent's own situation as well. Intriguingly, those in the autonomous regions appear significantly lower in their perception of danger facing the country.

Expression of Outlooks Supportive of Democracy

Note that the questions used to construct this index are not measures of support for democratic institutions, even less of support for vague ideas such as 'democracy' or of the people labelled as 'democrats'. Rather, the index measures acceptance of certain outlooks which, when distributed widely among a populace, have been found to be helpful for democratic consolidation. Table 6.1 shows that Russian women are distinguished from Russian men in their democratic outlook, as they are with the other attitudinal indices. In this case, they are significantly less likely to evince a democratic outlook. Older Russians, those with less educational achievement and blue-collar workers are also less likely to reveal these orientations. Those living in large cities are more likely to hold a democratic outlook, as are those living in the autonomous regions. Educational achievement is the most powerful predictor.

3. POTENTIAL VOTING BLOCS AND SUPPORT FOR MAJOR PARTIES

The above analyses point to several key groupings of Russian citizens. Each grouping stands as a potential voting bloc whose support one or more political parties must pursue. We shall examine more closely gender, education level, age, whether the individual has a blue-collar job, urban and rural place of residence, whether the individual lives in an autonomous region, whether he or she lives in a city of more than one million inhabitants (including Moscow and St. Petersburg, which we separated out in Table 6.1), and the success of the region's economy. We change each of these variables into a dichotomy, then examine the differences across the dichotomy of Russians' attitudes and behaviour. Table 6.2 shows the results for the attitudinal measures analysed in Table 6.1, and also for several standard types of political behaviour. Although the presentation of patterns in attitudes tells the same story as the regressions in Table 6.1, the differences in average scores more readily convey the orientations of certain groupings.

Russian women, as we know from the figures shown in Table 6.1, are significantly less supportive of market economics, perceive significantly more danger and are significantly less likely to evince a democratic outlook. Yet Table 6.2 shows that they also have certain behavioural distinctions. They are significantly more likely to have voted in the 1995 legislature elections, although they less often report themselves as having discussed how to vote than men do. Russian women are significantly more likely to have contacted an official about a problem or other matter of concern and to have signed a petition.

Those Russians with at least some higher education represent roughly a fifth of our sample. This is nowhere near a majority but is a sizeable grouping nevertheless. They differ in almost every way from less-well-educated Russians: they are more supportive of the market, less concerned about increasing state power in Russia, less pro-communist, less worried for the country and more likely to hold attitudes supportive of democracy. They also vote more often and discuss politics more frequently. They sign petitions and join rallies at a higher rate. Their potential importance, therefore, extends beyond their strength in the electorate.

Russians aged 50 and above are more anti-market, more desirous of increased state power, more pro-communist, more worried and less democratic. They vote more often than the young yet discuss politics less often and are less likely to sign petitions and attend rallies. The latter characteristics of older Russians may decrease their political clout somewhat despite their constituting two-fifths of the populace.

The main thing that distinguishes Russian blue-collar workers from other Russians is that they are less participatory. Fewer have voted in recent elections and fewer report having contacted an official about a problem. The four remaining variables that indicate features of where the individual lives all show strong distinctions in attitudes, but few distinctions in behaviour (with the exception that Russians living in the countryside are more likely to vote).

What difference do these groupings make for an individual's orientation towards the major political parties? Table 6.3 provides some evidence to help answer this question. As in Table 6.2, both attitudes and forms of political behaviour are displayed. Respondents could rate a number of institutions and people on a seven-point scale, with a higher score indicating a more favourable assessment. Two of these questions asked about political parties, the CPRF and the LDPR. The two-way breakdowns of Russian citizens almost all make a difference for the rating of these two parties. The young, for instance, are significantly less approving of the CPRF than are older Russians. The same goes for females compared with males, rural Russians compared with urban residents, those living in smaller cities compared with larger cities, and those with poor economies compared with those in areas experiencing better economic performance.

Table 6.2 Cross-group differences in attitudes and behaviour

	Gender		Higher education		Age		Blue collar		Location		ASSR*		Big city		Regional economy	
	Male	Female	No	Yes	17–49	50+	No	Yes	Urban	Rural	No	Yes	No	Yes	Bad	Better
Ideological dimensions																
Pro-market	**0.08**	**0.08**	**-0.08**	**0.28**	**0.16**	**-0.28**	-0.02	0.01	**0.03**	**-0.15**	**-0.04**	**0.04**	**-0.04**	**0.03**	**-0.07**	**0.02**
State power	0.02	0.02	**0.03**	**-0.12**	**-0.04**	**0.07**	-0.01	0.03	-0.01	**0.04**	**0.03**	**-0.08**	**0.06**	**-0.09**	**0.09**	**-0.05**
Other attitudes																
Pro-communist	-0.01	0.01	**0.04**	**-0.15**	**-0.16**	**0.25**	0.01	-0.04	**-0.03**	**0.10**	0.01	-0.02	**0.05**	**-0.08**	**0.08**	**-0.04**
Danger	**15.5**	**15.9**	**15.9**	**15.1**	**15.6**	**16.0**	15.7	15.9	15.8	15.7	**15.9**	**15.2**	15.8	15.6	**15.9**	**15.6**
Democratic attitudes	**0.3**	**-0.2**	**-0.04**	**0.16**	**0.05**	**-0.08**	0.01	-0.03	**0.02**	**-0.06**	**-0.02**	**0.05**	**-0.03**	**0.05**	-0.01	0.02
Electoral behaviour																
Voted in 1995[1]	**0.61**	**0.67**	**0.61**	**0.76**	**0.57**	**0.77**	**0.67**	**0.58**	**0.62**	**0.70**	0.80	0.78	0.64	0.64	0.64	0.65
Round 1[2]	0.79	0.79	**0.78**	**0.86**	**0.75**	**0.86**	**0.80**	**0.76**	**0.78**	**0.82**	0.72	0.72	0.80	0.79	0.79	0.79
Round 2[3]	0.70	0.73	**0.70**	**0.81**	**0.66**	**0.81**	**0.74**	**0.66**	0.71	0.74	0.72	0.72	0.70	0.74	0.70	0.73
Talked politics[4]	**0.26**	**0.19**	**0.20**	**0.30**	**0.24**	**0.19**	0.22	0.23	**0.24**	**0.16**	0.22	0.22	0.22	0.22	0.21	0.23

Other behaviour[5]

Contacted the media	0.06	0.07	**0.05**	**0.13**	0.06	0.07	0.07	0.07	0.07	0.06	**0.07**	**0.05**	0.07	0.06	0.08	0.06
Contacted an official	**0.06**	**0.10**	0.08	0.12	0.08	0.09	**0.08**	**0.05**	0.08	0.09	0.08	0.10	0.09	0.09	0.09	0.08
Signed a petition	**0.16**	**0.22**	**0.17**	**0.29**	**0.24**	**0.13**	0.19	0.22	0.21	0.17	0.19	0.20	0.20	0.19	0.22	0.18
Joined a rally	0.11	0.09	**0.08**	**0.17**	**0.11**	**0.08**	0.09	0.12	0.11	0.08	0.11	0.07	0.10	0.10	0.11	0.09
Percentage of sample	41	59	80	20	60	40	74	26	74	26	74	26	60	40	39	61

Notes

* ASSR = Autonomous Soviet Socialist Republic.

Scores in the table are averages except when a variable has only two values (for example, having voted or not). In that case, the score represents the percentage of the sample in a given group. When a pair of scores is presented in bold type, that signifies that the scores were significantly different from each other using a *t*-test.

1 Did you vote in the 1995 parliamentary elections?

2 Did you vote in the first round of the presidential election in 1996?

3 Did you vote in the second round of the presidential election in 1966?

4 Did you, over the past year, talk to any people about why they should vote for a certain party or individual?

5 Have you, over the past year, …?

Table 6.3 Cross-group differences in orientations towards major parties and their leaders

	Gender		Higher education		Age		Blue collar		Location		ASSR*		Big city		Regional economy	
	Male	Female	No	Yes	17–49	50+	No	Yes	Urban	Rural	No	Yes	No	Yes	Bad	Better
Rate CPRF	**4.1**	**4.3**	**4.3**	**3.6**	**3.9**	**4.6**	4.2	4.1	**4.1**	**4.5**	4.2	4.2	**4.3**	**4.0**	**4.3**	**4.1**
Rate LDPR	**3.1**	**2.9**	**3.1**	**2.7**	**3.0**	3.0	**3.0**	**3.2**	**2.9**	**3.3**	3.0	3.0	**3.1**	**2.9**	**3.3**	**2.9**
Views are closest to:[1]																
Democratic Choice	0.02	0.02	**0.01**	**0.06**	0.02	0.02	0.02	0.01	**0.03**	**0.01**	0.02	0.01	**0.01**	**0.04**	**0.03**	**0.03**
CPRF	0.25	0.23	**0.26**	**0.16**	**0.18**	**0.34**	0.24	0.24	0.23	0.28	0.25	0.23	**0.27**	**0.20**	**0.28**	**0.22**
LPDR	**0.07**	**0.03**	**0.05**	**0.02**	**0.06**	**0.02**	0.04	0.06	0.04	0.05	0.04	0.04	0.05	0.04	0.05	0.04
Our Home is Russia	0.07	0.08	0.07	0.08	0.07	0.08	0.08	0.07	0.08	0.07	**0.09**	**0.05**	0.07	0.09	0.08	0.07
Yabloko	0.10	0.08	**0.07**	**0.19**	0.11	0.06	0.10	0.08	**0.11**	**0.05**	0.10	0.08	0.07	**0.13**	0.08	0.10
1995 party list voting:																
Democratic Choice	0.03	0.02	**0.02**	**0.08**	**0.02**	**0.04**	**0.03**	**0.01**	**0.03**	**0.01**	0.03	0.02	**0.01**	**0.05**	**0.01**	**0.04**
CPRF	0.19	0.18	0.19	0.16	**0.12**	**0.27**	0.19	0.16	0.18	0.18	0.18	0.19	0.19	0.16	0.20	0.17
LPDR	0.06	0.04	**0.05**	**0.03**	**0.06**	**0.03**	**0.04**	**0.07**	**0.04**	**0.06**	0.04	0.06	**0.05**	**0.03**	0.04	0.05
Our Home is Russia	0.08	0.09	0.08	0.11	**0.07**	**0.11**	**0.09**	**0.06**	0.08	0.11	0.09	0.07	**0.07**	**0.11**	0.07	0.09
Yabloko	0.07	0.08	**0.05**	**0.16**	**0.09**	**0.05**	0.080.	0.06	**0.09**	**0.04**	0.08	0.06	**0.06**	**0.10**	0.07	0.08

154

For whom voted in 1996 presidential election:

Yeltsin, Round 1	0.29	0.33	**0.30**	**0.38**	0.31	0.32	**0.33**	**0.28**	**0.30**	**0.36**	0.31	0.31	**0.30**	**0.34**	0.29	0.33
Yeltsin, Round 2	0.37	0.40	**0.36**	**0.50**	0.39	0.40	**0.41**	**0.35**	0.39	0.39	0.40	0.39	**0.36**	**0.44**	0.37	0.41
Zyuganov, Round 1	0.23	0.20	**0.22**	**0.17**	**0.14**	**0.32**	0.22	0.20	0.21	0.23	0.22	0.21	**0.23**	**0.19**	0.23	0.20
Zyuganov, Round 2	0.26	0.25	**0.26**	**0.20**	**0.19**	**0.35**	0.26	0.24	0.25	0.27	0.24	0.26	**0.28**	**0.21**	0.27	0.24
Lebed	0.14	0.12	0.12	0.14	**0.14**	**0.11**	0.12	0.14	**0.14**	**0.10**	0.12	0.13	0.13	0.13	**0.15**	0.12
Yavlinskii	0.03	0.05	**0.03**	**0.08**	**0.05**	**0.02**	0.04	0.04	**0.05**	**0.02**	0.04	0.04	**0.03**	**0.06**	**0.03**	**0.05**
Zhirinovskii	0.04	0.03	**0.04**	**0.01**	**0.04**	**0.02**	0.03	0.05	0.03	0.04	0.03	0.05	**0.05**	**0.01**	0.04	0.03
Percentage of sample	41	59	80	20	60	40	74	26	74	26	74	26	60	40	39	61

Notes: Scores in the table are averages except when a variable has only two values, in which case the score represents the percentage of the sample in a given group. When a pair of scores is presented in bold type, that signifies that the scores were significantly different from each other using a *t*-test.

* ASSR = Autonomous Soviet Socialist Republic.

1 On this card is a list of political parties. Is there one particular party on the list that expresses your views better than any of the other parties?

Our survey also asked which political party, if any, an individual believed best represents his or her views. The results for five prominent parties are given in Table 6.3. Russian men, for example, are significantly more likely than are Russian women to have indicated that the LDPR was their preferred party. Older Russians are much more prone to pick the CPRF and less likely to select either the LDPR or Yabloko.

Our survey also asked for whom the respondent voted in the 1995 legislative party-list vote, and both rounds of the 1996 presidential elections. Whether one has higher education, one's age, whether one works in a blue-collar job and whether one lives in a big city are the variables with the most numerous behavioural consequences. For almost all the parties and candidates, those with higher education differ from those without. Russians with higher education, for instance, are more supportive of Russia's Choice, less of the LDPR and much more of Yabloko. They backed Yeltsin in both rounds in 1996 more strongly than did those with less education. They were more likely to back Yavlinskii and less likely to back Zyuganov or Zhirinovskii.

Our results, then, do demonstrate the type of 'clustering' that presents parties with a variegated electoral environment. Russians in certain categories have tendencies towards holding certain attitudes and behaving in certain ways that set them apart from other Russians. Comparing Tables 6.2 and 6.3, moreover, suggests that Russia's leading parties have begun to have identifiable constituencies. Those groups – the elderly for example – that support communist ideas also vote for the CPRF in higher numbers (almost double the percentage: 18 per cent compared with 34 per cent).

4. ARRAYING RUSSIAN GROUPINGS BY SUPPORT FOR MARKETS AND DESIRE FOR A STRONG STATE

The placement of political parties along the two dimensions in Figure 6.1 (support for or opposition to market economics and support for or opposition to nationalist, assertive and anti-Western policies) was a rough estimation. We can, however, place the central tendencies of our groupings within the Russian public with more accuracy along these scales. Measuring each issue dimension in terms of deviations from the overall average, we can indicate to what extent a certain grouping, such as those with higher education, falls into a centrist or extreme position. Figure 6.2 shows a redrawing of the two dimensions from Figure 6.1 with scales indicated. For each of the two index variables that we use to tap the dimensions in Figure 6.2, we find the average score for various social groupings. The two scores for each group of Russians place it in one or another of the four quadrants.

Indicative of how different Russians' views of politics can be is the distance between older rural dwellers and younger urban citizens. The latter (almost twice as large a portion of society) are distinctly more supportive of the market and hostile to the nationalist and statist policies of the communists and nationalist parties. Women tend to be left of centre as regards economic policy, but do not show as much support for nationalist or statist ideas. They occupy, it seems, the position in this issue space that the Bloc of Ivan Rybkin was supposed to cover and that the party Women of Russia did try to cover. Rybkin's party never really became established, and Women of Russia has faded significantly.[19]

Note that the groupings exhibit the two-dimensionality we expected, with significant differences along both scales. Even so, Figure 6.2 also clearly has a southwest–northeast array. Among Russians, in other words, support for left-wing economic policies and for a strengthening of the state go together, as do right-wing economic policies and a lesser concern for strengthening the state. An ideological reason partially explains this, since a left-wing economic stance includes a preference for a stronger state role in the economy than a right-wing stance would prefer. However, what we are calling the desire for a strong state refers to other possible meanings of the term, so the link is not a necessary one. These two dimensions can be somewhat collapsed into one spectrum for political reasons as well: in 1992 and 1993, and to varying degrees since then, President Yeltsin has supported Western-orientated economic and state-building policies. Hence, opposition to Yeltsin stems from concern with either or both of those aspects of Yeltsin's regime. Also, the connection is to some degree a product of active campaigning by left-wing parties to present themselves as defenders of

19. On the question of why this area of the political spectrum (also known as 'social democracy') has not achieved a higher profile in Russian politics, see Fish, 'The Advent of Multipartism'.

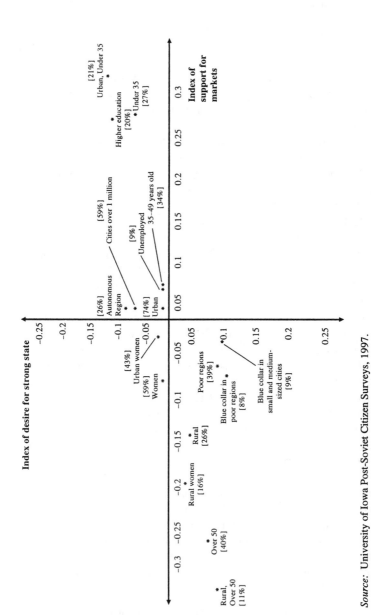

Source: University of Iowa Post-Soviet Citizen Surveys, 1997.

Figure 6.2 Distribution of Russian groupings in two-dimensional issue space (percentage of sample)

a strong state, not just of left-wing economics. (Marxism, including Soviet-style Marxism–Leninism, has both more nationalist and more internationalist strains, so the CPRF could have found ideological rationales for either approach; only one seemed likely to be helpful in attracting voters, however.)

The lack of sizeable groupings in the southeast quadrant of Figure 6.2 may clarify why the LDPR's support has been declining. Although it has staked out a prominent and extreme position in favour of putting Russia first, fighting crime and getting back land that belongs to Russia, the LDPR's economic stance is much less well defined. The CPRF, offering similar statist themes together with a more widely known economic orientation, did much better than the LDPR in 1995, as Zyuganov did over Zhirinovskii in 1996.

What President Yeltsin accomplished in his re-election campaign in 1996 was to cross from the northeast quadrant some of the way into the southwest quadrant, leaving the CPRF leader, Zyuganov, with support from the elderly, the rural and those living in the worst-off regions – all three minority categories. In many respects, such a 'movement' on the part of a successful candidate in any country with winner-take-all elections is a standard pattern. Yeltsin knew that those located to his northeast would have no choice but to back him over the communist candidate. Note, though, that for Yeltsin to capture the centre, he had to 'move' (position himself) in both a southerly and a westerly direction. In other words, he had to attend to issues of nationalism and statism as well as to distance himself from the least-popular pro-market policies. To capture the presidency in future elections, the CPRF candidate would need to outdo his rival in capturing votes from urban women and others near the centre of these two axes.

5. CONCLUSIONS

Russians' views are evolving in response to their place in a changing society. Where they live, what background they have, what their position within the new economy is – these all constrain their reactions to events, politicians, institutions and policies. The variety in Russians' lived experiences provides a complex electoral geography for Russian parties to master. Although our results indicate that the process of matching party platforms with likely constituencies has begun in Russia,[20] Russian political parties have much work left to do. Some parties which would seem to be well positioned to attract a reasonably sized core of supporters have failed to garner this support (Russia's Choice is the prime example).

A fascinating aspect of electoral politics is why one presidential candidate captures the heavily populated middle ground and another, also intent upon doing so, fails. By the same token, how political parties cast themselves and appeal to potential voters for support remains central to representation in electoral democracies. Just as leadership is partly a function of the leader and partly of the led, so a party's electoral success is a function of both the party and the public. Using survey data to clarify attitudinal and behavioural patterns within Russian society provides a support structure for those seeking to understand parties' behaviour and to explain their success or failure.

20. For evidence of increasing congruence between the attitudes of party politicians and members of the public who support the same party, see Arthur H. Miller, William M. Reisinger and Vicki L. Hesli, 'Mass–Elite Linkage Through Political Parties in Post-Soviet Russia', manuscript, University of Iowa.

APPENDIX 6A   QUESTION WORDING AND INDEX CONSTRUCTION

Index of Pro-market Orientation

Questions used

There are different sectors of society that could have ownership of various resources in Russia: the government, the employees of the enterprise, or private individuals. For each of the types of enterprises I will read, please tell me whether in your opinion, the government, the employees or private individuals should own such enterprises:

A. *Former kolkhoz and sovkhoz property (farms and farmland)*
   1 = government ownership, 2 = employee ownership, 3 = private ownership

B. *Large industry*
   1 = government ownership, 2 = employee ownership, 3 = private ownership

C. *Now we would like to get your feelings towards certain groups using a seven-point scale, where 1 indicates a very negative view and 7 a very positive view. You may use any number between 1 and 7 to tell me how favourable or unfavourable your feelings are for each group. ...*
   private enterprises 1 = low, 7 = high

D. *There should be a mechanism regulating income such that no one earns very much more than others.*
   1 = strongly disagree ... 5 = strongly agree

E. *Economic reform must be pursued, even if it means significant hardship for the people.*
   1 = strongly disagree ... 5 = strongly agree

F. *Some people think that certain groups in society have too much influence on society and politics in Russia and that other groups don't have as much influence as they deserve. For each group listed on this same card, please tell me if they have too much, too little or the right amount of influence on society and politics ... Businessmen*
   1 = too much, 2 = about right, 3 = too little

G.   Some people say the central government of the Russian Federation should guarantee everyone work and a high standard of living; others argue that every person should look after him- or herself. On this card is a scale from 1 to 7, where 1 signifies that the government guarantees everyone work and 7 that every person should look after him- or herself. You may select any number from 1 to 7.

1 = government guarantees work ... 7 = every person looks after self

H.   Some people believe that large business profits should not be allowed; others believe that business profits should be allowed to be as large as possible. For the growth of the economy, which is closest to your view?

1 = no large profits, 2 = large profits are OK

I.   Some people believe that companies should fire workers who do not work hard enough; others think everyone should be guaranteed a job as long as they try to do their best. Which of these do you agree with?

1 = guarantee a job, 2 = it depends, 3 = fire those who work poorly

Index construction
Questions were recoded so that, for each, a high score indicates a more pro-market orientation. Then each was standardized (mean = 0, standard deviation = 1). The index variable consists of the average, for each respondent of his or her standardized scores on the nine component variables. If the respondent did not answer from one to seven of the questions, the score was the average of the remaining two to eight variables. That is, the index variable has a missing value only if the respondent did not answer eight or nine of the questions.

Index of Preference for Strong State Power

Questions used
I am now going to read you a number of statements. For each statement, would you please indicate whether you agree with each fully or partially or disagree partially or fully.

A. *The Russian government should use force, if necessary, to preserve the unity and integrity of the Russian state.*
1 = strongly agree ... 5 = strongly disagree

B. *I almost always feel proud when I see the Russian flag.*
1 = strongly agree ... 5 = strongly disagree

C. *Russia has always given other countries more than it got in return.*
1 = strongly agree ... 5 = strongly disagree

Some people think that, in order to strengthen relations between Russia and the former republics of the USSR, it is necessary to make certain changes to current policies. Some people would like these changes to occur within the next three years; others are completely opposed to such changes. For each of the possible changes listed on this card, please tell me if you fully agree, agree, disagree or fully disagree that it is necessary to carry out such changes.
1 = fully agree ... 5 = fully disagree

D. *Our country should have joint military structures with other republics of the former USSR.*

E. *Our country should have joint political structures (legislatures) with other republics of the former USSR.*

Now we would like to get your feelings towards certain groups using a seven-point scale, where 1 indicates a very negative view and 7 a very positive view. You may use any number between 1 and 7 to tell me how favourable or unfavourable your feelings are for each group.

F. *The Army*   1 = low, 7 = high

G. *The Police*   1 = low, 7 = high

H. *If you had to choose, which do you think is the better way for us to keep peace by having a very strong military so other countries will not attack us or by working out our disagreements at the bargaining table?*

Index construction

Questions were recoded so that, for each, a high score indicates an orientation more supportive of strong state power. Then, each was standardized (mean = 0, standard deviation = 1). The index variable consists of each respondent's average across the standardized scores on the eight component variables. If the respondent did not answer from one to six of the questions, the score was the average of the remaining two to six variables. That is, the index variable only has a missing value if the respondent did not answer seven or eight of the questions.

Index of Pro-communist Orientation

Questions used

A.   Although the Soviet Union no longer exists, some people still think of themselves as Soviet, whereas others have stopped thinking of themselves in those terms. To what extent would you say you think of yourself as a Soviet person?
1 = not at all ... 4 = a great deal

B.   These days Stalin is not given adequate credit for building of socialism
1 = strongly disagree ... 5 = strongly agree

C.   Our society is made up of many different kinds of people. Next we would like to ask you some questions about the many different groups that are part of our society. Any individual may have a great deal in common with some of these groups and very little in common with other groups. On this card is a list of various social groups of people. I would like to find out how much you have in common (share their ideas, interests, their outlook on different events) with these different sorts of people ... communists.
1 = nothing ... 4 = a great deal

D.   Now we would like to get your feelings toward certain groups using a seven point scale, where 1 indicates a very negative view and 7 a very positive view. You may use any number between 1 and 7 to tell me how favourable or unfavourable your feelings are for each group ... The Communist Party of the Soviet Union/Russian Federation
1 = low ... 7 = high

Index construction

Questions were recoded so that, for each, a high score indicates a more pro-communist orientation. Then, each was standardized (mean = 0, standard deviation = 1). The index variable consists of the average, for each respondent of his or her standardized scores on the four component variables. If the respondent did not answer one or two of the questions, the score was the average of the remaining two or three. The index variable only has a missing value if the respondent did not answer three or four of the questions.

Index of Perception of Danger to the Country

Questions used

What in your view is the most dangerous, that is, leads towards destabilization in our country? For each item I will now mention, evaluate the degree of danger with numbers from 1 to 7, where 1 means no danger at present and 7 means the highest danger:

A. *The growth of economic inequality among citizens*
B. *Unemployment*
C. *The growth of crime*

Index construction

Each variable had one subtracted from it so that it ranged from 0 to 6. The three variables were then added together, producing a variable ranging from 0 (no perception of danger) to 18 (highest perception of danger).

Index of Outlooks Supportive of Democracy

Questions used

I am now going to read you a number of statements. For each statement, would you please indicate whether you agree with each fully or partially or disagree partially or fully.

A. *It is very important to stop crime, even at the risk of violating the rights of the accused.*
    1 = strongly agree … 5 = strongly disagree

B.   Participation of the people is not necessary if decision-making is left in the hands of a few trusted, competent leaders.
   1 = strongly agree ... 5 = strongly disagree

C.   It is better to live in an orderly society than to allow people so much freedom that they become disruptive.
   1 = strongly agree ... 5 = strongly disagree

D.   The government has the responsibility to see that the rights of all minorities are protected.
   1 = strongly disagree ... 5 = strongly agree

E.   Right now, Russia needs strong leadership more than it needs democracy.
   1 = strongly agree ... 5 = strongly disagree

F.   Any individual or organization has the right to organize opposition or resistance to any governmental initiative.
   1 = strongly disagree ... 5 = strongly agree

Index Construction
Questions were recoded so that, for each, a high score indicates an orientation more supportive of democracy. Then, each was standardized (mean = 0, standard deviation = 1). The index variable consists of the average, for each respondent of his or her standardized scores on the six component variables. If the respondent did not answer from one to seven of the questions, the score was the average of the remaining two to five variables. That is, the index variable only has a missing value if the respondent did not answer five or six of the questions.

7. Ideology and Russian Mass Politics: Uses of the Left–Right Continuum

Timothy J. Colton

Ideology, a mainstay of Soviet studies, has fallen into disuse in research on the post-Soviet political process. Nowhere is this more so than in the mass arena. Analysts rely heavily on the opinions of citizens to account for voting decisions and other acts and omissions. But mostly they take them to be either points of view on discrete issues, large and small, or positions within a two-dimensional or multidimensional space whose bearings are exogenously fixed by the scholar.[1] The shared assumption is that integrative and internally 'constrained' systems of belief, causally prior to particular attitudes and more or less consciously held – in other words, ideologies – do not exist in contemporary Russian society, cannot easily be tapped by survey methods, or do not have much to do with political outcomes.

In the stable democracies of the United States and Western Europe, by contrast, social scientists will typically postulate that ideological leanings make – or at a minimum *can* make – a big difference. The language delineating them differs some from country to country,

---

1. For good examples of two-dimensional schemes for classifying political beliefs, see M. Steven Fish, 'The Advent of Multipartism in Russia, 1993–1995', *Post-Soviet Affairs*, Vol. 11 (October–November 1995), pp. 340–83; Herbert Kitschelt, *Party Systems in East Central Europe: Consolidation or Fluidity?*, Studies in Public Policy No. 241 (Glasgow: University of Strathclyde, 1995). The first full-length monograph on voting in Russia contains much useful information about 'political attitudes' and their relation to electoral choice but generally avoids ideological categories: see Stephen White, Richard Rose and Ian McAllister, *How Russia Votes* (Chatham, NJ: Chatham House, 1997).

depending on history and linguistic convention: Americanists assign 'liberal' and 'conservative' labels, and Europeanists 'left' and 'right' labels.[2] Whatever the markers, students of public opinion and voting in all these countries have for a generation or longer tried to map the predispositions to which they refer and to probe for effects on individual behaviour.

When it comes to the unconsolidated proto-democracy found in the Russian Federation after communism, it is possible to deduce a compelling brief arguing the irrelevance, or, alternatively, the massive importance, of ideology to Russian mass politics. On the negative side, we hear incessantly that the collapse of the Soviet regime and of its utopian Marxism–Leninism has engendered a moral vacuum and pervasive cynicism about all things political. On the positive side, we are assured no less regularly that some political business is transacted largely as it was before 1991 or 1985 and that a subtle restoration of pre-*perestroika* habits and routines may have been under way for some time. Whether or not the latter claim is justified, it stretches credulity to suppose that seven decades of state socialism, to say nothing of its dramatic exit from the scene, would have left no residue at all on how people reason about public issues. Moreover, it plainly is the case that much of the rhetoric spouted by Russia's present-day political leaders, during and between election campaigns, is couched in terms of general values and orientations.

I approach the question of ideology in this study not deductively but inductively, exploiting valuable bits of empirical evidence gleaned during an election survey of the voting-age Russian population in 1996.

2. See, especially, Angus Campbell, Philip E. Converse, Warren E. Miller and Donald Stokes, *The American Voter* (New York: Wiley, 1960), esp. Ch. 9; Philip E. Converse, 'The Nature of Belief Systems in Mass Publics', in David E. Apter, *Ideology and Discontent* (New York: Free Press, 1964), pp. 206–61; Jean A. Laponce, 'Note on the Use of the Left–Right Dimension', *Comparative Political Studies*, Vol. 3 (January 1970), pp. 481–502; Hans D. Klingemann, 'Measuring Ideological Conceptualizations', in Samuel Barnes et al., *Political Action: Mass Participation in Five Western Democracies* (Beverly Hills, CA, and London: Sage, 1979), pp. 215–53; Philip E. Converse and Roy Pierce, *Political Representation in France* (Cambridge, MA: Harvard University Press, 1986), Ch. 4; Dieter Fuchs and Hans D. Klingemann, 'The Left–Right Schema', in Kent Jennings et al., *Continuities in Political Action* (Berlin: de Gruyter, 1989), pp. 203–34; and Ronald Inglehart, *Culture Shift in Advanced Industrial Society* (Princeton, NJ: Princeton University Press, 1990).

The data show a majority of the country's citizens, albeit a slight majority, to give signs of understanding the ideational scheme most relevant to contemporary Russia – one ranging political orientations from a left to a right pole – and to be able to apply it to concrete political situations. Although the ideological factor's impact on electoral choice is modest, except for the most sophisticated participants, it merits close scrutiny as public opinion and political competition evolve in the years ahead.

1. HOW CITIZENS MAP THE TERRAIN

It would make little sense to expect ordinary Russians to warm to the Anglo-American constructs 'conservative' and 'liberal', since they are recent imports into the tongue and seldom feature in political debates. 'Left' (*levyi*) and 'right' (*pravyi*) are a different matter. Embedded in Russians' everyday speech, these words refer, as in other languages, to the human anatomy (left arm, right leg, and so forth) and more generally to the organization of space and motion. They have been utilized metaphorically in political communication since the late imperial period. The early Bolsheviks and then the Communist Party of the Soviet Union (CPSU) instinctively dubbed themselves a party of the left or a vanguard of the 'leftist forces' in Russian society. And indeed they did exemplify in grossly exaggerated form the two hallmark characteristics of European radicalism: a devotion to bringing about the improvement or perfection of the social order, rather than its preservation or management; and a commitment to carry out that task through purposive expansion of the sphere of government activity. When the hegemonic party momentarily harboured militant and moderate dissidents from the general line before Joseph Stalin tightened his control in the 1920s, they were aptly referred to as leftist and rightist groupings: a 'left opposition' which proposed advancing as rapidly as possible and a 'right opposition' content to 'creep at a snail's pace' towards socialism, as one of its leading lights put it.[3]

Generations later, as innovators within the CPSU and eventually agitators outside it challenged Soviet orthodoxy and the party's

3. Nikolai Bukharin, quoted in Stephen F. Cohen, *Bukharin and the Bolshevik Revolution: A Political Biography, 1888–1938* (New York: Knopf, 1973), p. 187.

monopoly on power in the 1980s, it is understandable that the insurgency would be widely cast as originating on the political left. Standing on the left in Russia a decade ago connoted a desire to accelerate the pace of reform and steam at full throttle towards a multiparty democracy and, for many adherents, towards a market economy; the political right was associated with a more cautious attitude towards change and, on the extreme right edge of the spectrum, with a reactionary attachment to the Brezhnevite status quo or even with neo-Stalinism.[4] But the left–right vocabulary was not always employed with ease. The vacillating general secretary of the CPSU, Mikhail Gorbachev, had his speech writers enclose the adjective 'leftist' in quotation marks when referring to Boris Yeltsin and others, insinuating that their radicalism was bogus or illegitimate. While the new democratic opposition could logically enough think of itself as occupying a strategic position on the 'left', in that it was an agent of disruption of the established order, its embrace of market economics put it at odds with the reflexive socioeconomic programme of most leftist movements, which have advocated the use of state power to curb the injustices of capitalism and not, as in the USSR, to dismantle socialism.

The collapse of the Soviet Union and the birth of the independent Russian state prompted a shift in perspective and a slackening of the tension between the several meanings of left and right. Now that the erstwhile ruling party (reborn as the CPRF, Communist Party of the Russian Federation) was in the political wilderness and Yeltsin and its

---

4.   A survey of residents of the European USSR in May 1990 suggested that many ordinary people approached the left–right distinction the same way. About 60 per cent could place themselves on a left–right scale, and those seeing themselves as 'left' were more likely than persons on the 'right' to favour radical social transformation. Since the survey did not ask respondents directly how they defined left and right, conclusions about the meanings attached must be arrived at indirectly: see Lauren M. McLaren, 'Ideology in the Former Soviet Union: Defining Left and Right in a Non-Western Context', unpublished paper, Department of Political Science, University of Houston, 1994. Eurobarometer surveys done in Russia in 1991 and 1992 found the same correlation between self-location on the political left and support for creation of a market economy, whereas in many countries in Eastern Europe the reverse was true: Jürgen Hofrichter and Inge Weller, 'On the Application of the Left-Right Schema in Central and Eastern Eurobarometer Surveys', report prepared for Eurobarometer Unit, Commission of the European Community (Mannheim, April 1993).

one-time tormentors were in at the helm of the state – and were using it aggressively to promote economic liberalization and privatization – it was natural for public discourse to drift towards the traditional European usage. This was quite evident during the 1995 and 1996 election campaigns, when the communists argued for both political innovation (replacement of Yeltsin's government) and a greater state role in the economy.

A few Western analysts, noting the trend, have picked up the revamped terminology. For example, Jerry Hough and two collaborators wrote in a preview of the 1996 presidential election:

> In the past few years, Russian political commentators have begun to move towards western nomenclature by using the terms *Left* and *Right* in their western meanings. The Communists and those close to them are the Left (or, pejoratively, the Reds), while the strong pro-market forces are the Right. As in the West, the strongly nationalist Right does not fit easily in this spectrum, for these parties are usually more pro-market than the Communists but still have a strong element of economic populism. Nevertheless, because these labels begin to put Russia in a meaningful comparative context, we will use them in this book.[5]

Hough went on to discuss Our Home is Russia, Democratic Russia's Choice, and Yabloko as 'right-wing parties' and the CPRF, Agrarians, and related groups as 'left-wing parties', reserving separate niches for the nationalists and centrists.

For certain purposes, therefore, the left–right typology may well serve as an expedient shorthand for Russian pundits and foreign scholars alike. It will not provide independent explanatory power for the study of mass political behaviour, however, unless it can also be demonstrated to have resonance at the grassroots level. To what extent, it is proper to ask, are rank-and-file Russians at home with left–right imagery? Can their fundamental beliefs, their opinions and predilections on current controversies and their assessments of their electoral options be rendered on this dimension? Do left–right differences within the population have any demonstrable connection with choices in the polling booth?

The survey material that this chapter examines was collected in the

5.   Jerry F. Hough, Evelyn Davidheiser and Susan Goodrich Lehmann, *The 1996 Russian Presidential Election*, Brookings Occasional Papers (Washington, DC: Brookings Institution Press, 1996), p. 47.

summer of 1996, in country-wide interviews after the presidential election that returned Yeltsin for a second term. Any points made here cannot automatically be transferred to the setting of a parliamentary election, where voting choices are different and political parties are more directly involved in framing them. None the less, the exercise does yield some clues which can be pursued in subsequent research.[6]

About three-quarters of the way through the interview, the following question was read out to all respondents:

> Sometimes, in describing other persons, people say, 'This is a person of left political views' or, 'This is a person of right political views'. Imagine a scale from 1 to 7, where 1 denotes persons with views on the far left [*s samymi levymi vzglyadami*] and 7 persons with views on the far right [*s samymi pravymi vzglyadami*]. Where on this scale are you?

The interviewer handed the subject a card depicting the seven-point scale, with far left and far right labelled in words and the intermediate locations, 2 to 6, simply numbered. The self-location question was followed by requests to situate the five major presidential candidates (Boris Yeltsin, Gennadii Zyuganov, Aleksandr Lebed, Grigorii Yavlinskii and Vladimir Zhirinovskii) and seven national parties (the CPRF, LDPR, Our Home is Russia, Yabloko, Congress of Russian Communities, Russia's Democratic Choice, and Agrarians) on the same scale. Finally, we asked our informants an open-ended question about the meaning of left and right: 'What, in your opinion, are the most important differences between left and right?'. The verbatim responses to this

6.   The post-presidential election survey was the last in a three-wave panel study supervised by William Zimmerman of the University of Michigan, as co-investigator, and myself. It was carried out by the survey group at the Institute of Sociology of the Russian Academy of Sciences headed by Polina Kozyreva and Mikhail Kosolapov, with the collaboration of Michael Swafford. Generous funding for the project came from the MacArthur Foundation and the Carnegie Corporation. Respondents were selected in a multistage area probability sample with 35 primary sampling units (towns and raions found in five republics and 27 *oblasts* and *krais*) and three self-representing units (St. Petersburg and Moscow city and *oblast*). Of the 3,579 adults drawn into the sample in 1995, 2,841 were interviewed in advance of the State Duma election of December 1995, 2,776 were re-interviewed after that election, and 2,456 were interviewed for a third time in July–August 1996, subsequent to the second round of the presidential election. The data have been weighted by household size, to correct for the over-representation of single persons and members of small households resulting from the sample design. The weighted *N* for the presidential wave, which is used in this chapter, is 2,472.

query were written down by the interviewer, transcribed in Moscow, and later numerically coded for content by myself.

How conversant are Russians today with the left–right distinction? In our sample, a slight majority, 56 per cent, were prepared to reply to the initial question regarding their personal views; 44 per cent could not say or declined to answer. This is a response rate substantially less than the 80 or 90 per cent recorded for similar questions in Western Europe, or than the 65 to 80 per cent for queries about liberal versus conservative beliefs in the United States.

Ideological self-knowledge is distributed unevenly within the population. Russians who happen to be highly aware of political phenomena in general have a considerably larger chance than the politically unaware of being self-conscious in left–right terms. In our 1996 survey, 34 per cent of those in the least informed quintile of the electorate managed to locate themselves on the left–right scale, whereas 71 per cent of the most knowledgeable quintile did so.[7] Formal education, which is highly correlated with political awareness in the Russian Federation, as in many other nations, shapes left–right consciousness in its own right, presumably because of the cognitive sophistication (as distinct from the substantive knowledge) it imparts in men's and women's formative years. While only 30 per cent of those in our sample who had fewer than four years in the classroom could cope with the left–right scale, and 50 to 60 per cent of those with intermediate levels of schooling, 74 per cent of citizens with a post-secondary diploma could.

7.   The awareness index is a simple additive scale with values from 0 to 16, constructed from 14 survey items posed in the first two waves of the panel survey, in late 1995. Taking the lead of John R. Zaller, *The Nature and Origins of Mass Opinion* (Cambridge: Cambridge University Press, 1992), I base it on factual knowledge of politics. One item in the scale, having three values, gives the survey interviewer's evaluation of the respondent's understanding in the interview preceding the Duma election. All other items were scored as 1 or 0 and came from questions put in the subsequent, post-Duma election interview. They asked the positions occupied by five national leaders (Viktor Chernomyrdin, Pavel Grachev, Ivan Rybkin, Vladimir Shumeiko and Anatolii Chubais); ability to evaluate four lesser politicians (Sergei Kovalev, Boris Nemtsov, Anatolii Sobchak and Yuri Luzhkov); the countries led by Jacques Chirac and John Major; and recognition of the International Monetary Fund and of Russia's membership of it. Alpha reliability for the scale is 0.86. It has a mean of 8.67 and a standard deviation of 4.01.

The combined effects of political awareness and education on ideological self-consciousness are plotted in Figure 7.1. Note that at each step of public awareness educational attainment has an autonomous impact on the likelihood of citizens locating themselves on the left–right line. Eighty-one per cent of informants who were simultaneously in the most political aware quintile of the population and had

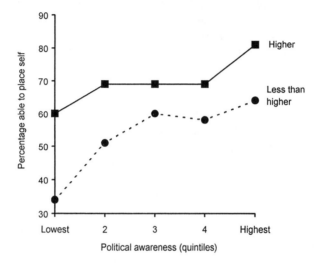

Figure 7.1   Effects of political awareness and education on ability to place self on left–right scale

graduated from a university or institute could say where they belonged on the left–right scale. This was about two-and-a-half times the ratio among less-educated citizens in the least knowledgeable quintile of the mass public.[8]

---

8.   Other individual-level characteristics also had some effect on ideological self-knowledge. There was a gap of 13 percentage points in the ability to locate oneself on the scale between men and women, 13 points between residents of Moscow and St. Petersburg and others, and 14 per cent between former members of the CPSU and persons who were never members of the party. Generationally, self-placement on the scale was most frequent among individuals in their thirties and forties and fell off considerably after the age of seventy, especially among the least informed and the most poorly educated citizens.

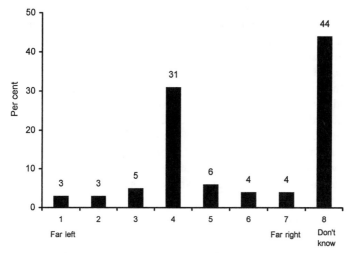

Figure 7.2 Self-locations on left–right scale

Figure 7.2 displays the distribution of the left–right designations which our respondents chose for themselves. Apart from the large number of non-responses, the striking feature of the bar graph is the dominance of category 4, the mid-point of the scale. The middle-of-the-road score outnumbered all other actual responses combined, with right-of-centre responses finishing several points ahead of left-of-centre responses, but coming to barely 40 per cent of the centrist replies. The extreme left and right positions, 1 and 7, attracted a mere 7 per cent between them. The syndrome of eschewing the fringes and cleaving to the centre, endemic to many political systems, is found particularly strongly in post-Soviet Russia.[9]

For ideological preferences to make a difference in a democratic election, the citizens who hold them must ultimately link them to the stances of the politicians and organizations seeking their support in the

9. Converse and Pierce, *Political Representation in France*, pp. 128–9, found French citizens who located themselves at the neutral point on a left–right scale to be disproportionately uninterested in and uninformed about political issues. There is little evidence of this being the case in Russia, especially for knowledge. The mean score for political awareness for respondents who located their views at 4 on the scale was 9.4, only marginally below the average for all respondents who answered the question (9.5).

campaign. According to our data, most Russians who could categorize themselves on the left–right continuum in 1996 could do the same for all or most of the major presidential candidates. Left–right self-identifiers on average placed 3.9 of the five heavyweight candidates mentioned in the interview somewhere on the seven-point scale; respondents who could not formulate a position of their own placed 0.8 candidates on average. Fifty-four per cent of our sample pinpointed Yeltsin and Zyuganov, 52 per cent Lebed, 50 per cent Zhirinovskii, and 47 per cent Yavlinskii. A similar pattern may be detected for the political parties. The mean number of parties placed on the seven-point scale was 4.8 out of 7 for respondents who had located themselves on the scale and 0.9 for respondents who had not.

Table 7.1   Placement of presidential candidates and political parties on left–right scale (percentages)[a]

Candidate or party	Position on scale							
	1 (Far left)	2	3	4	5	6	7 (Far right)	Don't know
Candidates								
Boris Yeltsin	6	3	4	13	6	6	16	46
Gennadii Zyuganov	24	5	3	5	4	3	9	46
Aleksandr Lebed	2	3	6	18	8	7	8	48
Grigorii Yavlinskii	2	3	6	17	7	7	5	53
Vladimir Zhirinovskii	9	6	6	9	5	6	9	50
Parties								
CPRF	24	6	3	4	3	4	9	47
LDPR	7	5	8	8	5	6	8	53
Our Home is Russia	3	3	6	13	6	6	10	53
Yabloko	3	3	6	15	7	6	6	54
Congress of Russian Communities	3	4	7	10	6	4	4	63
Russia's Democratic Choice	3	3	6	10	7	6	9	55
Agrarian Party	6	6	7	10	5	2	4	61

Note: [a] $N = 2,472$.

Table 7.1 depicts exactly where our informants placed the ideological coordinates of the five presidential contenders and the seven political parties in 1996. Let us concentrate here on the candidates for president, as the parties were not in the forefront in the presidential election.[10] The centripetal tendency so prominent in the ideological self-locations portrayed in Figure 7.2 is considerably weaker in the assessments of the candidates, implying that voters have some comprehension of the variety of the choices confronting them. Number 4 is the modal position ascribed to just two of the five presidential contenders, Lebed (at 18 per cent of all respondents) and Yavlinskii (17 per cent). Much about the summary profile for Gennadii Zyuganov seems true to life, inasmuch as 32 per cent of all respondents (61 per cent of those respondents who could locate him) placed him to the left of the centre spot. Realistically, right-of-centre scores for Grigorii Yavlinskii, the first-tier candidate arguably the most remote from Zyuganov on concrete issues, outnumber left-of-centre responses, and the same applies to Boris Yeltsin.

Other aspects of Table 7.2, it has to be said, may baffle the detached observer. Popular perceptions of Vladimir Zhirinovskii, for example, were trimodal in 1996, with almost exactly equal proportions of the citizenry holding him to be an extreme *rightist*, a perfect *centrist*, and an extreme *leftist*. In a well-ordered European polity, the consensus surely would consider Zhirinovskii to be a representative of the extreme, fascist-tending right, in the mould of a Jean-Marie Le Pen in France or a Jörg Haider in Austria. The dispersion of the Zhirinovskii ratings is far from the only anomaly in the table. Note, for instance, that more voters saw Yeltsin as an extreme rightist (position 7) than put Zhirinovskii in the same position. General Lebed, the closest thing to a centrist candidate in 1996, was situated to the right or left of the centre position by twice as many voters as put him in dead centre. And a healthy subgroup of our respondents considered the Moscow intellectual Yavlinskii, the epitome (understandably) of the 'strong pro-market' spokesman in Jerry Hough's taxonomy, to be a man of the left.

Some of this confusion of categories is no doubt a product of limited knowledge and lack of finesse. As Figures 7.3 and 7.4 show for the reputations of the presidential finalists, Zyuganov and Yeltsin, more

10. This applies even to Zyuganov, the leader of Russia's largest and best-organized party, the CPRF. He was nominated by, and formally ran his campaign through, an electoral 'front' representing a number of socialistic groups.

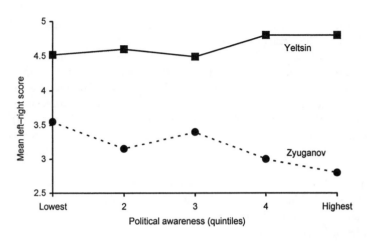

Figure 7.3 Effect of political awareness on placement of Yeltsin and Zyuganov on left–right scale

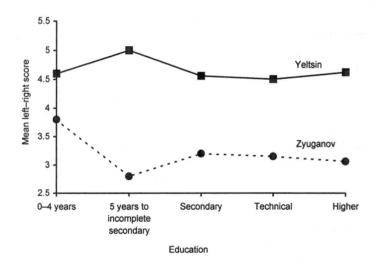

Figure 7.4 Effect of education on placement of Yeltsin and Zyuganov on left–right scale

politically astute and better-educated Russians in 1996 were more inclined than their fellow citizens to impute left-of-centre views to Zyuganov and right-of-centre views to Yeltsin. Figure 7.5 suggests further that psychological projection was also at work, although it manifested itself in different ways for the two principal candidates. Voters of a leftist persuasion not unexpectedly tended more than other respondents to categorize Yeltsin as an extremist of the right. Somewhat surprisingly, they attributed a more left-leaning position to Zyuganov than other respondents did, thereby inflating the perceived ideological distance between him and the anti-communist incumbent.[11]

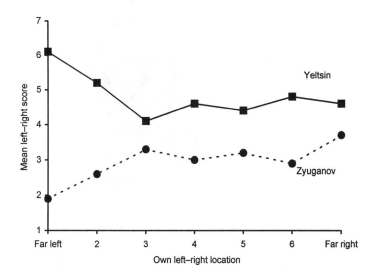

Figure 7.5 Effect of citizens' self-location on placement of Yeltsin and Zyuganov on left–right scale

11. Compare with the tendency for French voters who identify with the radical left to locate parties of that type closer to the political centre than other citizens do: Converse and Pierce, *Political Representation in France*, pp. 124–5.

2. POPULAR UNDERSTANDING OF LEFT AND RIGHT

We can add texture to the picture of left–right differences by folding into it the qualitative comments of our respondents. As mentioned, all those surveyed in the summer of 1996 were asked to verbalize what constitute 'the most important differences' between left and right. My rendering of the results is given in Figure 7.6.

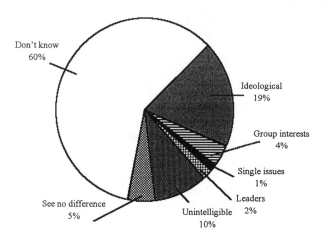

Figure 7.6 Meaning respondents attributed to differences between left and right

It is significant, first of all, that 60 per cent of our sample could *not* provide an answer to the definitional question. Many declined without comment; others volunteered that they knew nothing of such esoteric things or that, the world having been shaken to its foundations, they did not know which way was up:

> I cannot imagine how they [left and right] can be distinguished, but it seems to me that the further away you get from politics the better.
> Before, everybody was a party [CPSU] member, but now everything has been turned around and I cannot understand who is who. All of them only chatter and make promises.
> Now everything has been messed up. You cannot know who is right and who is left. In our time the leftists were communists.

Without question, outright ignorance of the generic meaning of left and right is widespread in the Russian electorate and is considerably more commonplace than lack of consciousness of the individual's own left–right position (the incidence of which was 44 per cent in our sample). Not surprisingly, inability to distinguish left from right was much higher among respondents who could not venture their own left–right location (86 per cent) than for those who could (40 per cent).

The tableaux of left–right differences offered by the 40 per cent of our informants who felt in a position to do so cover a broad front. To impart some order to them, I adapt the level-of-analysis categories for mass political understanding introduced in the classic *The American Voter* and amplified in studies of West European public opinion.

Of most interest to us are the 19 per cent of all respondents to the survey who tied left–right differences to general principles of government, history or social organization. Their comprehension can fairly be characterized as ideological in the full sense of the word, in that it reflects not only recognition of the left–right continuum but its connectedness to underlying normative questions about public affairs and the state. Most frequently, individuals in this group associated a leftist approach with communism and the Soviet regime and rightism with the transformation of Russia into a democracy and market economy. For example:

> Leftists are in favour of our former Soviet life. The rightists are in favour of democracy and the market.
> Leftists want to return to communism, and the rightists want to continue reforms.
> Leftists are communists and rightists are democrats.
> Leftists put a brake on reforms and want to push the country backward. The rightists stand for the rebuilding of our society.
> Leftists are for socialism and rightists are for capitalism in the country.
> Rightists are all for what is new, for democracy. The leftists want to bring back the old times and communism.

As with self-location, the ability to anchor the definition of left and right in abstract notions is much more prevalent among better-informed and better-educated Russian citizens than in other quarters. Thinking about political differences in global, ideological terms was positively associated among our 1996 respondents with both political awareness and higher education (see Figure 7.7). Note, though, that in contrast to

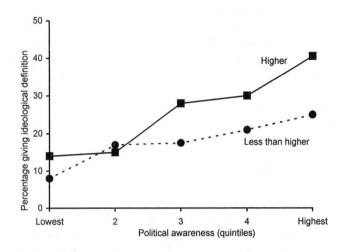

*Figure 7.7 Effects of political awareness and higher education on
ability to give ideological definition of left and right*

Figure 7.1 (which traces left–right self-placement) the educational
effect becomes relevant only for persons with average or above-
average levels of political awareness. Formal education helps bring
about greater ideological sophistication in Russia only when the citizen
– quite apart from his or her reasoning capacity – has moderate or high
levels of substantive knowledge about the political world.

Approximately one citizen in five among our sample formulated an
answer to the question about left–right differences which did not
invoke ideas and abstract concepts. A sprinkling of them related left
and right to social categories (a much more popular answer in Western
Europe), to positions taken on particular issues, or to political leaders
and their styles.[12] Five per cent insisted there is in the end no difference
to speak of between left and right. Responses in this vein often
conveyed cynicism and despair about the condition of Russian political
life:

> Some of them [politicians] chatter about one thing and the rest of them
> chatter about something else, but they all do nothing.

12. Most often, respondents linked either left or right (usually right) to President
    Yeltsin and assigned the other direction to the opposition to him.

There is no difference at all. This kind of division is necessary only for the sake of an election campaign.
They all follow the same policy and there are no particular differences.
They all promise that we will live well, and nothing comes of it.
They may have different political views, but neither one nor the other cares about simple people like me. It's all the same what is left and what is right. Who cares what people call themselves?
The extreme rightists and extreme leftists are almost the same. They differ only in slogans.
Every party does what it promised not to do and does not carry out what it promised. So I don't see any difference.

Then there were the 10 per cent of respondents who gave unintelligible answers, responses that disclose at best the glimmering of an understanding that left and right are differentiable categories, yet with or without moral value: 'different views of life', 'different positions on the development of Russia', 'good and bad', 'worthy and unworthy', and the like. Many individuals made an etymological link between the political right wing and Russian words for goodness and authenticity drawing on the same root. Such declarations were often coupled with confessions of ignorance about the true meaning of 'left':

Rightists are righteous (*pravednye*) and leftists are unrighteous.
The rightists are correct (*pravil'nye*), they are taking the correct path. I don't understand the left parties.
The rightists are for doing the right thing (*za pravoye delo*). I don't know about the leftists.
The rightists are just (*spravedlivye*) and the leftists are unjust.

Let me note, finally, that confusion was not confined to individuals who gave non-ideological responses. A sizeable minority of those who voiced definitions of left and right drawing on philosophical propositions either gave a distorted or eccentric explication of those principles or betrayed evidence of great uncertainty about how to translate them into Russian circumstances. Consider the following remarks:

The leftists are against communism and the rightists are communists.
The leftists are 'red–brown' and the rightists are old communists.
The leftists are more liberal and softer towards people in their decisions and laws. The rightists are extremists – by historical association, like the Left SR's [Left Socialist-Revolutionaries, an early twentieth-century party

dissolved after the Bolshevik Revolution], of whom there are many among the intelligentsia.
The leftists are for democracy and progress. The rightists are for stagnation, terror, and blood.
The leftists are nationalists who urge us to go to war. The rightists are those who struggle against all that.

A particular source of confusion, in my view, is what to do about the category 'right', and especially about the segment of the left–right continuum between what we would conventionally call centre-right and the extreme right. Here Russians' confusion mirrors a confused reality, and perhaps a deep-seated problem in applying a universal scheme without modification to local conditions. Many citizens who perceive the CPRF as left wing and the liberal parties as right wing see, say, Zhirinovskii as a *left-wing* politician. To the extent that Zhirinovskii and populist nationalists like him rail against the status quo and promise to shake it up in forceful fashion, they look to many rank-and-file Russians not unlike the communists.

To be sure, it may be possible for individuals to articulate an explicit interpretation of the meaning of left and right that is disjointed or nebulous, or perhaps to shy away from such a scheme altogether, and at the same time to nurse in the back of their minds an *implicit* conception of left and right that correspondents meaningfully to some external compass points. To see whether this might be so for post-Soviet Russians, it is useful to juxtapose left–right self-placements with opinions ascertained during the survey interview about more concrete issues facing the country. Correlations between the left–right scale and responses to sixteen questions about concrete policy preferences are set out in Table 7.2.

The table demonstrates convincingly that subjective formulations of the left–right continuum among the Russian electorate do have a systematic bearing on other preferences. For all sixteen issues, the correlations between the given issue opinion and the individual's left–right score are massively unlikely to have occurred because of mere chance. The signs of the correlation coefficients, moreover, are all in the predicted direction. The higher (that is, the more rightist) the respondent's left–right score, the more likely she or he was in 1996 to favour liberal economic policies, the less likely to prefer a large state role in social policy, the less likely to favour political authoritarianism, and the less likely to favour an assertive foreign policy *vis-à-vis* the West and

Table 7.2   Associations between left–right self-placement and issue opinions[a]

Issue	Correlation *(r)* with left–right score
Economic	
Allow private trade in land	0.190†
Rapid transition to market economy	0.186†
Prefer private to state property	0.125†
Encourage foreign investment	0.088†
Principal component for all 4 items	0.208†
Social	
Tariff production for Russian firms	−0.122†
Government control of food prices	−0.101†
State over individual responsibility for welfare	−0.109†
Controls on incomes of rich	−0.086†
Government guarantee of job for everyone	−0.081†
Principal component for all 5 items	−0.142†
Political	
Fight crime and corruption at all costs	−0.145†
Better to have strict order than too much freedom	−0.085†
Republics should be able to secede freely	0.068*
Principal component for all 3 items	0.158†
Foreign relations	
Western credits have too many conditions attached	−0.119†
Oppose NATO enlargement	−0.102†
Promote integration with former USSR republics	−0.072†
Increase defence budget	−0.072†
Principal component for all 4 items	−0.140†

Notes

† $p < 0.01$ (two-tailed test).   * $p < 0.05$ (two-tailed test).

[a] *N* for battery of questions is 1,395 (that is, the number of responses to the open-ended question about the meaning of left and right). Missing values for other questions excluded pairwise.

the former Soviet republics. When principal component scores are generated to summarize economic, social, political and foreign-policy opinions, the left–right index has a higher correlation with each component than with the individual items, again pointing to some consistency in attitudes.

A closer reading of Table 7.2 also brings out sobering lessons about the contribution of the left–right distinction to the understanding of

Russian mass politics. First, it must be kept in mind that the correlations catalogued here apply to a bare majority – 56 per cent – of the
electorate. For a very large minority, there is no correlation whatsoever
because the individual is not capable of locating him- or herself
ideologically on the left–right scale. Second, the strengths of the
relationships revealed are not high. For opinions on separate issues, no
correlation with the left–right measure exceeds 0.200 in magnitude and
only two (for private ownership of land and pace of transition to a
market economy) exceed 0.150; seven of sixteen coefficients are lower
than 0.100.

3. LEFT–RIGHT DIFFERENCES AND VOTING BEHAVIOUR

The acid test of measures of left–right orientation is whether they help
us predict mass political behaviour, and in particular voting in national
elections. The high-stakes presidential election of 1996 furnishes a
critical test. If the left–right yardstick has any analytical power, we
would expect it to be manifested in the tendency to vote for or against
the candidate affiliated with the most overtly ideological political force
in Russian politics – the CPRF. The candidate in question is Gennadii
Zyuganov, who attracted 32.0 per cent in the first round of the election
and 40.3 per cent in losing the run-off to Boris Yeltsin. Does the left–
right variable add to our understanding of who voted for and against
Zyuganov?

Table 7.3 gives some intriguing answers. It presents the results of an
ordinary least squares regression of first-round votes for Zyuganov
against two explanatory variables: our seven-point left–right measure,
re-scaled to measure from 0 to 1, with missing values set at the mid-
point of the scale; and the five-value measure of attitude towards state
versus private ownership of property, re-scaled from 0 to 1 and with
missing values re-coded to the mean of the distribution. I chose the
property indicator to perform the test because I know it to have quite a
strong bivariate relationship to voting choice in 1996[13] and because the

13. A mere 4 per cent of voters who believed all economic property should be in
     private hands voted for Zyuganov in the first round of the election, while 61 per
     cent of those who preferred exclusively state property voted for him.

Table 7.3 *Effects of left–right score and opinion about private property on vote for Zyuganov in first round of presidential election (OLS estimates)*

Explanatory variable	Least aware voters[a]		Moderately aware voters[b]		Most aware voters[c]		All voters	
	B (SE)	Beta	B (SE)	Beta	B (SE)	Beta	B (SE)	Beta
Left–right	-0.114 (0.107)	-0.042	-0.393 (0.098)	-0.148	-0.726 (0.076)	-0.313	-0.449 (0.053)	-0.176
Property	-0.805 (0.099)	-0.320	-0.837 (0.094)	-0.327	-0.813 (0.089)	-0.300	-0.823 (0.054)	-0.318
Constant	0.654 (0.059)		0.730 (0.060)		0.897 (0.047)		0.781 (0.031)	
Adjusted R^2	0.107		0.127		0.212		0.144	

Notes: [a] $N = 600$. [b] $N = 644$. [c] $N = 741$.

property issue was much stressed by the contestants during the campaign. The regression was performed for our entire sample of the electorate and, to probe for sophistication effects, for subsets of the electorate partitioned into thirds by degree of political awareness.

In the sample as a whole, both the left–right scale and the opinion about property are quite solid predictors of the vote for Zyuganov, with sizeable coefficients significant at an extremely high level. Taking the standardized coefficient (Beta) as the best measure of explanatory weight, the left–right score has considerably less influence on the vote – a little bit more than half – than opinion about property ownership. If the question is whether left–right ideology or preference on the discrete issue of property ownership is the most illuminating predictor of the vote, then the property issue wins hands down.

The other feature of the regression, deserving at least as much emphasis, is the sharp difference in the results obtained for voters at different levels of political awareness. The standardized and unstandardized coefficients for opinion on private property remain virtually flat across plateaux of political awareness. For this relationship, it seems to matter little whether the voter is relatively ignorant of public issues or richly informed. But the coefficients for the left–right scale behave very differently. They *increase* conspicuously from the least aware third of the electorate, where they are so tiny as to fall below the usual threshold of statistical significance, to the most aware third. In fact, for the most attuned citizens the standardized coefficient for the effect of left–right placement on the vote is slightly *larger* in magnitude than the coefficient for attitude on property. For this relationship, it clearly matters a great deal how knowledgeable the voter is.

4. CONCLUSIONS AND IMPLICATIONS

The evidence of this chapter suggests in total that we should award ideological values, as captured in the terminology of left and right, a modest but nowhere near a determinative place in our understanding of Russian mass politics. Their pertinence seems greater than in Russia five or ten years ago, but not nearly as great as in most Western democracies. A slight majority of citizens today recognize the words 'left' and 'right'; nearly as many Russians do not. Only 40 per cent of survey respondents in 1996 could articulate what they thought the nomenclature means, and many of them did so in a fuzzy and undiscerning manner or in terms incompatible with international usage. And for the electorate as a whole, single-issue opinions seem better suited than any left–right scale to explaining how individuals vote.

This having been said, the demonstrably greater familiarity with left–right imagery evinced by the more politically aware segment of the population, and the much more intimate relationship of ideological beliefs to voting choice in these quarters, may well point to the likelihood of ideology's assuming a greater role in mass politics in the future. To the extent that electoral competition proves in due course to be the school of citizenship that many classics of democratic theory suggest it should be, we can expect Russians to become gradually more at home with seeing the political struggle as turning on some, if not all, of the same contested values that are at issue in many established democratic polities. Our research programme for Russia and similar countries in the years ahead should make room for discovering whether this conjecture is borne out in reality.

8. The Mystery of Opponents of Economic Reform among the Yeltsin Voters

Jerry F. Hough and Susan Goodrich Lehmann

The 1996 Russian presidential election has been interpreted in a number of different ways. For some, Yeltsin and the various right-wing parties are synonymous with democracy and economic reform. While many Russians are dissatisfied with the course of reform, Russia, in this view, has 'a polarized electorate' that is divided between 'those for "reform," however defined [and] those against'. From this perspective, the vote for Yeltsin was one for 'moving both from authoritarian to democratic rule and from a communist to a market system'. Yeltsin won precisely because he moved to solidify his support among the reformers.[1]

For others – for example, Gavriil Popov – Yeltsin won not because he was a democrat, but because he was not: the average Yeltsin supporter was a patriarchal traditionalist voting for an authoritarian tsar.[2] Indeed, a television advertisement of General Aleksandr Lebed, run when he was being supported and financed by Yeltsin forces, stated that he and Yeltsin were real tsars, but that Gennadii Zyuganov and Grigorii Yavlinskii could not be imagined in this role and hence did not deserve support.

The distinguished correspondent of the *Financial Times*, Chrystia Freeland, expressed a similar opinion in her last report before the first

---

1. Michael McFaul, 'Russia's Presidential Election', *Post-Soviet Affairs*, Vol. 12, No. 4 (October–December 1996), pp. 321 and 344.
2. *Argumenty i fakty*, 1996, No. 8, p. 3.

round of the election: 'Nearly 1000 years of Tatar overlords, autocratic tsars and communist dictatorships have left Russians accustomed to abasing themselves before their rulers. Tomorrow, as they grit their teeth and vote for a president few trust or admire, many Russians will be vowing that it is the last time'.[3]

Our 1996 election survey yields support for each interpretation. Authoritarianism is difficult to define and measure, but when three simple questions were added into a scale, there was a −0.23 correlation between authoritarianism and support for Yeltsin and a −0.31 correlation between support for economic reform and authoritarianism, crudely defined. Support for economic reform correlates strongly with support for Yeltsin in a Yeltsin–Zyuganov contest: a +0.52 correlation on scales constructed from our pre-election study.[4]

On the other hand, our surveys, including one of 24- and 32-year-olds conducted in March 1997, show no evidence of polarization of opinion on economic reform among Russians. Instead we find a bell-shaped distribution of views, albeit with an abnormally long tail on the right-wing or 'radical' side of the spectrum; the top of the curve lies well to the left-wing (or conservative) side.[5]

This moderate character of Russian opinion is evident from answers to questions other than economic reform. As the data presented in Appendix 8A show, our election studies have consistently demonstrated that a strong majority of Russians thought that the breakup of

3. *Financial Times*, 15–16 June 1996, Weekend Section, p. 2.
4. Our survey included the question 'How do you react to the following candidates for president?'. As in 1993, the answers suggested that the respondents treated the questions as a surrogate for a subtle question on voting intention. Thus, in the pre-election survey, if 'undecided' are excluded, 33.4 per cent evaluated Yeltsin 'positively' and 20.1 per cent 'more positively than negatively', and 29.5 per cent evaluated Zyuganov 'positively' and 13.0 per cent 'more positively than negatively'. The 'positive' answers for both candidates were very close to their first-round vote and the 'more positively than negatively' very close to their respective incremental gains on the second round. For this reason, an index with some spread can be created by adding the two sets of answers, with one of them reversed. That we have done. The economic reform scale is discussed on pp. 202ff of this chapter.
5. Only a quarter of the voters thought that Russia was on a correct path, up from 10 per cent six months earlier, and Yeltsin received 96 per cent of their vote. The quarter who were not sure were conservative in their economic views, but Yeltsin won 73 per cent of their vote and even 31 per cent of those who thought Russia was on an incorrect path. If Zyuganov had won 96 per cent of the last group he would have won easily.

the Soviet Union was harmful, but they do not want to reunite the former Soviet Union by force. Instead, they want a tolerant federation or confederation. The Russian public is a strong supporter of democracy, but unhappy with democracy as it is developing in Russia.

The purpose of this chapter is to begin exploring the mystery of the voter who disapproves, often strongly, of the economic reforms and other policies pursued by Yeltsin over the past six years, but who still voted for him. The pro-reform Yeltsin voters turn out to have the characteristics we all expect – younger, better educated, inhabitants of large cities, and the like. Yet, the pro-reform voters comprise only a quarter of the electorate and only 40 per cent of Yeltsin's vote. One might think that the other Yeltsin voters were also younger, better educated and more urban, but simply doubted the efficacy of his economic policy. In fact, this turns out not to be the case. The conservatives on economic reform who vote for Yeltsin turn out to be similar to Zyuganov voters across a range of characteristics and views. In that sense, both the McFaul and the Popov and Freeland positions accurately point to real groups of voters among Yeltsin supporters.

This point has major implications for an understanding of Russia. Scholars studying Russia typically rely on regression analysis in trying to ascertain the characteristics of the supporters of different candidates and parties. Yet when we analyse the victory of Bill Clinton in the United States in 1996 and Tony Blair in Britain in 1997, we do not focus on their core left-wing supporters and their success in mobilizing them, but on their ability to move to the centre and win more moderate voters. This phenomenon is not well caught in the typical regression analysis.

From this perspective, the existence of two distinctive groups of Yeltsin supporters is of major importance. No one doubted that Yeltsin had a core group in the electorate who would support him against any conservative candidate or that this group possessed the characteristics found in the most pro-reform quarter of the sample. But Yeltsin's problem was to pick up those voters more towards the centre of the spectrum. From a theoretical point of view, it would be highly unusual if he succeeded in doing this, as McFaul suggests, by emphasizing the economic reform of Anatolii Chubais.

Part of the explanation lies in Yeltsin's obfuscation of his own position on economic reform in the early part of the campaign and his offering of subsidies to every group and region he visited. Another part was the ability of state television to place Zyuganov on a more extreme part of the spectrum than he actually occupied and thereby make Yeltsin seem more centrist. But the kind of factors that Popov and Freeland emphasized should not be ignored, nor should Yeltsin's ability to use social appeals to add to his economic ones.

In this respect, as in others, we need to begin to think of Russian politics in more comparative and theoretical terms. The US Republican Party, for example, wins by combining basically secular, high-income, pro-choice 'Country Club' voters with fundamentalist, low- and middle-income, pro-life members of the Religious Right. When the Republican Party was formed in the 1850s, it was based on a similar combination of the 'respectable' Protestants and the supporters of the nativist Know Nothing Party. Franklin Roosevelt put together a winning coalition of liberals, Catholic immigrants from the North, and anti-Catholic segregationists from the South. It should not be surprising if successful Russian politicians too must learn to put economic and 'social' issues together in such a way as to attract contradictory groups.

1. THE DIFFERENCE BETWEEN YELTSIN AND ZYUGANOV VOTERS

A wide variety of Russian and Western surveys have defined the basic characteristics of the core Russians who have supported the reform parties and Yeltsin in comparison with those voting communist. As Table 8.1 indicates, our surveys confirm the basic conclusions of this other work: age, education, income, evolution of economic situation, occupation, and size of population of place of residence, are all correlated with voting behaviour in the expected manner. But these statistics can be seen in another way. Even when he failed to gain a majority from them, Yeltsin received an unexpectedly large number of votes from those who had incomplete secondary education or income under 300,000 rubles a month, who were unskilled workers or were over 50 years old, who lived in rural areas or towns under 10,000, and from those who thought their economic situation had worsened in the previous year.

The situation with respect to place of residence is especially important. All studies have noted that respondents living in rural areas

Table 8.1   Percentage of Yeltsin vote in the second round, by selected demographic and economic characteristics

Education

	Respondent's	Father's	Mother's
Elementary	36.6	36.4	41.2
Incomplete secondary	43.5	49.6	49.0
Complete vocational secondary	63.2	53.6	54.6
Complete general secondary	60.3	72.0	69.4
Complete specialized secondary	63.3	74.4	70.6
Incomplete higher	71.0	65.9	74.4
Complete higher	69.1	72.6	73.0

Age

18–29	30–39	40–49	50–59	60+
75.9	67.7	58.3	47.7	43.2

Economic condition over past year

Improved significantly	75.4
Improved somewhat	84.2
Remained unchanged	68.8
Worsened somewhat	56.7
Worsened significantly	37.4

Size of place of residence

0–9,999	43.5
10,000–199,999	59.8
200,000–999,999	60.9
Over 1 million	74.9

Occupation (including former occupation)

	Age under 60	Age over 60
Higher manager	78.9	62.9
Middle manager	68.5	46.0
Lower manager (supervisor)	56.6	32.6
Professional	70.4	54.0
White collar	64.4	51.8
Skilled worker	57.9	40.9
Unskilled worker	57.8	40.4
Peasant	34.3	39.7
Private business	85.1	100.0

Table 8.1 continued

Monthly income in basic job, if employed

Less than 300,000 rubles	49.9
300,000–599,999 rubles	60.3
600,000 rubles and over	71.0

Note: The undecided are excluded, and hence the Zyuganov percentage can be obtained by subtracting the given figure by 100. Only likely voters are included in this table and later tables.

and smaller towns have had more conservative views and voting behaviour than those in the larger cities. Since economic reform has scarcely touched the countryside and small towns, since below-market prices are paid in the agricultural sector in order to maintain subsidized food prices in large cities, and since incomes in smaller towns and the countryside are lower and paid more tardily, the attitudes and voting behaviour in these areas have not been a surprise.[6]

Russian scholars working with the Central Electoral Commission emphasized Yeltsin's success in the 100 largest cities as the key to his victory in the 1996 election, and Westerners have generally followed their lead. And, in fact, 63 per cent of those who voted in such cities in the second round voted for Yeltsin, compared with 30.8 per cent for Zyuganov. Nevertheless, the fact remains that Yeltsin received a total of 40.2 million votes and that he won only 18.8 million of them in the 100 largest cities.[7]

In fact, Yeltsin won because he did much better in the small towns and the countryside than might have been expected. In our survey, 47.3 per cent of those living in the countryside and towns with fewer than 25,000 inhabitants voted for Yeltsin in the second round and 58.6 per cent of those living in towns with a population in the range 25,000–200,000 voted for him. One might worry about a sampling problem,

6. See Jerry F. Hough, Evelyn Davidheiser and Susan Lehmann, *The 1996 Russian Presidential Election* (Washington, DC: Brookings Institution, 1996), pp. 5–8, 37, and 56–8; and Ralph S. Clem and Peter R. Craumer, 'Urban–Rural Voting Differences in Russian Elections, 1995–1996: A Rayon-Level Analysis', *Post-Soviet Geography and Economics*, Vol. 30, No. 7 (September 1997), pp. 379–95.
7. Calculated from *Vybory Prezidenta Rossiiskoi Federatsii, 1996: Elektoral'naia statistika* (*Presidential Elections of the Russian Federation, 1996: Electoral Statistics*) (Moscow: Ves' mir, 1996), pp. 183–5 and 280.

but Table 8.2 is drawn from the official electoral data released by the Electoral Commission and shows a similar pattern.[8]

Table 8.2   Percentage of vote for Yeltsin and Zyuganov, by percentage of urban population in electoral section and the size of its largest town and city, 1996 presidential election

Size of largest town or city	Number of electors (million)	Percentage urban							
		<25		25–49		50–74			75+
		Ye	Zyu	Ye	Zyu	Ye	Zyu	Ye	Zyu
		First Round							
Rural	9.6	29.1	47.6	28.6	41.5	39.5	26.8	33.7	33.1
1,000–9,000	12.3	26.9	45.6	26.6	45.3	33.7	33.7	38.2	23.5
10,000–24,999	11.3	25.2	48.0	25.2	48.2	28.7	38.4	33.7	28.4
25,000–49,999	10.4			26.5	45.3	29.6	39.4	33.5	30.7
50,000–199,999	19.4					33.0	33.8	35.0	31.1
200,000–999,999	24.5							35.4	27.4
One–two million	8.8							47.1	21.8
St. P. and Moscow	9.9							59.5	15.2
		Second Round							
Rural	9.7	42.8	54.0	43.5	52.2	60.5	34.0	54.2	40.2
1,000–9,000	12.4	42.8	53.4	41.2	54.8	50.1	45.0	59.1	34.2
10,000–24,999	11.4	37.1	59.3	39.4	56.9	46.4	48.8	54.8	39.2
25,000–49,999	10.4			41.6	55.1	47.7	47.9	54.0	40.4
50,000–199,999	19.5					51.6	43.5	54.8	39.8
200,000–999,999	24.5							56.7	37.1
One–two million	8.8							64.5	30.2
St. P. and Moscow	9.7							76.9	18.8

Note: This table is based on some 1.6 to 1.8 million fewer electors than officially announced. Electors living abroad or in Chechnya or Ingushetia are excluded, as are those in a few districts in which boundaries were changed from 1995. Their exclusion should not affect the results.

8.   The data on size of largest city or town in the electoral districts (*uchastki*) and the percentage of urban population was added by the authors to the official data set.

The data from our survey and the electoral commission are not strictly comparable, for votes 'against both' have been removed from our own, but not from the official data. Moreover, in the official data, almost all villages and towns smaller than 10,000 people and a large number of those between 10,000 and 25,000 are in districts with mixed rural and urban population, although by definition 'urban' in these areas denotes very small towns. Our survey data separate the two categories.

But, whatever the division between rural and 'urban' in these areas where towns had fewer than 25,000 people, Yeltsin won one-quarter of his total vote in them, and nearly 55 per cent in villages, towns, and cities with less than 200,000 population. He defeated Zyuganov by 3.5 million to 3.2 million in districts whose largest town was between 10,000 and 25,000 population and by 7.2 million to 5.1 million in those whose largest town had between 25,000 and 200,000 inhabitants.

Although three of our surveys were conducted at the time of the 1993, 1995 and 1996 elections, respectively, the general purpose of our work has been not the study of electoral behaviour, but documentation of the social structure that existed at the end of the communist period and the evolution of attitudes and values in the aftermath of a great revolution. Hence, our questionnaires have included 60 demographic and economic questions, many of them seldom found in election studies.

A book which we are writing with Evelyn Davidheiser explores the relative impact on political attitudes of earlier social experiences and cultural attitudes and of the contemporary economic and social situation. Table 8.3 includes two such questions – education of father and mother – and they correlate with support for Yeltsin by +0.21 and +0.23, respectively, and with support for economic reform by +0.36 and +0.39, respectively. Respondents' own education correlates only +.17 with support for Yeltsin and +.31 with support for economic reform.

Similarly, the size of the town in which the respondent grew up also correlated with support for Yeltsin – and, again, somewhat more strongly than the size of town in which he or she lives at present (+0.22 compared with +0.18) and also more strongly with support for economic reform (+0.27 against +0.13). Yet, as Table 8.3 indicates, the two factors strongly interact: those living in larger cities who grew up in the countryside or smaller town support Yeltsin less than those in similar cities who were raised in larger cities; those raised in the country or smaller town and living in large cities are more supportive of Yeltsin than those of similar background who live in smaller towns.

Table 8.3   Support for Yeltsin and Zyuganov, by size of settlement in which respondent lives and was raised, second round, 1996 election

Size of settlement in which respondent lives	Size of settlement in which respondent was raised	Vote for Yeltsin (%)	Vote for Zyuganov (%)
Under 10,000 inhabitants	Over 10,000 inhabitants	52.0	48.0
	Under 10,000 inhabitants	42.8	57.2
10,000–199,000 inhabitants	Over 10,000 inhabitants	68.3	31.7
	Under 10,000 inhabitants	48.7	51.3
200,000–999,000 inhabitants	Over 200,000 inhabitants	70.5	29.5
	10,000–199,999 inhabitants	63.7	36.3
	Under 10,000 inhabitants	47.8	52.2
Over 1 million inhabitants	Over 200,000 inhabitants	81.7	18.3
	10,000–199,999 inhabitants	74.3	25.5
	Under 10,000 inhabitants	59.9	40.1

There is other evidence in our surveys showing the impact of traditional cultural values. The General Social Survey, the major annual national sociological survey in the United States, includes questions on attitudes about preferred values for children, partly as a base for the construction of authoritarianism scales. Some of these questions were included on the between-election survey in 1996, but at the suggestion of the junior author, the questions were divided into separate questions for values of boys and girls.[9] As the hard numbers in Table 8.4 indicate, the difference in values that Russians valued in girls and boys is striking.

The percentage figures indicate that answers with respect to boys did not correlate with support for Yeltsin if we control for respondents'

9.   The basic questions about desired values were included at the request of Karen Stenner of Duke University for her work on authoritarianism. Lehmann believed (quite rightly, it turned out) that Russians have very different views of proper traits for men and women.

*Table 8.4 Yeltsin vote in the second round by attitude towards
economic reform and number of 'independent' answers to
questions about ideal values for boys and girls*

Number of independent values	Total	Attitude towards economic reform		
		Pro-reform	Moderate conservative	Conservative and Arch-conservative
Boys				
0	–	–	–	–
1	48.4	91.8	73.9	31.4
	(136 of 281)	(41 of 44)	(37 of 50)	(59 of 188)
2	60.0	91.6	75.4	37.4
	(266 of 443)	(101 of 111)	(79 of 105)	(85 of 227)
3	61.9	94.4	71.4	34.5
	(403 of 651)	(168 of 178)	(139 of 195)	(96 of 279)
4	60.3	96.8	68.3	34.2
	(145 of 241)	(64 of 67)	(42 of 62)	(38 of 112)
Girls				
0	52.3	92.1	71.9	29.6
	(258 of 493)	(89 of 97)	(87 of 121)	(81 of 275)
1	56.1	90.1	71.3	33.3
	(296 of 527)	(106 of 118)	(100 of 140)	(89 of 268)
2	63.9	98.1	71.9	38.1
	(250 of 391)	(109 of 111)	(73 of 102)	(68 of 178)
3	71.4	95.3	76.7	47.5
	(147 of 206)	(70 of 73)	(37 of 48)	(40 of 84)
4	–	–	–	–

attitude towards economic reform. The situation with respect to ideal
traits in girls is more complex. There is no meaningful correction in the
case of those with a pro-reform or moderate conservative attitude
towards economic reform, but people with 'modern' ideas about
women's values and conservative views on economic reform do
support Yeltsin more than those not cross-pressured. The key fact of
Table 8.4, however, is the very substantial number of people who were
authoritarian by this measure and very conservative on economic

reform, but who still voted for Yeltsin. If Zyuganov had won 90 per cent of the conservatives and arch-conservatives who chose no or only one independent value for girls, he would have won the election even if nothing else changed.

By some cultural indicators, Yeltsin actually did better than Zyuganov among those usually considered traditional. The most obvious are the religious. Religious believers in Russia have become quite diverse in character. The older believers have long been among the most traditional elements of Soviet society, but now it has become fashionable for young people to believe in God, although not to practise religious observance. For this reason, religious belief tends not to correlate highly with other variables. As Table 8.5 indicates, however, religious belief is associated with voting for Yeltsin among those aged under 30 and those over 50. The young may have become believers because they were radical in other spheres, but this is scarcely likely to be the case for those over 50 years old. The differences between Yeltsin's supporters among believers and non-believers of this age group is significant. If believers over 50 had voted as did the non-believers of that age, Zyuganov would have won one-sixth of the extra vote that he need for victory. Of such atoms is a winning molecule built.

Table 8.5   Support for Yeltsin and Zyuganov, by age and religious belief (per cent)

Age	Belief	Vote for Yeltsin	Vote for Zyuganov
18–29	Believer (44.9%)	80.2	19.8
	Non-believer (42.9%)	73.1	26.9
30–39	Believer (47.6%)	69.5	30.5
	Non-believer (42.7%)	68.2	32.8
40–49	Believer (46.2%)	57.2	42.8
	Non-believer (44.7%)	59.9	40.1
50–59	Believer (53.0%)	52.5	47.5
	Non-believer (37.3%)	49.9	50.1
60+	Believer (63.3%)	51.2	48.8
	Non-believer (31.4%)	44.7	55.3

2. ATTITUDES TOWARDS ECONOMIC REFORM

By far the strongest correlations with support for Yeltsin reported so far in this chapter have been among those with attitudes towards economic reform. The only demographic factor to be correlated with voting behaviour nearly as strongly is age, but it is less robust, at +0.37 instead of +0.52. One might think this resulted either from strong support for Yeltsin's economic reform or at least from a fear of criticizing it, but, in fact, respondents in June 1996 answered in a very disenchanted manner about the course of economic reform, not to mention the specific measures that economists such as Anatolii Chubais were advocating.

In order to judge the evolution of attitudes over time, we repeated a number of the same questions in election surveys conducted in Russia in 1993, 1995 and 1996 and in a survey of those aged 24–32 conducted in March 1997. The results for a number of questions are presented in Appendix 8A, with separate tables for those aged 24–32 so that data from the youth study may be utilized. These tables show that public opinion on policy matters has been relatively stable from 1993 to 1997. The number of people supporting radical economic reform has been declining, but so too has the number who are totally against reform. (Paradoxically this was probably the effect of Zyuganov's moderate campaign.) Members of the public have become much more negative about the privatization of large enterprises, but somewhat more accepting of the sale of land – although one wonders in the latter case whether they were thinking of major urban and farm land or mainly *dacha* and vegetable garden land.

While young people are more supportive of economic reform, the tables show that it would be a grave mistake to think that only the old resist reform as defined by the International Monetary Fund (IMF) or that any increase in conservative views is limited to older respondents. For example, Table 8.6 shows answers to questions concerning attitudes towards the privatization of large enterprises given by respondents between the ages of 24 and 32.

Only the 1996 pre-election survey had questions from previous surveys, but the 1996 between-election survey included a number of new questions, and the answers to them point in exactly the same direction as those in the pre-election survey. To the basic question,

Table 8.6   Do you support privatization of large enterprises?

	1993	1995	1996	1997
1. Completely support	23.1	11.4	12.5	8.0
2. Support on the whole	28.1	21.3	17.5	23.3
3. Do not support it on whole	15.4	19.8	23.2	22.9
4. Completely against it	13.2	20.6	22.3	22.8
5. Hard to say	19.4	26.6	23.9	22.3
6. No answer	0.5	0.2	0.5	0.7

'What in your opinion ought to be done in the present economic situation in the country?', 10 per cent answered, 'Hold to today's course of reform'; 55 per cent, 'Continue reforms, but introduce serious changes in carrying them out'; and 20 per cent, 'Return to a planned economy, to state supply, and regulation of prices'.

In the between-election survey, 74 per cent of respondents either completely or generally agreed that privatization brings more use to the mafia and speculators than to honest people. Only 14 per cent completely or generally agreed that the name of Lenin should be removed from all geographic points and organizations in Russia. Sixty-eight per cent agreed that the government does not take public opinion into account when it makes decisions. Seventy-six per cent of respondents completely agreed that 'the government should guarantee work to everyone who needs it', and an additional 16 per cent generally agreed. This, it should be noted, is in a sample of respondents, 49.8 per cent of whom said they would vote for Yeltsin on the second round and 24.7 per cent for Zyuganov, with the rest saying they would not vote or were undecided.

A number of questions on the 1996 pre-election questionnaire dealt with detailed aspects of economic reform, and ten of them have been combined into an index. The 'reform' position as understood in the West is given 10, the moderate reform position 20, the moderate conservative position 40, and the most negative position 50. 'Don't know' answers were coded as 30. The answers were simply added, and hence a respondent who answered all questions with the answer approved by the IMF and Yegor Gaidar would receive a total score of 100. One who always took the moderate reform option would have a total score of 200 and one halfway between the reform and conservative positions

Table 8.7 Number of respondents with different economic reform scores

Reform score	Number	Percentage
120–145	15	0.4
150–195	137	3.6
200–245	352	9.3
250–295	634	16.8
300–345	813	21.5
350–395	930	24.6
400–445	632	16.7
450–500	267	7.1

would have 300. The results are given in Table 8.7. Only 5.2 per cent of the respondents received a score of 200 or less, and 33.2 per cent a score of 300 or less.

Given the fact that the moderate reform position (200) was vague and easy to answer (for example, support foreign investment or the sale of land but with restrictions), the 'don't know' responses are likely to be more conservative than their placement on the scale indicates. This can be illustrated by examining responses to two general questions on economic reform asked in the pre-election questionnaire, which were not included in the index: (1) 'Are things going in a correct or incorrect direction?'; and (2) 'Should the transition to the market be quick, gradual, or opposed altogether?'. Approximately a quarter of the respondents answered 'don't know' to each question.

Those who answered 'don't know' to either general question favoured housing privatization in a ratio of 53:24 per cent with 23 per cent undecided, but opposed privatization of big enterprises by 56:14 per cent, with 30 per cent undecided. They thought the West was trying to weaken Russia with its economic advice by a 59:15 per cent margin, with 33 per cent undecided. Ten per cent thought food prices should be determined by the market, 36 per cent that they should be restricted but not strictly controlled, and 60 per cent that they should be strictly controlled. Sixty-six per cent thought the income of the rich should be limited, 22 per cent not, while 15 per cent did not know. All these positions were somewhat more conservative than the sample as a whole.

The scores of the economic reform scale are not a reflection of abstract ideology, but rather of the conviction that the policies followed by Yeltsin were not working well. In December 1995, only 10 per cent of the population thought things were going in a correct direction, and, despite the strong tendency for the voter in 1996 to see the question as a referendum on the presidential election, this figure only rose to 23 per cent in 1996.[10] As Table 8.8 shows, scores on the economic reform are closely associated with judgement about whether things are going in a correct direction in Russia.

Table 8.8   Attitude to economic reform among likely voters, by answer to 'Are things going in a correct direction?'

	Economic reform score	Percentage of respondents	Correct	Incorrect	Hard to say
Pro-reform	100–275	22.9	57.6	18.3	24.1
Moderate conservative	280–345	26.7	25.2	41.1	33.7
Conservative	350–400	26.7	12.2	61.0	16.8
Arch-conservative	405–500	23.6	3.6	82.5	13.8
Total			24.0	51.0	24.9

3.   IDENTIFYING THE YELTSIN VOTERS

Clearly whatever the precise interpretation of the index scores, a large number of individuals who opposed the economic reform and other programmes of the Yeltsin government still voted for him as president instead of the candidate whose views seemed far closer to theirs. This is the key problem to explain, but it is not a simple task.

First, Russian election studies face a little-recognized methodological difficulty. Virtually all election surveys in the United States show more respondents claiming to have voted than actually did so; they also

10. For the 1995 data, see Hough, Davidheiser and Lehmann, *The 1996 Russian Presidential Election.*

feature over-reporting of the vote for the victor. In Russia, an analogous, but not identical, phenomenon occurs: too high a percentage of respondents report having voted, but not necessarily too high a percentage that they voted for the winner. Instead, Russian surveys report excess support for best-known respectable candidates or parties, regardless of whether they won.[11]

In some surveys, over-reporting of the support for respectable candidates may result from sampling problems, but this is not the only possibility. We need to remember a simple mathematical fact often forgotten in election analysis: percentages are obtained by dividing a denominator into a numerator. When the percentages of votes reported for Zyuganov or Zhirinovskii are too low, we usually assume that the problem is in the numerator – that is, that the support for these men is under-reported.[12] In reality, in our own surveys in 1993, 1995 and 1996, the problem lay in the denominator.

A sample can be treated as a real replica of the electorate, and we can calculate the number of respondents in the sample who should have gone to the polls and voted for each candidate if the sample were perfect. For example, 64.8 per cent of the electorate were officially reported to have cast a valid ballot in the second round of the 1996 election. That means that 2,450 out of 3,781 respondents in our pre-election survey should have voted in the second round. If those who deliberately voted against both candidates in the second round are excluded, Yeltsin received 57.2 per cent of the vote in the run-off and Zyuganov 42.8 per cent. That means 1,401 respondents in our pre-election sample should have voted for Yeltsin and 1,049 for Zyuganov.

In fact, when asked in the pre-election survey whom they would vote for in a contest between Yeltsin and Zyuganov, 61.8 per cent of those with a concrete choice answered Yeltsin and 38.2 per cent Zyuganov – an under-reporting of 4.6 percentage points for Zyuganov. However, 1,105 actual respondents named Zyuganov, an over-

---

11. Occasionally, surveys done in Russia show results that correspond almost exactly to the actual results. Given the near universality of over-reporting in the West, the question is whether precise results in the occasional Russian study reflect a particularly accurate random sample or one achieved in the field or institute through a quota sample.

12. Vladimir Shlapentokh, 'The Polls – A Review: The 1993 Russian Election Polls', *Public Opinion Quarterly*, Vol. 58 (1994), pp. 579–602.

reporting by 56 respondents, not an under-reporting![13] The problem was that 1,773 respondents named Yeltsin – 372 more than was proper. This meant that the denominator totalled 2,878, not 2,450 as it should have, and, consequently, the percentage for Zyuganov was smaller than it would have been with the correct denominator.

We strongly suspect that a large number of the excess Yeltsin voters were respondents who said they would vote when they had little intention of doing so. American respondents who make a false claim of voting in order to appear respectable to the interviewer can then make the quite respectable claim to have voted for either the Republican or the Democratic candidate or can simply boast that they supported the winner. But Russian respondents know that television and, probably, the interviewer think some leading candidates highly disreputable. Respondents who falsely claim that they voted in order to avoid interviewer disapproval scarcely want to claim falsely that they voted for a disreputable candidate. The 'natural' false answer for non-voters was Yeltsin in 1996, quite apart from reasons of fear.[14]

There are a number of confirmations of this hypothesis in our data. For example, those who said that they voted in the 1995 election and named a particular candidate said that they would vote for Yeltsin by a 58:42 per cent margin, almost exactly the correct percentage. By contrast, those who said they did not vote in 1995, or could not remember for whom, reported a preference for Yeltsin by a 68:32 per cent margin. Similarly, respondents were asked four questions about how often they talked about politics with friends or followed the campaign on television or radio, or in newspapers. Those who showed little interest in politics (they answered, several times a week or less on the average) said they voted for Yeltsin by 66:34 per cent, while 57 per cent of those

13. Actually, the reported vote is even more accurate than seems on the surface. Four per cent of the ballots were reported to be invalid – 98 of our respondents if they were a perfect sample. Some invalid ballots were, no doubt, deliberate, but many who cast an invalid vote did not realize what they had done and thought they had actually voted for a candidate. It would not be surprising if many of the vote counters were looking for invalid Zyuganov ballots to discard.

14. We find the same phenonomen in our 1993 and 1995 election surveys. For example, precisely the proper number of respondents said they had voted for Zhirnovskii's Liberal Democratic Party, but far too many claimed to have voted for Yegor Gaidar's Russia's Choice in 1993. We explore this elsewhere.

who reported greater interest said they voted for Yeltsin, again the correct percentage.

The false reports of support for Yeltsin create problems not only for forecasts, but also for later political analysis. Those who falsely claim to have voted for Yeltsin may well be different from those who actually voted for him. If they are disproportionately located among those who, for example, take an anti-reform position on economic reform, they may seriously distort our understanding of the reasons so many in this group voted for Yeltsin.

As stated above, the 1996 pre-election survey asked respondents whether they had voted in the 1995 Duma election and, if so, for whom. In response, 2,737 individuals (72.4 per cent) claim to have voted in that election, but 473 of the purported voters said they did not remember the party for which they had voted and another 60 refused to answer. If the latter two groups are also considered probable non-voters, the remaining pool of voters in 1995 proved to have preferences in a hypothetical Yeltsin–Zyuganov run-off that proved very close to the final results: 53.5 per cent were for Yeltsin, 38.9 per cent for Zyuganov, and 7.6 per cent undecided. If the undecided are excluded, the result was a 57.9:42.1 per cent Yeltsin victory – almost precisely right.

Since the 1995 voters were, in fact, the most likely voters in 1996 and since their reported vote for Yeltsin was so accurate, we have decided to use them as the sample of respondents for analysis of conservative Yeltsin voters. The resulting percentages are presented in Table 8.9. Since this group is 30 per cent smaller than our hypothetical 2,441 respondents, we have increased the various Ns by the requisite per cent to maintain the same ratios in order to have concrete numbers for illustrative purposes in the discussion.

Table 8.9 dramatically shows the meaning of the +0.52 correlation between attitude on economic reform and attitude to Yeltsin and Zyuganov reported in our introduction; yet it also dramatically shows that correlational and regression analysis can obscure understanding. If we cross-tabulate the position of the respondent on the economic-reform scale with his or her support for Yeltsin in a Yeltsin–Zyuganov run-off, we find very strong support for Yeltsin not only in the generally pro-reform and moderate conservative groups, but even in the conservative and arch-conservative ones.

Table 8.9　Support for Yeltsin and Zyuganov, by attitude towards economic reform

| | Economic reform score | | Intend to vote in run-off for | | | |
| | | | Yeltsin | | Zyuganov | |
	Score	N	%	N	%	N
Pro-reform	100–275	607	91.8	556	8.2	51
Moderate conservative	280–345	622	70.3	435	29.7	187
Conservative	350–400	623	46.8	291	53.2	332
Arch-conservative	405–500	598	20.1	119	79.9	479
Total			57.2	1,401	42.8	1,049

Note: The data on intention to vote in the second round comes from the pre-election survey. The table is based on those who claim to have voted in the 1995 election and named the party for which they voted. This group 'voted' for Yeltsin 58:42 per cent, and the Yeltsin figures in each category have been reduced by 0.8 of 1 per cent and the Zyuganov raised by a like amount to correct them to a 57.2:42.8 per cent total. The hard numbers of respondents in each category are the number who would have voted in the designated way if the sample were a perfect replica of the population.

The concrete numbers in the column of Yeltsin voters also allow us to judge the proportion of Yeltsin voters in each group. Forty-per cent (556) of his voters were pro-reform, 31 per cent (435) fell into the moderate conservative group, and 29 per cent (410) into the conservative and arch-conservative group. Only 25 per cent of moderate conservatives thought Russia was on a correct course, compared with 41 per cent identifying an incorrect course, but the equivalent figures were 8 per cent and 71 per cent, respectively, for the 410 conservative and arch-conservatives together.

If our survey were a microcosm of the electorate, 2,441 cast a valid vote for either Yeltsin or Zyuganov in the second round. One can go further. The winning candidate needed 1,221 respondents to win. Zyuganov received only 1,044 and all he needed for victory was to shift 180 respondents. According to Table 8.9, he lost 119 arch-conservatives, and another 291 conservatives, not to speak of those who did not vote. This is the mystery to be explained.

4. THE CHARACTERISTICS OF TWO TYPES OF YELTSIN VOTERS

Who were these different groups of Yeltsin voters? Not surprisingly, the pro-reform third of Yeltsin's supporters had the characteristics we have all come to associate with support for the radical political parties. Table 8.10 permits us to compare the Yeltsin pro-reform voters with the Zyuganov voters across a series of demographic variables. They are, of course, younger and better educated. More of them live in the larger cities, and more of them were born and grew up in the larger cities. To use an indicator that Lehmann has been emphasizing, Yeltsin supporters were born and raised in the larger cities in far larger numbers.[15] Far more of them think that their economic condition has

Table 8.10 Demographic characteristics of Zyuganov voters and Yeltsin voters of different types

	Yeltsin pro-reform voters	Zyuganov voters	Yeltsin anti-reform voters
Gender (% male)	51.8	47.8	32.6
Under 40 years old	63.7	26.9	31.7
Raised in city of 200,000 or larger	41.4	18.2	21.0
Live in city of 200,000 or larger	54.7	32.4	37.1
Complete or incomplete higher education	38.8	16.1	11.0
Life has improved over past year	39.3	9.0	21.3
Income in basic job (rubles per month)	906,377	516,593	555,420
Always or usually paid on time	68.4	33.4	50.4

Note: 'Anti-reform' combines the 'conservative' and 'arch-conservative' categories of other tables.

15. We forget that the childhood of Russians of different ages is a reflection of Russian history. If 80 per cent of Russia was rural then in 1927, then 80 per cent of today's 70-year-olds were born in the countryside, and the same association is found for any year of birth. Those in the cities who were born in the countryside are more conservative than those born in the city. In part, this is an effect of age, but it is also true if we control for age: see Susan Goodrich Lehmann, 'The Mystery of the Urban Vote in the 1995 Russian Election', paper delivered at the annual conference of the American Political Science Association, 29 August 1996.

been improving over the past year or, at worst, has remained unchanged.[16] In fact, their income in their basic job was slightly over 900,000 rubles a month, more than 75 per cent larger than the average Zyuganov voter.

Table 8.11 Psychological characteristics of Zyuganov voters and
Yeltsin voters of different types (per cent)

	Yeltsin pro-reform voters	Zyuganov voters	Yeltsin anti-reform voters
Believe improvement of life depends on self	47.4	10.8	22.2
Inculcate boys with independent values (at least 4 of 5 'yes' answers)	45.7	29.0	32.1
Inculcate girls with independent values (at least 4 of 5 'yes' answers)	15.4	5.4	8.7
Inculcate girls with independent values (3 of 5 'yes' answers)	33.5	12.9	21.1
Elections give average people some influence	80.2	65.0	56.8

As Table 8.11 shows, the Yeltsin pro-reform voters were also psychologically more 'modern'. Nearly half thought that an improvement in their life depended on themselves, compared with 11 per cent of the Zyuganov voters. (Of course, the American liberal does not think that the Depression era American poor who believed that improvement in their lives depended on government action had an unhealthy dependence on government, but rather that they had avoided unhealthy self-blame.) When asked in five questions which of a pair of values they preferred in boys (for example, independence or obedience), nearly half of the Yeltsin pro-reform voters chose the more independent variable in at least four out of five cases. Although only 15 per cent of the Yeltsin pro-reform voters chose the more independent option for girls in four out of five cases, another 33.5 per cent did so in three out of five. Both figures were far higher than those for Zyuganov voters. Indeed, if Yeltsin pro-reform voters outnumbered Zyuganov's by a

16. This indicator is suspiciously stable in our data over a four-year period, and we increasingly wonder if it really is a reflection of real economic conditions or whether it is an indicator of economic confidence or morale.

Table 8.12 Views on economic security of Zyuganov voters and Yeltsin
voters of different types

	Yeltsin pro-reform voters	Zyuganov voters	Yeltsin anti-reform voters
For strict control of food prices[1]	10.2	68.3	78.4
For state limitations on income of the rich	13.3	75.9	85.7
Priority to principle of:			
1. Freedom of choice	56.2	22.1	27.1
2. Traditional values	21.9	22.3	24.4
3. Equality	18.6	47.2	42.1

Note: [1] The middle option in this question is to restrain prices, but not strictly control them, so the choice of the option indicated in the table eschews the easy price control option.

46:29 per cent margin with respect to boys, they outscored them 49:18 on girls.

The Yeltsin pro-reform respondents included by definition those who answered the questions on economic reform in a more favourable manner, while the Zyuganov voters covered the entire range of views. Since the two questions on economic policy in Table 8.12 were in the index, the difference between respondents on those questions is to some extent a product of methodology. However, they are included to give the reader a sense of the enormous size of the concrete differences that can lie behind a general scale. However, the broader question about the trade-off between freedom and equality was not included in the index and thus is independent of it. It shows a striking and probably conscious indication of a basic difference in values.

Questions about support for dictatorship and a strong central government are often seen by Westerners as a sign of basic authoritarianism. Unfortunately, respondents in contemporary Russia often give these questions a contemporary meaning. Yeltsin is usually labelled a 'democrat', and hence a question about 'dictatorship' is often interpreted by respondents to mean the overthrow of Yeltsin by a nationalist or communist, not the extent to which Yeltsin (or another leader) should rule with a strong hand. Similarly, questions about a strong role for the central government are often interpreted as asking about a strong Yeltsin government, not about abstract constitutional matters.

As a consequence, answers to questions about 'authoritarianism' often correlate strongly with support for or opposition to Yeltsin, independently of the general orientation of the respondent. In our 1993 data, therefore, it turned out that the communist voters were far less democratic than Russia's Choice voters when words such as 'democratic' were used, but that the communists were more democratic in answers to some specific questions – for example, the popular election of governors – which touched on Yeltsin's power.[17] The same is true of our 1996 data. If readers look at the top three items in Table 8.13, they will see an authoritarian side of the Yeltsin pro-reform voters that is not picked up in many types of questions.

Table 8.13   Views on nationality questions of Zyuganov voters and Yeltsin voters of different types

	Yeltsin pro-reform voters	Zyuganov voters	Yeltsin anti-reform voters
Prefer *guberniya* (i.e. abolish republics)	46.5	15.6	22.6
Believe strong rule by Centre (Moscow) needed for order	39.0	29.8	30.6
Believe strong regions needed for order	7.2	23.4	30.6
Prefer ruler who restores the USSR	1.5	50.3	21.6
Completely agree that country should live in accordance with traditions	19.3	40.7	42.7
Russia is Motherland (*Rodina*)	66.9	26.3	46.7
The West is trying to weaken Russia with economic advice	25.9	78.8	71.4

The most difficult question to analyse is the difference between Yeltsin pro-reform and Zyuganov voters on questions pertaining to ethnicity and nationalism. The pro-reform Yeltsin voters are classic Westernizers, and they identify with Russia rather than with the Soviet

17. See Jerry F. Hough, 'The Russian Election of 1993: Public Attitudes Toward Economic Reform and Democratization', *Post-Soviet Affairs*, Vol. 10, No. 1 (1994), pp. 16–18.

Union. Nevertheless, the great majority of young Russians have wanted blue jeans, jazz, rock-and-roll and Western films since the 1950s, and the 20-year-old of 1953 is now 64 years old. Most of the pre-retirement Zyuganov voters have high school diplomas, and they surely were not greatly different from other high school graduates of their time in their interest in these aspects of mass Western culture. Hence, they should not be looked upon as anti-Western in the old sense of the term. They are, however, deeply suspicious of Western governments. Moreover, their nationalism, whatever other features it has, is not associated with Russia, but with the Soviet Union.

So far, of course, we have been analysing only the difference between the Yeltsin pro-reform voter and the Zyuganov voter. Even the dullest of readers must, however, have noted that each of our tables contained three columns rather than two. Those taught in their youth to be independent and adventurous have probably even stolen a look at the unmentioned column and noticed that those Yeltsin voters who are

Table 8.14 Percentage support for Yeltsin in second round by age, gender, and views on economic reform (per cent)[1]

Age	All likely voters		Pro-reform and moderate conservative likely voters		Conservative and arch-conservative likely voters	
	Male	Female	Male	Female	Male	Female
18–29	74.0	77.7	84.8	87.2	39.4	50.2
30–39	66.3	69.1	76.9	83.7	40.0	49.1
40–49	56.5	60.0	80.2	85.0	29.7	34.4
50–59	39.0	54.3	75.8	81.6	17.6	39.9
60+	37.4	46.5	76.5	77.7	22.5	35.6
Total	55.8	60.2	79.7	83.8	27.2	39.6

Notes: [1] Undecided voters are excluded and hence the Zyuganov vote in each case is the given figure subtracted from 100 per cent.

'Likely voters' are defined as in Table 8.1. If all respondents were counted, then the male and female support for Yeltsin would be:

18–29 – 77.8% male and 78.4% female; 30–39 – 68.3 and 68.8 per cent; 40–49 – 58.5 and 58.7 per cent; 50–59 – 75.8 and 81.6 per cent; 60+ – 76.5 and 77.7 per cent.

conservative on economic reform are also far closer to the Zyuganov voters in their demographic profile and social-cultural views than to the pro-reform Yeltsin voters.

A sophisticated analysis of the Yeltsin anti-reform voters is far more complex than can be attempted in a short initial chapter. We have, of course, noticed the very low education level of the conservative Yeltsin voters, and especially the gender difference between pro-Yeltsin reform and pro-Yeltsin conservative voters and between the conservative male and female voters. Table 8.14 documents the point dramatically. Yet women are more conservative on economic reform than men on the average: a score of 342 on the economic reform scale compared with 329 for men; a score of 345 for probable women voters against 334 for probable men voters. Yeltsin's support among women is scarcely explained by his support of radical economic reform.

5. CONCLUSION

Whatever the psychological, cultural or combination of reasons behind the decision of the conservative Yeltsin voter to support the president, the key political point is obvious even without sophisticated analysis: 30 per cent of Yeltsin voters are either conservative or arch-conservative on economic reform, and they are very close to the Zyuganov voters in their demographic profile and their cultural values. A great many of them live in the countryside and small towns where everyone concedes that support for reform is weak. Still others were born in the countryside and moved to the city, but retain many of the traditional values associated with the countryside.

We have not yet analysed the Yeltsin voters in the moderate conservative group, but it should be remembered that their average score is on the conservative side of the economic reform scale – and in some cases considerably so. Their scores on questions in Tables 8.10–8.13 probably lie between the pro-reform and anti-reform Yeltsin voters, but a fair number of them have characteristics similar to the latter.

There are many possible explanations for conservatives' support of Yeltsin. First, the possibility of misreporting of the vote count should not be totally dismissed. The official electoral data at the *oblast*, republic and electoral district (*uchastok*) levels do sometimes raise questions. Thus, Zyuganov defeated Yeltsin by 511,000 to 231,000 in the first round in Dagestan, but lost to him in the second round in the republic by 471,000 to 401,000.[18] There were other republics in which analogous, if not so dramatic, changes occurred.

Dagestan may well be a special case,[19] but there is nothing in the results of our national survey as a whole – or in the surveys done by others – to suggest any large-scale counting fraud that affected the nation-wide results. The question, to use the language of the analysts of the Central Electoral Commission, is the extent to which we should speak of a 'managed electorate'. The Central Electoral Commission uses the phrase to refer to districts, usually rural districts, where the population was presumed to be responsive to the instructions of local authorities and voted in one direction to a suspicious degree.[20]

The more interesting possibility is suggested by the vote in Sarov, Nizhnegorod *oblast* – the atomic city near Arzamas. Few cities have suffered more from the changes of the past decade, but it voted for Yeltsin in the second round by a 54:39 per cent margin. Responding to indications of great hostility, Prime Minister Viktor Chernomyrdin had visited the city during the campaign to promise changes. Many voters may have been sceptical about these promises, but they had to wonder whether the opposite might be true – whether a victorious Yeltsin would punish the city if it voted against him.

In the 1993 referendum, Ivanovo *oblast* voted strongly for Yeltsin's economic policy even though it stood to lose heavily from it. But the head of *oblast* administration had stated that the *oblast* factories depended on Yeltsin for subsidized cotton, and he hinted at possible retaliation for a negative vote. In 1996, Yeltsin forces were very eager to win the first round even by a few points, and they may have thought that many voters would vote for the likely victor on the second round for tactical reasons because of central control of finances. Hence the impression of inevitability was crucial.

Yet, while this factor is probably much more important than scholars generally recognize, it is hard to avoid the conclusion that the Popov-

18. A.A. Sharavina (ed.), *Vybory prezidenta Rossiiskoi Federatsii 1996 goda: itogi i vyvody* (*Election of the President of the Russian Federation 1996: Results and Conclusiong*) (Moscow: Voenizdat, 1996), pp. 33–4.
19. Earlier, Dagestan reported that in one of its National Assembly elections not a single voter voted against all candidates.
20. *Vybory Prezidenta Rossiiskoi Federatsii.*

Freeland hypothesis is correct for part of the electorate. One of our questions asked, 'What kind of president is more necessary to Russia today, a strong and decisive one or a democratic one?'; 70.4 per cent responded 'a strong and decisive one', 18.8 per cent 'a democratic one', and 10.8 per cent that they did not know.

On the first round, as Table 8.15 indicates, those who thought that a democratic president was necessary voted heavily for Yeltsin in the first round, but those who thought that a strong and decisive president was necessary went marginally for Zyuganov. In the second round, not surprisingly, Yeltsin picked up most of the rest of the voters who preferred a democratic president, but also over 60 per cent of those who thought the country needed a strong, decisive one. Some have considered authoritarianism an inherent part of Russian national character, but this interpretation in any crude form is very difficult to reconcile with Russian voting behaviour in the late 1980s and early 1990s. However, the theory of authoritarianism has always emphasized the role of severe insecurity in creating a propensity 'to escape from freedom'.[21] Hannah Arendt's *Origin of Totalitarianism*[22] pointed to the tendency of highly insecure people in an atomized society to identify with an authoritarian dictator. The destruction of institutions in Russia and the failure of solid institutions – political parties, interest groups, trade unions, churches with practising members, enterprises with stable employment – to develop has created the type of atomized society about which Arendt wrote, and the problem was intensified by the high economic insecurity.

The analysis of authoritarianism is highly complex, but in one sense the explanation for the phenomenon of the conservative Yeltsin voter is not crucial. The first purpose of this study was to explore the question posed in our opening section. Was McFaul correct in asserting that Yeltsin's election was a victory of 'those for "reform," however defined [over] those against', or were Popov and Freeland right to suggest a more authoritarian explanation? The evidence we have presented suggests that both positions are correct. The pro-reform third of Yeltsin's voters clearly do not deserve the kind of language used by Popov and

21. Erich Fromm, *Escape from Freedom* (New York: Rinehart, 1941); and Theodore Adorno, *The Authoritarian Personality* (New York: Harper, 1950).
22. Hannah Arendt, *The Origins of Totalitarianism* (London: Allen & Unwin, 1967).

*Table 8.15 Support for Yeltsin and Zyuganov, by preference for a
democratic or a strong president, first and second round,
1996 election*

Preferred type of president	First round				Second round			
	Yeltsin		Zyuganov		Yeltsin		Zyuganov	
	%	N	%	N	%	N	%	N
Strong decisive	33.0	403	36.2	442	51.1	593	48.9	567
Democratic	60.9	198	9.3	30	87.3	269	12.7	39
Don't know	35.5	55	33.3	51	59.6	88	40.4	58

Freeland. But by the same token, the most conservative third of his voters scarcely deserve the kind of language that McFaul employs.

But it is not enough to say that Yeltsin needed both groups to win. No doubt, any analysis of the 1997 British election would show that most of Tony Blair's voters were long-time supporters of the Labour Party. Yet, analysts correctly emphasized not his base, but rather the increment to his base, in explaining why he won. The classic scholarly analysis of this point – and the explanation of the logic behind it – was made by Anthony Downs in his *Economic Theory of Democracy*,[23] but Downs merely formalized what practical politicians always understood.

The great mystery of Yeltsin's presidency is that he did not respond to his political position after 1992 in the manner of President Clinton and Prime Minister Blair. He was a construction manager from the military–industrial complex of Sverdlovsk, and he had been conservative on economic reform and the rewriting of history while Moscow first secretary in 1986 and 1987. Yeltsin's top two lieutenants from his Sverdlovsk days, Oleg Lobov and Yuri Petrov, were Gaidar's major opponents in his entourage, and it seemed politically natural – and, from the perspective of the senior author, substantively preferable – for Yeltsin to use Gaidar as the scapegoat for economic difficulties after 1992 and adopt a state-directed capitalist model of transition and economic growth.

The senior author is inclined to see Western financial assistance and

23. Anthony Downs, *An Economic Theory of Democracy* (New York: Harper & Row, 1957).

the opportunities for corruption it provided as the major explanation for Yeltsin's unnatural choice, but this is not the place for such an argument. For our purposes in this chapter, the crucial point is that, for whatever reasons, Yeltsin did not behave as the Downs model would have predicted and did not move to the economic centre. The Downs model suggests that the natural consequence of Yeltsin's behaviour should have been a victory for Zyuganov.[24]

But how, then, did Yeltsin achieve his victory? The pro-reform Yeltsin voters were going to vote for Yeltsin in almost any circumstances. Three-quarters said they were very afraid of a Zyuganov victory, and only a handful said that they were not afraid of one. Once Yeltsin did not convincingly move into the centre on economic issues, he needed other appeals in order to build a winning coalition. It is our hypothesis that just as American Republicans need to use social issues to win the support of a large group of voters whose economic position should incline them in a Democratic direction, so Yeltsin used the appeals emphasized by Popov and Freeland to pick up voters inclined in the direction of Zyuganov.

Yeltsin's appointment of Lebed shortly after the first round of the election symbolized this side of his appeal, but Popov published his analysis before then. It referred to an aspect of Yeltsin's behaviour that was always visible: his dramatically contemptuous public treatment of Gorbachev and then of the Russian legislature, the court nature of high politics, his use of grants to win the support of the elite, his populist offering of gifts to his subjects and his Manichaean treatment of opponents, be they 'the centre', the Russian Congress, or later the communists.

For his most democratic supporters, these were simply the negative side of Yeltsin's personality and rule; for his conservative supporters, they were part of his appeal. Since his conservative supporters were the crucial 'centre' that Yeltsin needed to pick up (or neutralize into not voting) in order to supplement his natural economic base, Popov and Freeland are right to emphasize its crucial character.

From a Western perspective, the unfortunate aspect of the choice of Yeltsin is that it does nothing to reduce the economic frustrations of the

---

24. Indeed, the logic of such a hypothetical victory by Zyuganov was presented in Hough et al., *The 1996 Russian Presidential Election*.

broad electorate until the economy turns around dramatically, but it strengthens and legitimates their conservative inclinations in other respects. The policy has produced the kind of atomized society that another leader with a more dangerous policy may exploit.

But we shall have to see. Revolutions work themselves out slowly. It was 13 years after the American Revolution before George Washington was inaugurated, 12 years between the French Revolution and Napoleon, 14 years between the German democratic revolution and Hitler, 12 years between the Mexican Revolution and the consolidation of rule by the Partido Revolucionario Institucional, and 12 years between the Bolshevik Revolution and the Stalin Revolution of 1929. Unless we date the beginning of the revolution to 1985, we still are in the period of the Russian Articles of Confederation, and we have no idea what 2004 will bring – a George Washington, a Napoleon Bonaparte, or something else.

APPENDIX 8A

Total Population

J11. Is the West following the goal of weakening Russia with its economic advice?[25]

	1993	1995	1996
1. I am sure of it	28.0	35.4	33.3
2. Probably yes	24.1	23.6	26.1
3. Probably not	14.3	13.6	14.2
4. I am sure not	11.1	6.9	7.2
5. Hard to say	21.9	20.1	19.0

24–32-year-olds (except for 17s = 17-year-olds)

J11. Is the West following the goal of weakening Russia with its economic advice?

	1993	1995	1996	1997	17s
1. I am sure of it	15.1	22.7	22.4	22.8	19.9
2. Probably yes	27.5	25.7	27.1	33.7	37.8
3. Probably not	18.6	21.1	19.7	17.4	15.6
4. I am sure not	16.6	11.3	10.4	7.0	7.5
5. Hard to say	21.7	18.8	20.2	18.9	18.8
6. No answer	0.6	0.4	0.2	0.2	0.3

Total Population

E2. What do you think about the transition to a market economy in Russia?

	1993	1995	1996
1. Should be rapid	13.6	6.5	6.6
2. Should be gradual	43.6	44.7	52.7
3. Against a market economy	17.9	22.5	16.7
4. Hard to say	23.9	25.8	23.7
5. No answer	1.0	0.5	0.3

25. All figures are percentages.

24–32-year-olds (except for 17s = 17-year-olds)

E2. What do you think about the transition to a market economy in Russia?

	1993	1995	1996	1997	17s
1. Should be rapid	18.6	9.2	9.8	10.3	12.2
2. Should be gradual	51.3	55.3	62.4	54.3	60.9
3. Against market economy	10.7	11.8	7.8	12.1	7.1
4. Hard to say	18.1	23.0	19.3	22.7	19.4
5. No answer	1.3	0.8	0.7	0.7	0.5

Total Population

E3 Do you support privatization of big enterprises?

	1993	1995	1996
1. Completely support	17.3	6.2	7.7
2. Support on the whole	20.6	14.0	14.9
3. Do not support it on whole	14.2	18.0	20.0
4. Completely against it	21.5	35.1	32.6
5. Hard to say	25.4	26.2	24.6
6. No answer	–	–	–

24–32-year-olds (except for 17s = 17-year-olds)

E3. Do you support privatization of big enterprises?

	1993	1995	1996	1997	17s
1. Completely support	23.1	11.4	12.5	8.0	14.0
2. Support on the whole	28.1	21.3	17.5	23.3	27.2
3. Do not support it on whole	15.4	19.8	23.2	22.9	19.7
4. Completely against it	13.2	20.6	22.3	22.8	12.6
5. Hard to say	19.4	26.6	23.9	22.3	25.9
6. No answer	0.5	0.2	0.5	0.7	0.6

Total Population

E4. What is your attitude towards the free purchase and sale of land by private persons?

	1993	1995	1996
1. Should not be limited	14.4	11.0	15.9
2. Should be restricted	36.1	37.8	41.8
3. Do not support	39.2	40.0	31.8
4. Hard to say	9.9	11.0	10.3

24–32-year-olds (except for 17s = 17-year-olds)

E4. What is your attitude towards the free purchase and sale of land by private persons?

	1993	1995	1996	1997	17s
1. Should not be limited	22.1	15.0	22.0	21.2	24.7
2. Should be restricted	43.8	48.9	53.1	49.9	53.1
3. Do not support	24.3	25.7	17.4	16.7	10.4
4. Hard to say	8.9	10.1	7.3	11.9	11.5
5. No answer	0.6	0.3	0.2	0.4	0.3

Total Population

D14. Should the state limit the incomes of rich citizens?

	1993	1995	1996
1. Yes, it should	53.6	58.6	57.0
2. No, it should not	34.5	27.2	30.4
3. Hard to say	11.4	13.9	12.4
4. No answer	0.6	0.3	0.1

24–32-year-olds (except for 17s = 17-year-olds)

D14. Should the state limit the incomes of rich citizens?

	1993	1995	1996	1997	17s
1. Yes, it should	38.8	43.9	42.9	41.4	–
2. No, it should not	49.7	42.9	44.9	42.7	–
3. Hard to say	11.0	13.1	12.3	15.6	–
4. No answer	0.6	0.1	0.0	0.3	–

Total Population

J10. Do you support foreign investments in the economy of Russia?

	1993	1995	1996
1. Completely support	12.9	9.2	13.8
2. Support under strict control	42.3	38.2	40.6
3. Sometimes useful, but more harmful	11.9	14.1	13.9
4. Completely against	17.4	18.9	16.5
5. Hard to say	14.9	19.2	15.0
6. No answer	0.5	0.4	0.2

24–32-year-olds (except for 17s = 17-year-olds)

J10. Do you support foreign investments in the economy of Russia?

	1993	1995	1996	1997	17s
1. Completely support	19.2	12.7	18.1	10.9	14.6
2. Support under strict control	49.7	47.1	45.4	47.4	45.5
3. More harmful	12.9	14.3	15.1	14.9	15.8
4. Completely against	7.4	10.3	12.0	12.3	8.4
5. Hard to say	10.2	14.8	9.4	14.2	15.4
6. No answer	0.6	0.4	0.0	0.2	0.3

Total Population

J1. How do you evaluate the disintegration of the Soviet Union?

	1993	1995	1996
1. Useful	9.5	5.0	7.7
2. More useful than harmful	10.2	8.8	11.7
3. More harmful than useful	18.1	20.7	20.6
4. Harmful	51.3	56.0	48.9
5. It is hard to say	10.5	9.2	10.9
6. No answer	0.6	0.3	0.2

24–32-year-olds (except for 17s = 17-year-olds)

J1. How do you evaluate the disintegration of the Soviet Union?

	1993	1995	1996	1997	17s
1. Useful	9.0	5.5	9.4	8.0	10.9
2. More useful than harmful	19.5	14.6	18.0	19.1	22.6
3. More harmful than useful	29.5	28.2	24.1	28.6	28.0
4. Harmful	41.8	41.0	33.9	28.1	18.8
5. It is hard to say	10.1	9.5	14.1	16.0	19.5
6. No answer	0.1	0.2	0.5	0.3	–

Total Population

J2. What is your Motherland (*Rodina*)?

	1993	1995	1996
1. The USSR	28.8	34.1	29.2
2. Russia	50.6	38.1	43.6
3. The republic or *oblast* where I live	15.9	23.5	24.0
4. Hard to say	4.3	4.1	3.1
5. No answer	0.4	0.2	0.2

24–32-year-olds (except for 17s = 17-year-olds)

J2. What is your Motherland (*Rodina*)?

	1993	1995	1996	1997	17s
1. The USSR	26.6	26.4	20.0	16.7	9.1
2. Russia	49.2	42.9	45.1	41.6	46.3
3. My republic or *oblast*	21.4	25.1	32.1	36.9	40.0
4. Hard to say	2.5	5.6	2.4	4.5	4.2
5. No answer	0.3	0.0	0.3	0.2	0.5

The Data Sets

The data sets on which this chapter is based include a 1993 pre-election survey,[26] a 1995 pre-election survey, a 1996 pre-election and between-

26. The 1993 national election was a panel survey, and a post-election survey is

election panel study, and a 1997 study of those 17, 24 and 32 years old.

All these surveys are national random samples, stratified on a regional basis, of approximately 3,800 respondents. One hundred *raions* in 69 *oblasts* and republics across Russia were chosen at random by Timothy Colton, and with a few insignificant substitutions they remained the same throughout the various studies. Forty (later reduced to 38) respondents were chosen from each *raion*, with larger samples in 38-respondent units were chosen in larger cities. (Thus, Moscow had 240 respondents in the 1993 study and 220 in subsequent ones.) The work was carried out by interviewers under the supervision of a sociologist or political scientist in a local college or scientific institute in each region. The work in the Russian *oblasts* was supervised by Sergei Tumanov, director of the Centre of Sociology of Moscow University, and that in the Russian republics by Mikhail Guboglo, first deputy director of the Institute of Ethnography and Anthropology of the Russian Academy of Sciences. Drs Tumanov and Guboglo played an active role in the drafting of the questionnaires.

Efforts have been made to train the regional sociologists, to increase their sense of professionalism and to bring them together in annual conferences in Moscow to discuss their results and exchange experiences.[27] In addition, the Russian scholars were not only permitted, but encouraged, to publish from the data they have collected so that they will have a personal stake in the quality of data.[28] With these added incentives, the network conducts surveys for from one-quarter to one-third the cost of other polling agencies, and in our opinion it does higher-quality work. We recommend it most highly to other scholars, and, indeed, we hope that it will be used more widely not only because of the quality of its data, but because its use and further training is of

actually included in the data set. However, the questions on the post-election survey were entirely written by Timothy Colton, and, except for the marginals on support for the parties in 1993, the post-election data will not be utilized in this chapter.

27. A chapter on the youth survey was held at Moscow University on 23–24 June 1997, and books are coming out in Russian edited by Sergei Tumanov and Mikhail Guboglo.

28. See, for example, Mikhail Guboglo, *Razvivayushchiisya elektorat Rossii. Etnopoliticheskii rakurs* (*Russia's Developing Electorate: The Ethno-political For-shortening*) (Moscow: Institut etnologii i antropologii RAN, 1996), 3 vols.

major value in improving the social sciences in the provincial universities and colleges across Russia.

The December 1993 election study, in addition to the above-mentioned panel study of 3,800 respondents, included regional pre-election studies of 1,000 respondents, randomly selected and conducted in each of 35 *oblasts* and *krais* and 16 of the ethnic republics within Russia.[29] The survey of the Russian republics was the first in Soviet or Russian history in which a single questionnaire was administered to all former autonomous republics, and it permits detailed comparisons of subjects such as language use and religion.[30]

Ideally we would have liked 1,000-respondent surveys in all *oblasts*, but some of the regional sociologists were unwilling to conduct a large survey for the rather limited amount of money per questionnaire at our disposal. Yet, in practice, when the data from the *oblasts* was merged into a 35,000-respondent data set, the biases within it tended to cancel out each other, and the marginals on policy and campaign questions results proved very close to those in the national sample.[31] As a result, the 35,000-respondent data set can sometimes be used for some extremely fine-grained political and especially sociological analysis to supplement the national sample.[32]

29. The 51,000 respondents of the regional surveys made the study very expensive. The largest grants for the study came from the Carnegie Corporation and the MacArthur Foundation, but they were supplemented by two NSF grants (SBR-94-02548 and SBR-94-12051) and support by the Brookings Institution. The Principal Investigators were Timothy Colton, Jerry Hough and Susan Goodrich Lehmann. The questions on the pre-election survey were collectively written, but Colton had prime responsibility for the questions on the campaign, Hough for those on economic policy and democratization, and Lehmann for the 60-question sociological and demographic section. Colton alone drafted the questions for the post-election study.

30. For an article from these data on language use, see Jerry F. Hough, 'Sociology, the State, and Language Politics', *Post-Soviet Affairs*, Vol. 12, No. 2 (April–June 1996), pp. 95–113. For differences in religious attitudes in the five Muslim republics of Bashkortostan, Chechnya, Dagestan, Kabardino-Balkaria and Tatarstan, see Susan Goodrich Lehmann, 'Islam and Ethnicity in the Republics of Russia', *Post-Soviet Affairs*, Vol. 13, No. 1 (January–March 1997), pp. 78–103.

31. Too many of the republics had small, rural populations, and for this reason their inclusion in an overall data set would have created a major demographic imbalance.

32. Preliminary results on policy questions from this data set were reported in Hough, 'The Russian Election of 1993'.

The December 1995 election and the first-round presidential election studies contained most questions in the 1993 pre-election study. The 1995 study was financed by the National Science Foundation and sponsored by the Brookings Institution, while the study of the first round of the 1996 presidential election was financed by the MacArthur Foundation. The respondents in the first-round presidential study were revisited between the two rounds of the election, and 87 per cent agreed to participate in a between-election study. The between-election study was financed by the National Science Foundation.[33] The Principal Investigators of the NSF projects were Jerry Hough, Evelyn David-heiser and Susan Goodrich Lehmann, while those of the MacArthur Foundation project were Susan Lehmann and Jerry Hough.[34]

The 1997 youth study was conducted in March 1997 as the second part of MacArthur study mentioned in the last paragraph, with the funding of a study of the 17-year-olds, especially in the republics, funded by the National Council on Soviet and East European Research. A national survey was conducted among 1,068 17-year-olds, 1,382 24–25-year-olds, and 1,386 31–32-year-olds. The districts were selected by the same methodology as the election studies, but the individuals were chosen by a different methodology – randomly from the housing lists in the districts, stratified by year of birth. The 1997 questionnaire contains some of the questions on politics and economic reform from the election studies, but it had the purpose of surveying youth values more broadly defined. Much of the questionnaire was written by our Russian regional collaborators, often on the basis of questions used in earlier studies. The interviews of the 12,000 secondary school final-year pupils, half of them Russians and half non-Russians, in the capitals of 15 former autonomous republics were conducted in the classroom.

33. The decision was made to hold the second survey after the first round rather than the second for several reasons. First, it was feared that the dispersal of the original respondents after the second round in July would be much greater. Second, we did not expect the answers on presidential choice after the second round to be reliable, and we wanted to maximize the chances that the first-round vote and campaign exposure would be accurately remembered and reported.
34. The two NSF grants were SBR-96-00413 and SBR-96-01315, and they were supplemented by small grants from the United States Information Agency.

9. Consistency and Change among Russian Voters

Leonid Sedov

The parliamentary elections of December 1995 and the two rounds of the presidential elections of May and July 1996 give scholars an unprecedented opportunity to identify many typical features of Russian electoral behaviour and of Russia's party system and power system in general. This analysis is based on a series of poll results that identify which voters were consistent in their electoral choices, and which changed their mind over the three elections. The elections were held in close succession, so the behaviour of those who changed their sympathies in such a short period may be considered inconsistent. This chapter proceeds by converting percentages obtained in our polls into the equivalent numbers of votes in the actual elections. This helps us to identify distinct groups of voters, differentiated by both numerical strength and demographic characteristics.

We can establish schemes which show how voters ebbed and flowed between the various groups which we have identified. For example, we can see that, of the 1.8 million who had voted for former Vice-President Aleksandr Rutskoi's party *Derzhava* (Great Power), a quarter of a million then voted for Boris Yeltsin, 600,000 voted for Gennadii Zyuganov and another 300,000 for Aleksandr Lebed. We also learn that about 300,000 of those who had voted for Yeltsin in the first round then changed their allegiance and supported Zyuganov in the second round. Admittedly these are quite small groups of voters, but clearly their behaviour is far from consistent (See Tables 9.1 and 9.2).

The main observation that emerges from this analysis is that a large, consistent and relatively stable social group consists of non-voters, who number some 15 million. This group is disproportionately young: 24 per cent of eligible voters aged below 25, compared with just 7 per cent

Table 9.1   Voter movements between parliamentary and presidential elections

1995 vote		1996 round one vote (per cent of 1995 voters)			
Party	Total[1]	Yeltsin	Zyuganov	Lebed	Yavlinskii
Communist Party of the RF	15.4	3	82	5	0
Liberal Democratic Party	7.7	10	12	13	0
Our Home is Russia	7.0	64	4	7	2
Yabloko	4.8	33	4	8	33
Congress of Russian Communities	3.0	17	17	50	1
Party of Workers' Self-government	2.8	36	14	11	5
Russia's Democratic Choice	2.7	78	0	0	6
Russia's Women	3.1	32	10	23	10
Derzhava	1.8	14	33	17	0
Others	17.5	39	24	13	8
Against all	1.9	42	16	11	5
Non-voters	38.6	15	7	5	3

Note: [1] In millions.

Table 9.2   Movement of voters between rounds of the 1996 presidential election

First round		Second round vote (as per cent of first round vote)			
Candidate	Votes (millions)	Yeltsin	Zyuganov	Against both	Did not vote
Yeltsin	26.7	89	2	–	10
Zyuganov	24.2	3	92	–	5
Lebed	11.0	48	19	13	19
Yavlinskii	5.6	61	10	12	17
Zhirinovskii	4.3	21	38	8	33
Against all	1.2	17	8	33	42
Did not vote	32.9	12	5	2	82
Totals (million)		40.2	30.1	3.6	33.9

of those over the age of 55. Further analysis shows that they are in general young urban workers or the unemployed, and they are people who are either indifferent to politics or who are much less concerned about the state of affairs in the country than, say, Zyuganov voters. For instance, 40 per cent in the group believe that the majority of Russians have adjusted to the reforms, which is virtually the same proportion as among Yeltsin voters.

Those who manifest a consistent voting pattern with definite party allegiances number about 25 million. Almost half of this contingent – 12 million – belong to the communist electorate, and to that part of it which recognizes Zyuganov as their leader; this is about half of Zyuganov's first-round support. Another large portion of Zyuganov's first-round support (4 million) consists of those who had voted for small parties in the Duma elections. This includes the 4.5 million electorate of the extremist Working Russia Party, around 40 per cent of whom voted for Zyuganov. Around three million of Zyuganov's first-round supporters did not participate in the parliamentary elections. These were predominantly female workers, living in the countryside, and belonging to a younger age cohort than people in the other two groups mentioned above. Their income is extremely low, but a relatively larger proportion of them think that 'life is hard but endurable', and they are in general more optimistic in their views. These 'giddy village beauties' are particularly inconsistent in that only 36 per cent of them mention Zyuganov as a trusted politician, and they may mention Yeltsin or Gaidar as well. Although their trust in the media is much higher than that observed among other Zyuganov voters, at the same time they admit that they rarely follow politics or read political news (27 per cent as against 4 and 0 per cent in the other two groups, respectively). It is noteworthy that about 20 per cent of this group abstained from participation in the second round, and fully half of them were convinced that Yeltsin would win the election.

Those who preferred small parties in December 1995 tend to be good examples of inconsistent voters. As a rule they are younger than the bulk of the communist voters and more often they live in medium-sized and smaller towns. They are less traditional than other Zyuganov supporters, and in 1995 looked for alternatives to the CPRF such as Stanislav Govorukhin's bloc, Working Russia, the Agrarian Party and so forth. They dislike Lebed and do not think highly of his chances of becoming the next president. Rather than Zyuganov, many of them would have preferred the then prime minister, Viktor Chernomyrdin, the reformist former governor of Nizhnii Novgorod and later deputy prime minister, Boris Nemtsov, Aleksandr Rutskoi, or (especially) the mayor of Moscow, Yuri Luzhkov, but lacking that choice, and disliking Yeltsin, they gave their votes to the communist leader.

Yeltsin's supporters are much less likely than Zyuganov's to have a definite party orientation, as befits a politician who has been keen to cast himself in the role of national leader, standing above party politics. His supporters came from both major parties which proclaimed their support for Yeltsin. Our Home is Russia gave him 4.5 million votes out of its total of 7 million; 2.2 million of the 2.7 million who voted for Gaidar's Russia's Democratic Choice supported the president in the first round. However, in general terms, just a quarter of Yeltsin voters were party-orientated. Another half were the six million who had not participated in the parliamentary elections and a further six million who voted for various minor parties.

These distinct groups of Yeltsin's electorate differ from each other as well as from other electoral groups in many respects. The group identifying Yeltsin with the two pro-government parties is distinguished by its higher educational level, while the parliamentary non-voters are the least educated and the minor parties' supporters stand in the middle. There are also marked age differences between the groups, as can be seen in Table 9.3.

Table 9.3 Characteristics of the three groups of Yeltsin's first-round voters (per cent)

	Pro-government parties	Non-voters	Minor party voters
Age			
18–24	10	20	17
25–39	38	43	45
40–54	28	19	18
55+	24	18	22
Education			
College	26	20	20
Technical	54	52	65
Low level	20	28	15

There are also noticeable gender differences. Minor party voters who went on to vote for Yeltsin are more likely to be women than men (55 per cent of the total). This group also contains a large number of people who evaluate the situation in the country as extremely tense (71 per cent say so, which is as many as among Zyuganov's voters). It is interesting to note here, by contrast, that Zyuganov's voters who had not supported the CPRF and voted for other parties were predominantly male (58 per cent). Evidently these people had been looking for tougher opposition than the opportunistic CPRF.

The only other politician who has some party-orientated electorate behind him is Zhirinovskii, but the proportion who have chosen to vote for him as well as for his party is not great, at only some two million. Post-election surveys suggested that even among these, the LDPR leader's support was melting away, with just 73 per cent of consistent Zhirinovskii voters saying that they trusted him, and only 30 per cent believing that he could become president. As for the demographic features of the group, it is more male than female and includes very few more educated people or voters under the age of 25. Forty per cent are urban workers, and the unemployed and military are also over-represented. As a rule they are just as displeased with the current situation as Zyuganov's followers are, but their own life is not so destitute. They are not very interested in politics, have no great faith in the electoral process and show little confidence in the mass media. In the second round their votes were split almost equally among supporters of Yeltsin (34 per cent) and of Zyuganov (30 per cent) and those who either ignored the elections (17 per cent) or voted against both candidates (14 per cent). One-fifth of this group of staunch Zhirinovskii fans came from Western Siberia. Other regions where they are well represented are the Volga region and northern and northwestern Russia.

Those data suggest that most of the electorate are in what we may term 'Brownian motion': they easily change their commitments, switch from one party or candidate to another or take part in and then abstain from the elections. Their sheer numbers – more than 65 million out of an electorate of 100–110 million – attest to the imperfect state of the party system in Russia.[1] Of the major parties whose leaders were

1.   1995 voters for parties who had representatives in the 1993–95 Duma, such as Women of Russia, or for parties which existed in 1993 but were not allowed to

candidates in the presidential elections only four provided their leaders with consistent support: Russia's Democratic Choice (72 per cent of its electorate voted for Yeltsin), the CPRF (70 per cent for Zyuganov, the Congress of Russian Communities (65 per cent for Lebed), and Our Home is Russia (56 per cent for Yeltsin). Other party electorates proved to be inconsistent. For example, we observe a very major shift between the electorates of the Yabloko bloc and of its leader Grigorii Yavlinskii: out of 4.8 million Yabloko voters in 1995, its leader retained just 1.6 million as a presidential candidate in the following year, while a similar proportion (1.5 million) went to Yeltsin. None the less, in the first round Yavlinskii received even more votes than his party had done, precisely because of the 'Brownian motion' in the electorate (he gained 5.6 million votes, of which of which one million had voted for minor parties, one million had not participated in the Duma elections and so forth). In the same 'Brownian' manner Lebed's electorate was made up most prominently of abstainers in the parliamentary elections (2 million), minor party voters (3 million) and turncoats from the LDPR (1 million). In spite of its consistency of platform, his CRC party with its small electorate brought him only approximately 1.5 million votes.

We find that in Yeltsin's camp there were many more inconsistent voters (75 per cent) than in Zyuganov's (51 per cent), which is in line with Yeltsin's alleged role as a leader standing above all the parties. Inconsistent voters were found much more often among the more prosperous, and among those who thought things in the country were going quite well (77 per cent). These were not fervent anti-communists, but only a few of them would be pleased to see Yeltsin make any kind of pact with the CPRF. It must be especially emphasized that in spite of the general pro-communist trend in rural areas, a large proportion of the inconsistent vote also comes from the countryside: such voters are much more numerous in villages (71 per cent) than in Moscow (57 per cent), other big cities (61 per cent) and small towns (50 per cent). Curiously, St. Petersburg and the Far East exceed rural Russia, with 75 per cent each.

Let us take as an example one large (3 million strong) group of

participate in the elections, such as *Derzhava*, may be considered 'semi-consistent'. They number about 6.5 million voters, and their votes were widely dispersed among the presidential candidates.

inconsistent voters. These were people who had voted for pro-government parties in 1995 (90 per cent for Our Home is Russia), but then did not vote for Yeltsin in the first round, voting for Lebed (40 per cent), Zyuganov (32 per cent) or Yavlinskii (12 per cent), or against all candidates (11 per cent), and then in the second round either turning back to Yeltsin (41 per cent) or, almost as likely, voting for Zyuganov (34 per cent), abstaining (17 per cent), or voting against both candidates (6 per cent). Their voting behaviour in the parliamentary elections might have been explained by their special liking for Chernomyrdin, but his trust rating among them was not high, which at 7 per cent is much lower than that of Lebed (41 per cent), Zyuganov (28 per cent), Yavlinskii (27 per cent) or even Yeltsin (18 per cent). Their opinions are in many respects as inconsistent as their behaviour: they like Lebed and think his chances of becoming the next president are good, but would not like him to be vice-president alongside Yeltsin. Many of them think that Russians will never adjust to the changes, again raising the question of what had made them support Our Home is Russia.

One might expect that less consistent voting patterns would be more common among less-educated categories of electors, and our data confirm such a prediction: 70 per cent of the group consists of women who are mainly workers or clerks without specialized education, living in villages or medium-sized cities (from 50 to 100 thousand inhabitants), and who have a rather low or average income. They can rarely be met in Moscow, but much more often in the south of European Russia, especially the Northern Caucasus.

One more interesting subgroup of inconsistent voters comprises those who took part in only the second round of the presidential elections. These 'eleventh hour' voters were rather numerous (4.5 million) and predominantly pro-Yeltsin (72 per cent). Being on the whole in favour of the reforms, they do not pay much attention to politics and think that they have no means of influencing the situation in the country, which does not seem to trouble them too much. They think that most of the people have adjusted to recent changes, and are sanguine about the future. However the narrow gap between Yeltsin and Zyuganov in the first round motivated them to go to the polling station and support the president. This kind of behaviour was characteristic of young (under 25 years) city dwellers with secondary school or special technical education. It is notable that they like Yeltsin,

Chernomyrdin and Gaidar but do not trust Yavlinskii, who is rather more popular among more educated young people. In the group in question one can meet many small entrepreneurs and also military personnel and the unemployed; regionally they were over-represented in Central Russia and the Volga districts.

The process of redistribution of electoral sympathies seems to be continuous and continuing, since less than a year after the presidential elections the main competitors had preserved only about half of their supporters, as answers to questions on voting intentions show. Zyuganov stood out with 67 per cent remaining faithful, while Zhirinovskii had behind him 53 per cent of his former electorate, Yavlinskii retained 46 per cent, and Lebed had kept just 42 per cent, according to VTsIOM's polls of March 1997. Partly these changes may be explained by the inclusion in the list of suggested aspirants to the presidency of several who did not feature in the 1996 elections, most especially such politicians as Nemtsov and Luzhkov, whose popularity has risen rapidly. As of March 1997, Nemtsov had 'stolen' 12 per cent of the votes of both Lebed and Yavlinskii, and also a quarter of his following consisted of non-participants in 1996. Luzhkov's support came mainly from Yeltsin's electorate.

The figures for voting intentions suggested that Zyuganov's chances of victory in 2000 remained as small as they had been in 1996, even though he headed the list of potential candidates, with 18 per cent support, and is sure to repeat his success of getting to the second round. He is the only plausible representative from the left of the political spectrum, but managed to enlarge his support significantly only by attracting a small part of Zhirinovskii's (4 per cent) and Lebed's (11 per cent) voters. However, his reformist opponent – be it Nemtsov (10 per cent), Luzhkov (6 per cent), Yavlinskii (6 per cent) or Chernomyrdin (5 per cent) – would in the second round rally around himself the votes of the losers who had been disposed of in the first round. The analysis reveals that the latter candidates have almost the same type of electorate behind them, with small nuances such as that potential Chernomyrdin voters are more likely to be pleased with the present state of affairs, Nemtsov's supporters want further reforms (this comprises mainly the intelligentsia of larger cities), and Luzhkov's are concentrated mainly in Moscow. It is also evident that those who have not yet decided for whom they would vote for are not potential Zyuganov supporters: only 6 per cent of them mention him as a trusted politician, whereas Nemtsov is mentioned by 11 per cent, Lebed by 9 per cent, and so on.

What all these above data definitely attest to is the imperfect state of the party system. Russian political parties happen to be the least trusted social institution, with mass attitudes verging on contempt. When asked about their trust in the parties only 2 per cent of our respondents declared their complete confidence and 11 per cent more said that they had some level of trust, while 69 per cent described their views as mistrust, and 19 per cent could not say.[2] As we see, the number of those who in general evaluate parties positively is less than the number of consistent voters. It should be noted that a positive view of parties is found relatively more often among Zyuganov's (28 per cent), Yavlinskii's (28 per cent) and – strange as it might seem – Zhirinovskii's (34 per cent) followers. With the last the contradictory and antidemocratic nature of his electorate shows itself in the fact that the number of those who distrust parties is also the greatest among them. It can be deduced that trust is higher for those parties which have factions in the Duma. The fact that Chernomyrdin is recognized less as the party leader than as head of the government is reflected in the fact that his supporters trust parties less. The proportion who have no definite attitude to parties is highest among Lebed's supporters (since his relatively new party has not yet acquired a high public profile), and among potential Nemtsov voters, since the deputy prime minister belongs to no party.

The low confidence in parties seems to contrast sharply with a rather high estimation among respondents of elections as the means of expressing one's own will and of making personal choices. Those who approve elections in these terms stand at 54 per cent and those who do not number just 16 per cent. It is noteworthy that communists are less sure of the fairness of the electoral system, as they are accustomed to misunderstand the expression of views as their imposition. Thus, 52 per cent of those who think elections as not giving them an opportunity of expressing their will belong to Zyuganov's camp, and just 6 per cent to that of Yeltsin.

2. As of June 1996. By April 1997 parties' overall reputation had declined still further, the corresponding figures being 1, 4, 76 and 19 per cent. However, 31 per cent of the same respondents were able to name one (20 per cent) or several (11 per cent) parties whose ideas were close to theirs, although 47 per cent said that there were no such parties.

A negative attitude towards elections is just as widespread as mistrust of the democratic system of government in general. When asked whether Russia needs democracy or whether this brings harm to the country, 26 per cent of the respondents choose the second option while half as many again (41 per cent) give the first, more positive answer. The share of those who think democracy to be harmful is higher among the retired and uneducated, along with agricultural workers and collective farmers. The unemployed and military are typical of Russians as a whole. It also decisively depends on people's income, with support for democracy over three times higher among those who earn more than 500,000 rubles per family member monthly, and below average for those with monthly income of less than 100,000 rubles. Accordingly, 35 per cent of those who speak in favour of democracy voted for Yeltsin and only 10 per cent for Zyuganov, while just 11 per cent of those who rejected democracy voted for the president, while 43 per cent of them voted for Zyuganov. An anti-democratic feeling is predominant in Zhirinovskii's electorate as well. Locally it is more prominent in the Central Black Earth region (the famous 'Red Belt'), in the Northern Caucasus and Eastern Siberia and in rural areas in general. It may seem paradoxical, but there were more abstainers from the elections among the supporters of democracy: 32 per cent compared with 28 per cent among those who rejected democracy. On reflection, it becomes clear that this fact reflects the contrast between democratic freedom of choice, including the right to abstain, and the traditional communist treatment of voting as an obligatory rite.

A result still worse for democracy's prospects is obtained when people are asked about such an important element of democratic systems as multiparty elections. More than one-third of our respondents thought that they bring harm to the country and only 27 per cent recognized their usefulness. The remaining 36 per cent were not certain about them.

In conclusion it may be said that no stable and efficient democracy can be achieved without citizens' trust in democratic institutions, one of which – indeed, a crucial one – is a multi-party system. As White and his collaborators have perceptively expressed it,

> When the choice is between distrusted parties an election is only a choice between greater and lesser evils. Individuals can vote to turn out one group of rascals but the only result is that another group of rascals gains power.

Free elections remain valid even if there is a 'missing middle' of trusted parties, but the outcome is not representative government as this term is understood in established democracies.[3]

Under the existing Russian Constitution, the deliberate divorce of the parliament and the parties from any means of real influence on the executive power, in addition to the absence of any real grassroots work on behalf of the parties, suggests there is little hope that people's confidence in parties will grow and become a major factor of political and civic life in the short term. On the other hand, given the present correlation of forces in the country, too much democracy could lead to the overthrow of this same democracy, as happened in Germany in 1933, or Belarus in the present day. So the accent upon a strong semi-authoritarian executive branch may be justified, at least for the whole long period of transition which lies ahead of Russia, and it may last for the life-span of a generation or two.

As for the short-term prospects, it seems likely that the efforts of the Chubais–Nemtsov team to give a new impulse to the reforms will be blocked by the conservative part of the government and the retrograde managerial corps standing behind it. In the period up to the turn of the century, the struggle between 'conservatives' and 'radicals' inside the ruling elite will become the keynote of political and economic life until the time of the next presidential elections, which will coincide with the onset of a generational shift which brings new figures to the forefront of the political landscape. As of 1997, the country appeared ready to accept as a new political leader the young reformer Nemtsov, who occupied a prominent place in the list of presidential candidates immediately after being appointed a deputy prime minister (14 per cent of votes, exceeded only by Zyuganov's 15 per cent). Nemtsov ran ahead of Zyuganov in all age and social groups except pensioners and poorly educated inhabitants of villages and small towns. Nemtsov also took the upper hand against any possible second-round opponent. It seems likely that by the time of the elections many new faces will emerge as candidates.

Meanwhile the old elite appears unable to suggest any clear way out of the deepening crisis, and will have to leave the scene together with the present system of political parties, which will finally discredit

3. Stephen White, Richard Rose and Ian McAllister, *How Russia Votes* (Chatham, NJ: Chatham House, 1997), p. 131.

themselves. Competition for the presidential post will not be between party leaders but between professionals supported by banking and other business circles, with good chances for a young expert in economics or management (not necessarily Nemtsov) to be victorious.[4] As of mid-1997, when asked about their preference, 24 per cent of our respondents named communists, 16 per cent democrats, 4 per cent patriots and 2 per cent the 'party of power' (the incumbent administration), but 40 per cent said they did not sympathize with any political force. Everything remains to play for.

4. When asked about their confidence in politicians just 1 per cent said that they fully trusted them, 7 per cent partially trusted them, and as many as 56 per cent distrusted politicians. The picture is the opposite with scholars and experts, who are more trusted than even the Orthodox Church, with corresponding figures of 25, 43 and 17 per cent.

10. The CPRF: Towards Social Democracy or National Socialism?

Evelyn Davidheiser

Is the Communist Party of the Russian Federation (CPRF) moving towards social democracy or national socialism, or will it remain something peculiar to Russia? The answer to this question is crucial for understanding the evolution of the Russian political system. However, the difficulty faced in answering it reflects a weak theoretical understanding of the nature of electoral competition in transitional political systems. This study draws on comparative models of voting behaviour, contrasting spatial and mobilizational approaches, so as to understand the evolution of the CPRF as an electoral party. In order to develop a full picture of CPRF electoral performance, I examine both the supply of positions by the party and the demand of voters. I examine voter demand for particular policies by CPRF candidates on the basis of two mass surveys of the Russian electorate conducted during two very different electoral campaigns (1995 and 1996), and I examine the supply of policies on the basis of interviews with party workers and evaluation of party documents.[1] I argue that, while candidates seek to maximize votes, during the transition they face extraordinarily high levels of uncertainty. Candidates operate so as to minimize that uncertainty, treating this as the best strategy for maximizing votes.

---

1. The survey research was conducted in collaboration with Professors Jerry Hough and Susan Goodrich Lehmann, with the support of the National Science Foundation. Separate samples of 4,000 voters were interviewed during the 1995 parliamentary campaign and the 1996 presidential campaign. The 1996 survey was set up as a panel, with respondents interviewed a second time in between the first and second rounds. For a fuller description see Jerry Hough and Susan Lehmann's contribution to the present volume.

Gennadii Zyuganov emerged from the 1995 parliamentary election as the clear favourite in the coming presidential election. The 1995 survey data indicated that, while 34 per cent of the voters held a favourable impression of Zyuganov, only 16 per cent were similarly disposed towards Yeltsin. Polls conducted throughout the winter showed this margin narrowing, with Yeltsin finally outpolling his rival in late spring. In six short months Zyuganov's lead eroded, and by the second round of the presidential election, the victor of 1995 could muster only 40 per cent to President Boris Yeltsin's 54 per cent. Observers have offered a wide variety of explanations for this failure, ranging from popular fear of a return to the old system to a stronger media presence for Yeltsin. In developing an argument based on the problems posed by uncertainty in the transition, I contend that Zyuganov's loss reflected a misunderstanding of voters' preferences and that the survival of the party will require readjustment to reflect these preferences. This readjustment will determine the course of evolution of the party towards either national socialism or social democracy.

This chapter proceeds in three parts. First, I develop the explanations and predictions offered by contending models of electoral behaviour for the CPRF. I test these models in the Russian case by combining qualitative research on the positioning of parties and candidates with quantitative research on the positioning of voters. While each of the contending models helps clarify the Russian case, none fully explains the strategies adopted by the CPRF. To accomplish this, I present an alternative model of electoral competition designed to take into consideration the unique circumstances of the transition. The model focuses on the demands of voters and the supply of issues by candidates, in the conditions of intense uncertainty posed by the transition. The second section examines this model in the light of the continuing evolution of the CPRF. Finally, I suggest some implications for the evolution of Russia's communists, Russian party competition, and more broadly party competition in transitional political systems. Although the juxtaposing of these rival models of competition is useful for understanding the evolution of the CPRF, equally important are the insights for these models generated by the Russian case.

1. ALTERNATIVE MODELS OF ELECTORAL COMPETITION

Russianists frequently debate the probable evolution of the CPRF. The biggest source of confusion has emerged around the threat posed by extremist communists. While Zyuganov is generally viewed as moderate, his susceptibility to the influence of extreme nationalists or hard-line communists, such as Viktor Anpilov, has been a point of contention. Optimists, treating the CPRF as essentially a normal opposition party, argue that the CPRF and Zyuganov must remain moderate – or even move further towards the centre of the political spectrum – if they are to survive in a competitive electoral arena. By contrast, pessimists, treating the CPRF as an anti-system party, argue that Zyuganov will be swayed and the CPRF captured by more extreme elements, pulling it further from the centre.

This debate has been largely speculative, and the empirical evidence has offered support for both positions. In the 1995 parliamentary elections, the CPRF appeared to be dominated by moderates and moving in the direction of the centre (social democracy). In the 1996 presidential election, however, Zyuganov appeared to be pulled by the extremists to espouse a more virulently nationalist and anti-market position. This observation appears to run counter to the logic of competition under divergent electoral laws. Systems of proportional representation, and the resulting multipartism, should allow room for extremist positions, while winner-take-all elections, and the resulting duality of partisanship, should promote moderation. Hence, we would have expected Zyuganov's party to position itself further from the centre in the 1995 parliamentary contest than in the 1996 presidential contest. Instead, we observe the opposite behaviour.

The inability to resolve the debate stems from a failure to articulate the problem in terms of debates over the validity of spatial models of voting. Spatial models, from the classic presentation by Anthony Downs to Herbert Kitschelt's more refined discussion of competition in transitions, emphasize competition for the median voter.[2] Even in multiparty systems, extremists will be tempered by the need to woo

---

2. Anthony Downs, *An Economic Theory of Democracy* (New York: Harper & Row, 1957); Herbert Kitschelt, 'The Formation of Party Systems in East Central Europe', *Politics and Society*, Vol. 20 (1992), pp. 7–50.

moderate voters. Critics of spatial models argue that voters take their cues from political elites and are thus subject to extremist appeals. Thus, extremists within the party will exercise disproportionate influence over party programme and position.[3]

The classic spatial model of voting was offered by Anthony Downs in his *Economic Theory of Democracy* (1957). Downs contended that candidates seek to maximize votes and will position themselves in order to achieve this goal. Where voters are normally distributed along a single-issue continuum, candidates will move towards the centre, in order to maximize votes. This centrist tendency is reinforced in conditions of two-party competition. Where the distribution of voters is flat, possibilities for multipartism improve, and there is some room for candidates to adopt extremist positions. In either case, however, candidates respond to the demands of voters.[4]

Downs's argument suggests that the CPRF could afford some extremism during parliamentary elections but would pursue a more moderate course during the presidential race. To use the language adopted at the start of this chapter, Zyuganov and the CPRF might be expected to adopt an extreme national socialist position in 1995 and then to move towards a more moderate, social democratic position in 1996. From this perspective, in the presidential race Zyuganov should have been seeking alliances with groups such as Women of Russia, Svyatoslav Fedorov's Party of Workers' Self-management, the moderate Union of Labour, and even the weakened Democratic Party of Russia. He should have distanced himself from more extreme groups such as Anpilov's Working Russia or even Aleksandr Rutskoi's *Derzhava*.

Downs's presentation of electoral competition along a single dimension makes it somewhat difficult to assess competition which mixes dimensions. He acknowledged that the complexity of issues creates uncertainty for voters and argued that candidates will try to minimize

3. John Kessel, *Presidential Campaign Politics*, 4th edn (Pacific Grove, CA: Brooks/Coel, 1992), pp. 110–12; Benjamin Page, *Choices and Echoes in Presidential Elections* (Chicago: University of Chicago Press, 1978), pp. 102–7; Adam Przeworski and John Sprague, *Paper Stones: A History of Electoral Socialism* (Chicago: University of Chicago Press, 1986); G. Rabinowitz and S.E. Macdonald, 'A Directional Theory of Issues Voting', *American Political Science Review (APSR)*, Vol. 83 (1989), pp. 93–121.
4. Downs, *An Economic Theory of Democracy*, pp. 115–22.

the uncertainty voters face by focusing attention on a few salient issues. Opposition candidates will match incumbents on all but a handful of key questions. They will decrease voter uncertainty by focusing attention on those issues which allow them to differentiate themselves from the incumbents.[5] While this introduces the notion of a multi-dimensional issue space into Downs's argument, it does not explain the selection of issues. It seems a reasonable explanation of CPRF emphasis on the economy in 1995 or on nationalism in 1996 (although not extremism on this issue). When the two elections are juxtaposed, however, it offers no explanation for the shift in emphasis.

Mobilization theories of electoral competition offer an alternative to spatial theories. Mobilizational theories focus on voter uncertainty, arguing that, because voters have only a vague idea of where candidates stand in relation to one another or to the voters themselves, they will decide whom to vote for on the basis of the appeal of candidates on a single issue. Party elites operate as opinion leaders determining what that issue will be, as well as mobilizing voter support in favour of their candidate's position. Rather than seeing them as responding to voter demand, as spatial theories posit, mobilization theories treat parties and candidates as the creators of demand.[6] In a recent study of 37 European parties, Torben Iverson finds that directional theory provides the best explanation of electoral behaviour. Voters, having only a vague idea of where parties are positioned, respond to extreme positions taken on single issues.[7] Mobilization theories thus avoid simplifying the electoral arena into a single continuum, allowing multiple issues to enter the analysis.

Mobilizational theories tend to predict that the CPRF would position itself as far as possible from all alternatives. As the main opposition party, the CPRF (and its candidates) could be expected to focus on increasing the distance between themselves and the incumbents – Our Home is Russia in the parliamentary election or Yeltsin in the

5. Ibid., pp. 51–9.
6. John Aldrich, 'A Spatial Model with Party Activism', *American Political Science Reviews*, Vol. 77 (1983), pp. 974–90; J.D. May, 'Opinion Structures of Political Parties: The Special Law of Curvilinear Disparity', *Political Studies*, Vol. 21 (1973), pp. 135–51; Przeworski and Sprague, op. cit.; Rabinowitz and Macdonald, op. cit.
7. Torben Iverson, 'The Logic of Electoral Politics: Spatial, Directional, and Mobilizational Effects', *Comparative Political Studies*, Vol. 27 (1994), pp. 155–89.

presidential election. This alternative seems to offer a better explanation of Zyuganov's strategy in the 1996 presidential election than do spatial theories. While the extremism of Zyuganov's nationalism runs counter to spatial predictions about two-party competition, it can be explained as an attempt to mobilize opposition to Yeltsin. Mobilizational theories suggest that extremists amongst party activists would attempt to create demand amongst voters for a set of nationalist policies which were diametrically opposed to those pursued by the rival candidate. Communist activists would emphasize their candidate's anti-Westernism in contrast to Yeltsin's willingness to kowtow to the IMF. They would play up Soviet-era glories such as the victory in the Great Patriotic War and contrast it to the liberals' defeat in the Cold War. They would call for the preservation of national wealth and accuse the Yeltsin administration of selling Russia's natural resources in exchange for Snickers chocolate bars and Mercedes-Benz cars.

This explanation falls short on three counts, however. It cannot account for the failure of this strategy in 1996, nor can it account for the more moderate positioning which the party had adopted in 1995. While the CPRF vehemently attacked government economic policy during the parliamentary campaign, it was positioned to the centre of the more extreme alliance Communist–Working Russia–For the Soviet Union (known, by its Russian initials, as KTR). Equally problematic for mobilizational theory is its inability to explain the choice of issue to politicize. This is particularly problematic for understanding party competition in countries in transition. In these systems, candidates and voters face a complex issue space and much higher levels of uncertainty than in established democracies. Certainly, it is not new to talk of a threefold transition in Russia: from authoritarianism to democracy, from plan to market, and from empire to nation-state. Candidates and voters are positioned in this multidimensional issue space and are highly uncertain about where others are positioned. This uncertainty is likely to affect electoral behaviour. However, not all actors are equally uncertain. Asymmetries of information should also affect electoral behaviour.

Like spatial models, mobilizational models are unable to account for the CPRF's decision to target the economy in 1995 but to shift emphasis to issues of nationalism in 1996. Interviews with party activists reveal that they believed this strategy would improve support for Zyuganov by broadening his electoral base. Campaign strategists believed that the patriotic message would win Zyuganov votes from those who had supported the Liberal Democratic Party of Russia (LDPR), the Congress of Russian Communities, *Derzhava*, and Power to the People! in 1995.

From this perspective, activists believed that they were actually moving Zyuganov's programme in response to voter demands. They saw Zyuganov playing down a controversial, statist economic policy in favour of a broader 'patriotic' message which could attract nationalist voters who might oppose his statist economic policy. In other words, it reflected their understanding of the electorate and not the pull of extremists within the 'national–patriotic alliance'. Oddly, it suggests that the party was operating according to principles of spatial voting rather than according to mobilization theories. However, it also suggests that Zyuganov and his strategists misjudged the electorate.

Spatial models of voting have often been criticized for assuming perfect information on the part of voters and candidates. In stable democracies, this assumption, although imperfect, is at least reasonable. However, in countries in transition from authoritarianism to democracy, candidates and voters are more likely to suffer from uncertainty and imperfect information. Elections are not only about choosing leaders. They are also about party formation, and neither voters nor candidates may know in great detail where the other stands. In established democracies, asymmetries of information generally favour candidates over voters. While the candidates have fairly reliable information about the location of the electorate, voters are likely to have only limited information about the candidates. In transitional systems, asymmetric information is also a problem, but the advantage is likely to be reversed. Voters have a better, albeit still imperfect, understanding of candidates' location, but candidates have a limited understanding of voters' positioning.

The problem of intense uncertainty suggests a mixed model to explain electoral competition in transitional political systems. I hypothesize that, although the main goal of candidates is to maximize votes, their behaviour reflects attempts to minimize uncertainty. In transitional systems, high levels of uncertainty create conditions in which this behaviour may produce results very different from candidates' goals. The electoral process in transitional systems thus becomes a process, not only for choosing leaders, but also for conveying information about candidates and about voters. Candidates will adjust the programme they supply to reflect this new understanding of voter demand. As long as uncertainty remains high, candidates will continue to view minimizing uncertainty as the best strategy for maximizing votes.

Electoral competition is always part of the process of party formation, but this is even more pronounced during the transition to democracy when the party system is being created. In these conditions, the stakes are higher than in established systems. Both rewards for successful strategies and punishments for unsuccessful strategies are much greater. Success allows a party to establish itself as a prime contender in future elections and a viable option for voters. Failure often spells the political death of the party. Incumbency carries more than the usual advantages of tangible resources. It establishes the viability of the party as a choice for voters. In the 1995 Russian parliamentary elections, the only electoral organizations to overcome the 5 per cent threshold and win proportional representation seats were incumbent parties – three from the Duma (CPRF, LDPR, and Yabloko) and the governing party (Our Home is Russia – OHR).

Given the extraordinarily high stakes involved, candidates must be concerned with maximizing votes. The challenge consists in designing a strategy that will accomplish this. Much has been written about the problem of imperfect information for voters choosing among candidates. Relatively less attention has been given to the problem of uncertainty for candidates. Downs offers a series of factors that may create uncertainty in parties, but the location of the voters is not among these.[8] Lawrence Jacobs and Robert Shapiro consider this problem in their study of candidate use of private polling data in the United States,[9] but in transitional systems, uncertainty is fundamentally higher than in established electoral systems.

Candidates have two basic options available in order to decrease uncertainty, and these are consistent with contending models of electoral competition. Candidates can, first, attempt to create demand, as

8. Downs's list of factors creating uncertainty for candidates includes the behaviour of non-political actors, how government actions will influence voters, the consequences of policy, the influence of one voter over others, whether voters are aware of policy, and the policies of other parties (p. 80).

9. Lawrence R. Jacobs and Robert Y. Shapiro, 'Issues, Candidate Image and Priming: The Use of Private Polls in Kennedy's 1960s Presidential Campaign', *American Political Science Review*, Vol. 88 (1994), pp. 527–40.

mobilizational theory would indicate. Clearly, this is the best way to deal with uncertainty: a candidate who *creates* voters' preferences *knows* voters' preferences. Alternatively, a candidate may attempt to estimate voters' preferences through techniques such as opinion polling and focus groups. They may also estimate voters' preferences on the basis of feedback from previous elections. As spatial models suggest, communication with voters and learning on the part of candidates are the key to this strategy. Mixed strategies are also possible as Jacobs and Shapiro demonstrate in the United States' case. Candidates may decide how to mobilize voters (create demand) following an evaluation of voters' attitudes – a technique known as 'priming'.[10]

Because decreasing uncertainty is dependent on resources, asymmetries in candidates' resources will be reflected in asymmetries of information from one candidate to another. Creating demand is perhaps the most attractive strategy, since it is likely to decrease uncertainty to a greater extent than responding to estimates of demand. However, candidates will be constrained in their choice of strategy by the resources available to them.[11] The creation of demand requires greater resources than a strategy of estimating voters' preferences. Even the accuracy of estimation will be dependent on resources, and greater resources can provide more accurate estimates. In other words, parties are neither always takers of opinion nor always opinion leaders. Parties choose between strategies, and that choice depends, at least in part, on the resources available to the party.

The resources available to the communists were better suited to responding to estimated voter demand. In previous work, I have argued that internal resources can best be divided into two categories, the financial and the human.[12] While the party of power – be it Russia's Choice, OHR or Yeltsin – has dominated the former, the communists

10. Jacobs and Shapiro, op. cit., p. 527.
11. In previous work, I have argued that campaign strategy, and ultimately performance, will be influence by a mix of external constraints and internal resources. Evelyn Davidheiser, 'Left and Right in the Hard Opposition', in Timothy Colton and Jerry F. Hough, *Growing Pains: The 1993 Russian Duma Election* (Washington, DC: Brookings Institution, forthcoming); and Evelyn Davidheiser 'The Campaigns of the Communist and Nationalist Parties in the 1995 Russian Parliamentary Election', paper presented at the 92nd annual meeting of the American Political Science Association, San Francisco, 1996, p. 2.
12. Davidheiser, 'Left and Right in the Hard Opposition'.

have dominated the latter. Financial resources are particularly well suited to manipulating opinion through intensive media campaigns and to creating demand by supplying voters with issues which help them identify their preferred candidate. By contrast, human resources are better suited to responding to demand through canvassing and drives to 'get out the vote'.

The link between campaign resources and campaign strategy points us in the direction of spatial models for understanding the communist case, while simultaneously suggesting amendments to that theory. First, spatial models do not tell us why the party has chosen a given strategy; rather, they tell us why that strategy has succeeded or failed. Second, spatial models must be extended to allow study of multidimensional space. The simple left–right continuum employed by Downs does not capture the reality of the Russian political space. Candidates and voters exist in a multidimensional space.

In sum, during transitions, parties and candidates attempt to maximize votes by minimizing uncertainty. Parties and candidates dependent on human (rather than financial) resources, and forced to respond to perceived voter demand, will try to decrease uncertainty about that demand. This strategy will determine where the party positions itself in a multidimensional issue space. Because this space is multidimensional, candidates may use a strategy of coalition building to minimize uncertainty. Thus, positioning reflects an attempt to build a coalition of voters. Because multidimensionality also creates complexity for candidates, making it more difficult to gauge demand, candidates use elections to gather information about demand and to adjust supply accordingly. If those perceptions are correct, the party will win votes; if they are incorrect, the party will lose votes.

Russian communist candidates were compelled by internal resources to respond to voters' demands. They did this by positioning themselves in a multi-dimensional issue space, and attempting to build a coalition of voters. The party's starting position suggested two possible coalitions: a social democratic alliance with moderate voters or a national socialist alliance with nationalist voters. Information provided by the 1995 parliamentary election pushed them in the direction of the latter.

2. RUSSIAN VOTER DEMAND AND THE POSITIONING OF COMMUNIST CANDIDATES

In this section, I re-create – in a stylized fashion – the attempt by the CPRF and Gennadii Zyuganov to supply an electoral programme which they believed would meet the demand of a maximum number of voters. This approach relies on beginning with a relatively simple issue space and adding increasingly complex layers. I work between demand and supply, using the survey data to evaluate the former and qualitative techniques to evaluate the latter.

Although there has been significant debate over the role of economic factors in determining voting behaviour in Russia,[13] there is no question that debate over economic policy has been a key element in every election since 1991. The survey instrument contained a variety of questions dealing with economic reform, reflecting the contest between market and state. In order to determine the primary issues dividing voters, I performed a principal components analysis. The analysis evaluates common response patterns and identifies distinct dimensions in the responses. In this case, two were identified. The first captured attitudes about privatization, while the second captured attitudes about freeing prices. These were distinct from one another. While respondents might oppose both privatization and the freeing of prices, a substantial number also supported one – say, privatization – while opposing the other (freeing prices). In other words, the survey respondents treated these as separate issues. Principal-components analysis also assigns a factor score to each respondent on each dimension, with the median score equal to zero. This allows us to use the survey data to produce a picture of the distribution of attitudes in society. The further from zero, the more extreme the respondent's position (*relative* to the rest of the electorate). In this case, a negative score indicates opposition to privatization or freeing prices, while a positive score indicates the reverse, producing the familiar left–right continuum (see Appendix 10A).

13. Timothy Colton, 'Economics and Voting in Russia', *Post-Soviet Affairs*, Vol. 12 (1996), pp. 289–317; Jerry F. Hough, Evelyn Davidheiser and Susan Goodrich Lehmann, *The 1996 Russian Presidential Election* (Washington, DC: Brookings Institution, 1996), pp. 40–44; Stephen White, Richard Rose and Ian McAllister, *How Russia Votes* (Chatham, NJ: Chatham House, 1997), pp. 58–64.

The CPRF can also be located on these dimensions by assigning it factor scores based on the party's programme. To accomplish this, the programme was used to answer survey questions. Individual voters who responded in precisely this fashion were identified, and their factor scores were assigned to the party's programme.[14] The results of this exercise for the 1995 election are presented in Table 10.1.[15]

Table 10.1 Attitudes towards the economy and nationalism (factor scores, 1995)

	Support for privatization	Support for freeing prices	Anti-Westernism	Pro-Union
All voters	0.00	0.00	0.00	0.00
Maximum score	3.23	4.34	3.02	2.61
Minimum score	−2.89	−2.04	−3.68	−3.28
CPRF programme	−0.04	−0.71	1.67	1.13
Average CPRF voter	−0.51	−0.47	0.56	0.62
Average new CPRF voter	−0.48	−0.45	0.53	0.55
OHR programme	1.50	1.60	−1.15	−0.53
Average OHR voter	0.42	0.47	−0.42	−0.35
Average Yabloko voter	0.27	0.53	−0.61	−0.29
Average LDPR voter	−0.03	−0.21	0.34	0.07

Table 10.1 shows the *relative* positioning of groups of voters along a continuum defined by the attitudes expressed in the survey. Because the mechanics of principal components analysis place the median voter at zero, zero reflects attitudes which were actually expressed by voters in the centre of Russia's political space, rather than an objectively defined centrist policy. One can examine the responses of individuals who scored zero on a particular factor to evaluate where the centre lies. This is a useful exercise, for understanding the attitudes of the average Russian voter provides a snapshot of voters' demands. The survey data from 1995 showed that the median Russian voter believed that the

14. *Programma Kommunisticheskoi partii Rossiiskoi Federatsii* (*Programme of the CPRF*) (Moscow: Informpechat', 1995), pp. 2–11.
15. To improve the visual presentation, factor scores on the first dimension have been multiplied by −1. This allows opposition to privatization to fall on the left side of the diagram and support for privatization to fall on the right side.

country was on the wrong course. While supporting a gradual transition to the market, he or she was suspicious about the privatization of enterprises. The median voter also adopted moderately statist policies on collective farms, supporting their protection rather than their dissolution, opposing the purchase and sale of land, and calling for limited state control over food prices. Median voters also expressed the conviction that the state should limit personal incomes and wealth. Only on the issue of privatizing living space did the median voter express unabashed support for liberalization, approving enthusiastically privatization in this sphere.[16]

Table 10.1 is actually more useful as a way of assessing the positioning of various political actors with respect to the electorate as a whole. I have included the average factor scores for supporters of a series of major parties in the 1995 election. As expected, supporters of the CPRF fall well to the left of centre, although it may be argued that the average score is not an extremist score. New supporters of the CPRF (that is, those who did not vote for the party in 1993) stand to the centre of the average CPRF voter. Supporters of OHR stand nearly as far from the centre on the right as CPRF supporters stand on the left. More surprising is the positioning of LDPR voters in relation to the CPRF platform. On issues of privatization, LDPR voters stand squarely in the centre of the electorate. The CPRF programme also fell closer to the centre than did the average communist voter. The picture was different on issues of freeing prices, however: while LDPR voters were further to the left on this issue, they were still nearer to the centre than voters for any of the other major parties. The CPRF programme, on the other hand, fell to the left of the party's average voter, although still well to the centre of extremist voters.

In 1995 the CPRF programme placed economic issues of social

16. Note that claiming that the median voter evinced these attitudes is different from claiming that most Russian voters did. The median voter here is determined by factor score, which considers responses to each of the questions simultaneously. Twenty-seven median voters were identified (having factor scores between –0.01 and 0.01 on both factors) and used to create this profile. The percentage of respondents expressing the same position as the median voter on each of these issues was as follows: wrong path 65 per cent; gradual marketization 44 per cent; slow down or stop privatization 30 per cent; protect collective farms 76 per cent; oppose land market 39 per cent; some control over food prices 27 per cent; limits on personal wealth 59 per cent; privatization of living space 53 per cent.

welfare, the distribution of wealth, and the collapse of production centre stage. Like the median voter, CPRF candidates believed that Russia was on the wrong path. The party's programme was not wholly opposed to marketization, frequently referring to the period of the New Economic Policy as providing a viable model of economic organization. The transition which the programme envisaged, however, was both gradual and limited. Privatization of small-scale enterprises and of most of the consumer goods sector was acceptable (although the programme called for limits in the realm of foodstuffs). Large enterprises and the backbone of the heavy industrial sector, by contrast, should remain nationalized. The model frequently invoked by CPRF candidates was that of Austria, where a sizeable share of industry is state owned. The CPRF programme also called for substantial barriers to privatization in agriculture, supporting collective farms, opposing unfettered purchase and sale of land, and supporting subsidies to keep food prices under control while keeping the farms in business.

A large portion of the CPRF programme was devoted to the importance of a social welfare safety net. Guaranteed free health care and educational opportunities, barriers to unemployment, and raising pensions and the minimum wage (not to mention paying them), suggest redistributive policies which would limit incomes and personal wealth. The issues of maldistribution, income and privatization came together in the CPRF's vehement attacks on unnamed beneficiaries of the privatization process, who were accused of pillaging the country's wealth and productive capacity.

To the extent that nationalism featured in the 1995 programme it was largely with respect to these economic issues. The collapse of production was linked to the collapse of the Union and restoring production required restoring at least some aspects of that Union. The West was also blamed for economic difficulties facing the country, particularly Western-led economic organizations such as the IMF and the World Bank.[17]

This snapshot of voters' attitudes and of the CPRF programme on economic issues in the 1995 campaign suggests that the CPRF was moving in a centrist direction, in an effort to attract the median voter, as Downs would predict. The doubling of support for the CPRF between 1993 and 1995 further suggests that this was an effective strategy.

17. *Programma KPRF*, 1995, pp. 2–11.

Before proclaiming spatial models to be the best explainers of electoral behaviour in Russia, however, we must allow for the proportional representation electoral law and the decline in support for the LDPR, whose voters were closer to the centre than those of the CPRF. This is because, first, spatial models predict polarized, not centrist, platforms in multiparty systems, and clearly the 1995 race was multiparty thanks to the proportional representation component of the electoral law. Second, while LDPR voters stood at the centre on economic issues, the party received only 11 per cent of the vote.

The explanation for both these discrepancies lies in the nature of the Russian political space. As any observer of the Russian scene knows, economics is not the only dimension of competition. Nationalism has also generated serious debate across candidates and within the electorate. Support for the LDPR, and for other nationalist parties, has reflected less a demand for a centrist economic policy and more a demand for candidates espousing a strong nationalist line. A complete spatial model of Russian voting must introduce this second dimension.

Using the same technique of principal components analysis and independent evaluation of the CPRF platform, I assessed the distribution of voters attitudes on issues of nationalism. Once again, two dimensions emerged. One reflected voters' attitudes towards the 'far abroad' – particularly the West – and can best be labelled anti-Western-ism. The second reflected attitudes towards the 'near abroad', the former Soviet Union. These attitudes fall along a pro-Union–anti-Union continuum (see Appendix A). The distribution and comparison of group means is included in Table 10.1.[18]

The median Russian voter expressed attitudes which were more likely to be anti-Western than pro-Soviet; he or she agreed that Russia should follow its own path, not a Western one; foreign economic policy should be protectionist, but not autarkic; there should be tariffs to protect both agriculture and industry; the state should limit the export of raw materials from the country. He or she was willing to accept foreign investment in the country so long as it was controlled by the state. The median voter was extremely suspicious of the West, believing it had set

18. Again, in order to improve the visual presentation, factor scores on the second dimension have been multiplied by –1. This allows anti-Westernism and pro-Unionism to fall on the same sides of their respective diagrams and simplifies analysis.

out to ruin Russia with its economic advice. He or she was rather less concerned about the expansion of NATO, claiming to have heard little about it, but doubting that it could bring benefits to Russia.

On the issue of the Union, he or she expressed very mixed attitudes, seeing the breakup of the Soviet Union negatively, but being unwilling to support a Russian leader who would try to reconstruct the Union. He or she believed that the Russian government should defend Russians in the near abroad and supported the strengthening of ties between Russia and Ukraine. Median voters were divided, however, over whether their homeland (*rodina*) was the former Soviet Union or the Russian Federation; they were also ambivalent about the Federation, opposing the right of republics to secede, but willing to allow Chechnya to leave the Federation.[19]

Once again, the average scores of voters for most major parties fall where expected. CPRF voters are both more anti-Western and more pro-Union than the average Russian voter. New CPRF voters, on average, stand closer to the centre, however. Supporters of Our Home is Russia exhibit the opposite tendency. Once more, LDPR voters and the CPRF programme show up in more surprising places. While we might expect LDPR voters to express the most extreme views on issues of nationalism, the average LDPR voter stands closer to the centre than the average CPRF voter on both elements of nationalism. To be sure, this is not surprising on issues related to the Union: the LDPR is a Russian nationalist party, not a Soviet nationalist party, after all. It is more surprising, however, on the issue of anti-Westernism.

The position of the CPRF programme is perhaps most striking. It lies further from the centre than the average CPRF voter on both issues. Its pro-Union position places it well away from the centre, although still amid a substantial portion of the electorate, indicating that this position,

19. Thirty-seven median voters were identified to produce this profile (scoring between −0.01 and 0.01 on both factors). The percentage of voters expressing the same position as the median voter was as follows: Russia should follow own path 40 per cent; protect industry 62 per cent; protect agriculture 62 per cent; limit raw materials exports 63 per cent; control foreign investment 37 per cent; Western goal is to ruin Russia 59 per cent; NATO expansion is bad for Russia 36 per cent; the breakup of the Soviet Union was bad 76 per cent; support a leader who would develop Russia within current borders 47 per cent; defend Russians in near abroad 90 per cent; open borders with an independent Ukraine 25 per cent; homeland is the Russian Federation 39 per cent; homeland is the former Soviet Union 33 per cent; oppose secession 28 per cent; let Chechnya go 38 per cent.

while not moderate, falls short of extremism. Its anti-Westernism, however, is arguably extreme when compared to the average Russian voter. The 1995 CPRF programme went beyond simply rejecting Western forms and calling for a Russian solution to Russia's problems. It adopted a Zhirinovskii catch phrase, proclaiming that Russia should not be the site of social experiments. Like the median voter, the CPRF held Western economic organizations responsible for the country's problems. The IMF and World Bank were blamed for forcing policies on Russia which undermined its economic base. The party's programme called for both tariffs and quotas on imports to protect domestic producers – agricultural and industrial – and lashed out harshly against the policy of paying for imports with the export of the country's natural wealth (oil, diamonds, gold and the like). While not wholly opposed to foreign investment, the programme called for a more selective and controlled approach by the state.

Although with regard to the economic aspects of nationalism the CPRF programme did not differ dramatically from the attitudes of the median voter, on other elements it was more extreme. On the issue of NATO expansion, the programme was unequivocally opposed, viewing it as military extension of the economic conquest already wrought by the West. Similarly, on issues of the Union, the programme was more extreme than the median voter. Not only bemoaning the collapse of the USSR, the CPRF programme talked about the gradual reconstruction of the Union as inevitable. According to the programme, this would occur voluntarily but it was unarguably in the best interests of Russia. The programme took a similar position on the cohesiveness of the Federation. While it was critical of the regime's treatment of Chechnya, it opposed secession from the Federation. This combination of positions placed it well to the 'right' of the median voter on issues of nationalism. It suggests that a very different strategy was pursued by the CPRF on these issues when compared with economic issues. While the party courted centrist voters with its economic policy, it took an extremist position on issues of nationalism.

This strategy better fits spatial theories of competition under multi-partism. To prevent the loss of votes to more extreme candidates, CPRF candidates should have distanced themselves from the centre. If this were the strategy, we should have seen competition shifted away from economic issues and on to issues of nationalism, where the CPRF distinguished itself more dramatically. The problem with this line of argument is not only that the average new CPRF voter lay closer to the centre than repeat voters, but that the party itself did not emphasize nationalist issues in 1995. The focus of the CPRF parliamentary campaign was on economic issues, where centrist tendencies were more pronounced. Nor did the CPRF shift its strategy towards the centre in the presidential election in the manner that models of competition in two-candidate, plurality contests would predict.

In preparing for the 1996 election, the CPRF moved into a different kind of electoral competition. The presidential election was winner-take-all, carrying very different strategic implications from the proportional representation race of the previous winter. Spatial models of voting suggest that Zyuganov, as Yeltsin's undeniably main rival, should have attempted to maximize his votes by moving still more to the centre. Yet our initial impression is of behaviour that was quite the opposite. Table 10.2 positions voters and candidates on issues of economic policy and nationalism in 1996, using the same methods adopted for 1995. Zyuganov's programme remained fairly close to the median voter on issues of privatization, but it moved further from the centre on issues of prices. It was closer to the centre in degree of

Table 10.2 Attitudes towards the economy and nationalism (factor scores, 1996)

	Support for privatization	Support for freeing prices	Anti-Westernism	Pro-Union
All voters	0.00	0.00	0.00	0.00
Maximum score	2.93	4.39	2.76	2.63
Minimum score	–3.01	–1.92	–3.76	–3.03
Zyuganov programme	–0.16	–1.12	0.95	1.63
Average Zyuganov voter	–0.57	–0.43	0.46	0.53
Average new Zyuganov voter	–0.53	–0.35	0.44	0.43
Yeltsin programme	1.62	1.13	–0.24	–1.02
Average Yeltsin voter	0.43	0.15	–0.30	–0.29
Average Lebed voter	–0.11	–.08	0.15	0.09
Average Zhirinovskii voter	–0.35	0.13	0.10	0.01

anti-Westernism, but much further from the centre in its pro-Union stance.[20]

While precise elements of Zyuganov's programme changed only marginally between 1995 and 1996, two factors contributed to its change in location. One was shifting voter attitudes, partly in response to the campaign waged by Yeltsin (see below). Second, the rhetoric of Zyuganov and his supporters became more strident and the emphasis of the programme shifted dramatically from economic issues to questions of nationalism.

On economic issues, the median voter in 1996 looked little different from the median voter in 1995. Median voters remained suspicious of privatization and rapid change. They were critical of the course so far, but supportive of the idea of transition. The biggest change was a decrease in support for limiting personal incomes and wealth.[21] Over issues reflecting nationalism, more noticeable changes took place. On the first dimension, the median voter became just slightly more suspicious of the West, with a greater number expressing awareness and concern over the expansion of NATO. On the second dimension, however, the median voter showed less support for the former Soviet Union than had been the case in 1995. Most notably, a much greater share identified Russia – not the former Soviet Union – as their homeland, and a much greater share said that they would support a leader who would develop the country in its present borders, rather than a leader who would try to rebuild the Soviet Union.[22]

---

20. For Zyuganov's programme I used *Spravedlivost', Bezopasnost', Nezavisimost'* (*Justice, Security, Independence*) (Moscow: 1996), pp. 3–18. For Yeltsin's programme I used the summary version presented in *Izvestiya*, 31 May 1996, p. 1.

21. Thirty-seven median voters were included in compiling this profile. The percentage of respondents expressing the same position as the median voter on each of these issues was as follows: wrong path 49 per cent; gradual marketization 51 per cent; slow down or stop privatization 32 per cent; protect collective farms 71 per cent; oppose land market 33 per cent; some control over food prices 30 per cent; limits on personal wealth 57 per cent; privatization of living space 60 per cent.

22. Thirty-eight median voters were used to compile this profile. The percentage of the sample expressing the same view as the median voter on each of these issues was as follows: Russia should follow own path 42 per cent; protect industry 67 per cent; protect agriculture 64 per cent; limit raw materials exports 64 per cent; control foreign investment 39 per cent; Western goal is to ruin Russia 59 per cent; NATO expansion is bad for Russia 40 per cent; the breakup of the Soviet Union was bad 70 per cent; support a leader who would develop Russia within current borders 56 per cent; defend Russians in near abroad 92 per cent; open borders with an

Zyuganov's strategists, unaware of this shift in attitudes, pressed ahead with a nationalist message which included a strong pro-Union component. While the December platform tended to keep nationalism issues linked to economic issues, the June programme made little such attempt. Indeed, issues of nationalism were placed at the forefront and decoupled from economic issues. This shift was reinforced by Zyuganov's alliance with avowed nationalists, which loomed frighteningly in the Russian media. While the substance of his programme changed only slightly, the tone and emphasis changed dramatically. Zyuganov's direct rejection of social democracy, coupled with close association with leftist extremists and unsavoury nationalists, seemed to position him further from the median voter. Mobilizational models of electoral competition would explain this strategy in terms of demand creation. Yet this does not seem to capture accurately the understanding that party activists had of the competition.

Zyuganov and his strategists were adapting issues emphasized – and thus the programme supplied – to reflect their perceptions of voters' demands. But these perceptions were developed in conditions of extreme uncertainty. The party lacked not only the resources to create demand, but also resources to assess demand accurately. The lack of financial resources was reflected not only in Zyuganov's absence from the airwaves, but also in his inability to conduct sophisticated and accurate polling or methodologically sound focus groups. Instead, strategists for Zyuganov's campaign relied on information provided by the 1995 election and information provided by faithful party activists – that is, rank-and-file activists rather than rank-and-file voters. Each source carried its own difficulties for accurately assessing voter demand. Relying on the 1995 election to provide information about voters in 1996 is tantamount to generals preparing strategies designed to fight the last war. Furthermore, the outcome was subject to conflicting interpretation. At the same time, assessments of activists were subject to bias.

Multiple studies of electoral competition have shown party activists to be more extreme than the average voter for that party.[23] Indeed, this

independent Ukraine 35 per cent; homeland is the Russian Federation 43 per cent; homeland is the former Soviet Union 29 per cent; let Chechnya go 32 per cent.

23. Przeworski and Sprague, op. cit.; Rabinowitz and Macdonald, op. cit., p.111; and Kessel, op. cit., p. 82.

finding is one of the central challenges offered to spatial models of voting. While I have not conducted surveys of CPRF activists, there are indicators in the general survey that this holds true for the CPRF as well. Repeat voters for the CPRF expressed more extreme attitudes than the average CPRF voter. While previous membership of the CPSU did not increase extremism, CPSU membership and active engagement in the campaign were associated with increased extremism. Among loyal communist voters, those who claimed to have discussed the election with family and friends every day during the week prior to the interview were the most extreme. In 1995, their average score was -0.74 on privatization issues compared to -0.51 for all CPRF voters. On issues of nationalism, activists' average score was 0.59 for anti-Westernism and 0.64 for support for the old Union. These findings are highly suggestive of activists holding positions more extreme than the average CPRF voter and considerably more extreme than the average Russian voter. Since the party was dependent on human resources, it was dependent on an assessment of the electorate provided by these activists. These assessments suggested to party strategists that they should be emphasizing nationalist components of the programme.

The other major source of information was the 1995 parliamentary election. Unlike the information coming from party activists, information provided by the election was more ambiguous and subject to multiple interpretations. Between 1993 and 1995, the CPRF almost doubled its share of the proportional representation vote (from 12 per cent to 22 per cent) and increased the absolute number of votes won by an even greater 132 per cent (from 6,666,402 to 15,432,963). The CPRF could not be sure of the source of these new votes, however, and could assess the source only on the basis of aggregate data.

There were two reasonable explanations which could be offered for increased support. First, it could be coming from new voters, since turnout had increased by 9 percentage points between 1993 and 1995. Alternatively, new support may have come from former nationalist voters. In some ways, the biggest loser in 1995 was Vladimir Zhirinovskii's LDPR, which saw its support fall from 23 per cent in 1993 to 11 per cent two years later.[24] Each explanation carried potentially

---

24. In actuality, the CPRF received an estimated 35 per cent of its votes in 1995 from repeat communist voters, 12 per cent from former supporters for the LDPR, and 40 per cent from voters who either had not voted in 1993 or had forgotten which party

different implications for strategy in 1996. If increased support was coming from the nationalists, emphasizing the nationalist plank in Zyuganov's programme would maximize votes. If increased support was coming from new voters, the uncertainty was greater. Were new voters basing their support for the CPRF on the party's economic policy, the party's nationalist stance, or some combination of the two? Zyuganov's strategists simply did not know. Operating in conditions of high uncertainty, they acted so as to minimize that uncertainty. Three factors combined to suggest that emphasizing nationalism was the best solution to this lack of information. First, focusing on nationalists allowed Zyuganov to target a fairly well-defined audience, thereby minimizing uncertainty. Strategists knew what appealed to nationalist voters. They were less certain about what appealed to new voters, but they believed that at least some new voters would be attracted by a nationalist message.

Second, the results of the parliamentary elections provided some very clear information about the distribution of voters in the Russian political space. There were three fairly well-defined poles – communist left, liberal right and nationalist. Of the 43 organizations which contested the 1995 election, 17 fell into one of these three categories. Together these 17 accounted for 78 per cent of the vote.[25] This left a large portion of the electorate outside these three categories – voters who might be labelled 'moderates'. However, this group was far from cohesive, judging by the distribution of support across the 26 parties and blocs which did not fall into any of the other three categories. Party strategists expressed intense uncertainty about what kind of programme would appeal to this amorphous group of voters. The presence of nationalists as a dominant third pole was much clearer. Strategists minimized uncertainty by appealing to this comparatively well-defined third pole.

Finally, the information strategists received from party activists reinforced their faith in the wisdom of this plan. I explained above why this information would be skewed. However, it served the important function of reducing uncertainty by increasing the confidence within the

they had supported: see Evelyn Davidheiser, 'Russia's Transition to Social Democracy: Explaining Increased Support for the KPRF', paper presented at the conference on Economic and Political Liberalization, Duke University, February 1997, p. 26.

25. Figures can be found in Hough et al., op. cit., p. 53.

Zyuganov campaign that emphasizing nationalism was the optimum strategy for maximizing votes.

In deciding to emphasize the nationalist over the economic message, Zyuganov strategists were not so much changing programme as attempting to build a new and (they hoped) winning electoral coalition. To understand this strategy fully, we must move from simple spatial models, which invoke a single dimension, and examine the Russian electoral arena as multidimensional. As a simple next approach to this problem, I move to a two-dimensional issue space, defined by economic attitudes, on the one hand, and attitudes about nationalism, on the other. For heuristic purposes I have limited the visual presentation to one factor score for each of those dimensions. I have selected privatization as the indicator of economic position, because it was the most highly politicized aspect of economic reform, and anti-Westernism as the indicator of nationalism, because it reflects the dimension agreed upon by self-avowed nationalists. Combining these two factors, we can locate Russian voters in one of four quadrants in this two-dimensional issue space (see Figure 10.1).

It was within this issue space that Zyuganov's strategists operated to try to build a winning electoral coalition. They could emphasize nationalism to build a coalition with nationalist voters, or socialism to build a coalition with voters based on economic concerns. Attempting a coalition with the nationalists posed the lowest level of uncertainty. In emphasizing nationalism, however, Zyuganov's campaign highlighted issues on which its candidate stood quite far from the median voter. As Figure 10.1 indicates, Yeltsin's programme fell much closer to the median voter on this issue. In contrast, Zyuganov's programme was much closer to the centre on economic issues, while Yeltsin's fell a much greater distance from the mean.

The results were devastating. Zyuganov was unable to maintain the decisive lead he enjoyed early in the presidential race. Moderates flocked to Yeltsin, particularly in the second round of the election. Equally problematic, the coalition Zyuganov constructed was only partial. Even this two-dimensional issue space falls short of capturing the complexity of the Russian electoral arena. As we have seen, nationalism itself was two dimensional. Attitudes towards the West were coupled with attitudes towards the former Soviet Union. While communist voters tended to be anti-Western and pro-Union, supporters of nationalist candidates tended to be anti-Western but split in their

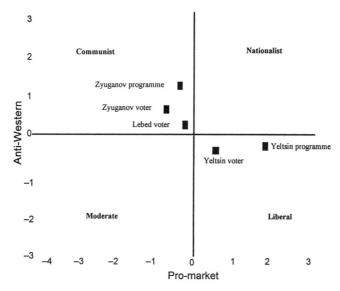

Figure 10.1 Location of Russian voters in two-dimensional issue space

attitudes towards the Union. This left the door open to a particularly nasty kind of competition during the election's second round, when both Yeltsin and Zyuganov targeted nationalist voters, that is, those who had supported either Aleksandr Lebed or Vladimir Zhirinovskii in the first round.

If we attach labels to voters in each quadrant of Figure 10.1, the implications of the competition and electoral coalition building emerge quite clearly. Competition for the nationalist vote in the second round pitted a national socialist coalition against what might be labelled an East Asian type of coalition of pro-market nationalists. Yeltsin was able to add the anti-Western, anti-Union voters to his coalition, while Zyuganov picked up the anti-Western, pro-Union nationalists who had not voted for him in the first round. Moderates were largely ignored in the second round. Whereas they had split fairly evenly between Yeltsin and Zyuganov in the first round, in the second round very few additional moderate votes went to Zyuganov (see Table 10.3).

Yeltsin achieved this on the basis of a final dimension in the Russian electoral space: democracy–authoritarianism. While communists and

Table 10.3   _Presidential election vote, 1996_

	First round					Second round	
	Yeltsin	Zyuganov	Lebed	Zhirinovskii	Yavlinskii	Yeltsin	Zyuganov
Communist	23	49	17	4	6	52	58
Liberal	62	9	12	3	12	88	12
Nationalist							
Anti-Union	53	18	14	5	10	79	21
Nationalist pro-Union	35	37	13	5	7	61	39
Moderate							
Pro-democracy	41	22	18	4	14	72	28
Moderate							
Anti-democracy	26	40	14	9	10	56	44

Table 10.4   _Attitudes towards democracy, 1996: average factor scores_

Quadrant	
Communist	−0.14
Liberal	0.20
Nationalist	−0.02
Moderate	−0.07

liberals were distant from one another on this dimension, 'moderates' and 'nationalists' fell closer to the centre of the electorate (see Table 10.4). Yeltsin's strategists were able to convince these voters that a victory for Zyuganov posed a threat to democracy. There was really nothing in Zyuganov's programme to suggest that he would restore authoritarianism in Russia, yet Zyuganov's own strategy strengthened Yeltsin's hand. His emphasis on nationalism, which combined anti-Westernism and support for the dissolved Union, suggested authoritarianism to voters. To be sure, in some instances, this boosted support for Zyuganov. Voters in the 'communist quadrant' of Figure 10.1 expressed attitudes more consistent with authoritarianism than did voters in the 'moderate quadrant' (see Table 10.4). An authoritarian reputation may also have strengthened Zyuganov's support among Zhirinovskii's former voters in the second round. However, it also strengthened Yeltsin's ability to shift attention away from the economy and to exploit his advantage over Zyuganov on the issue of democracy. Thus, in the first round, Yeltsin could generate support from pro-democracy moderates and nationalists; Zyuganov's loss of these voters in the first round left Yeltsin free to compete for the anti-Union, anti-Western vote in the second round.

Superior campaign resources allowed Yeltsin to identify the location of voters in this multidimensional issue space, and to set the agenda for the election accordingly. Setting the agenda was further facilitated by Yeltsin's commanding presence in the media. Thus, the incumbent was able to engage in the sort of 'priming' which Jacobs and Shapiro found occurring in US presidential races. Yeltsin kept the agenda focused on the issue of democracy and authoritarianism and on problems with the Soviet economy. The economy in 1996 was kept off the agenda. Zyuganov lacked similar resources and operated according to inadequate information about where the voters were positioned. His strategy played neatly into that used by Yeltsin. The emphasis on nationalism made Zyuganov look as extreme as Yeltsin said he was, and it allowed Yeltsin's strategy of taking the economy off the agenda to succeed.

From this perspective, Zyuganov lost the race, not in the second round, but in the first. His decision to target nationalist voters from the start might have worked in a single-round, two-candidate race, but it was a strategic blunder given the conditions he faced. Instead of forging a national socialist coalition in the first round, keeping the emphasis on the economy and building a social democratic coalition, as he attempted in 1995, might have produced higher levels of support for Zyuganov.

3. CONCLUSIONS AND IMPLICATIONS

Neither spatial nor mobilizational theories of electoral competition fully explain the behaviour or performance of the CPRF in 1995 and 1996. The transition to democracy produces higher levels of uncertainty than are seen in established democracies. Lack of information is a problem, not only for voters, as mobilizational models suggest, but also for candidates. In these conditions, it is difficult for candidates to know how best to maximize votes. Lacking this information, they can move either to create demand, as mobilizational theories predict that they will, or to decrease uncertainty. Candidates who lack resources to create demand will respond to perceived demand, in a manner predicted by spatial models. However, candidates face challenges associated with assessing the distribution of voters as well as those concerning which issue to emphasize in a multidimensional issue space. Wrong decisions can be devastating, particularly when those decisions play into the demand-creation strategy of one's opponent.

External and internal dynamics combined to push the CPRF towards national socialism rather than social democracy in 1996. The strength of the nationalist vote in the December 1995 election indicated that voter demand could best be met with a corresponding message. This fitted well with Zyuganov's natural predilections, but – more importantly – this strategy was confirmed by the constraints posed by internal party resources. Nationalists prevailed over moderates in debates over platforms because the nationalist strategy appeared the best one for maximizing votes, given the uncertainty faced by campaign strategists.

The CPRF resource base constrained Zyuganov to a strategy of responding to voters' demands, as spatial models would predict. However, simple spatial models fail to capture the more complex issue space in which the CPRF was operating. For the party, responding to voter demand meant not only attempting to move towards the median voter, but also choosing which issue to emphasize. This element of multidimensionality and choice of issues seems to suggest that mobilizational theories better explain the behaviour of the CPRF. Yet this analysis has attempted to show that simple application of mobilization theory is misleading.

The CPRF chose issues on the basis of its perceptions of voters' demands, rather than in an attempt to mobilize non-existent or ill-defined support for a new issue. The shift in emphasis from economic issues to issues of nationalism in 1996 thus reflected the party's understanding of the Russian electorate in the wake of the December 1995 parliamentary elections. Those elections had clearly demonstrated that the Russian voters were divided into four distinct segments: the communist left, the liberal right, nationalists, and ill-defined moderates. These were not points along a single continuum, but clusters of voters in a multidimensional issue space. While the CPRF tended to treat nationalism as a single dimension, even this issue was multidimensional, capturing both attitudes towards the West and attitudes towards the former Soviet Union. In responding to perceived voter demand, the CPRF chose issues in order to put together what it hoped would be a winning electoral coalition. The 1995 election pushed the CPRF into an alliance with nationalists because nationalists represented the strongest third pole in the electoral arena and because nationalists posed the major source of competition in that quadrant of the electorate from which the CPRF drew the bulk of its support. Zyuganov's decision to run as the 'national patriotic candidate' reflected elite coalition building. The leaders expected that voters would follow suit.

Zyuganov's use of this strategy was unsuccessful for two reasons. First, the distance from the median voter on this issue made it difficult for Zyuganov to continue to add support from moderate voters as the CPRF had done in 1995. These voters tended to turn to Yeltsin in the second round. Second, competition in the second round was focused on nationalist voters, with both Yeltsin and Zyuganov attempting to build coalitions with nationalists. Yeltsin and Zyuganov split the nationalist vote, with anti-Union voters supporting the president and pro-Union voters supporting Zyuganov.

The implications for the relative utility of competing models of electoral behaviour are important. In the context of the transition, elections provide important information to parties about voters' demands, and parties and candidates adjust the supply of issues to meet that demand. During the transition to democracy, as new parties are being created, uncertainty is much greater than in established democracies. Imperfect information – always a problem for spatial models – presents even more acute challenges for candidates in transitional systems.

Rather than reject spatial models outright, however, I have attempted to use the CPRF case to illustrate how candidates in this environment react to uncertainty. Candidates, or parties, with few financial resources cannot resort to pure mobilizational strategies. Instead, they must make their best guess about voters' demands and attempt to supply programmes which will fulfil those demands. The implications are obvious: when they err in estimating demand, they lose elections. Too many losses, or losses which are too severe, will eventually lead to the party's demise.

For the CPRF, the lesson learned in the summer of 1996 was a hard one. Becoming a 'catch-all party', capable of maximizing electoral support, requires emphasizing economic policies which are close to the median voter. The CPRF is likely to remain the dominant opposition party in Russia for the foreseeable future. If it continues to coalesce with nationalists, moving in the direction of national socialism, the party will find that it has at best relegated itself to the position of permanent opposition and at worst placed its very own survival in jeopardy. If it coalesces with moderates, moving in the direction of social democracy, it stands a better chance of moving out of opposition and into a governing position. The 1996 elections provided new information about the positioning of voters, decreasing uncertainty. This should help the party's leaders adapt the programme supplied to match voters' demand more closely.

APPENDIX 10A

Principal Components Analysis

Table 10A.1   Economic attitudes – rotated factor matrix

	1995		1996	
	Factor 1[a] Oppose privatization	Factor 2 Free prices	Factor 1[a] Oppose privatization	Factor 2 Free prices
Russia is on an incorrect course	0.29	–0.49	0.67	–0.03
The transition to a market economy should be slowed down	0.48	–0.49	0.62	0.07
The privatization of state property should be slowed down	0.78	–0.26	0.70	–0.29
I oppose privatization of large enterprises	0.74	–0.20	0.68	–0.27
I oppose the privatization of living space	0.69	0.01	0.49	0.40
Kolkhozes and *sovkhozes* should be dismantled	–0.10	0.69	–0.55	0.31
The purchase and sale of land by private individuals should be restricted	0.42	–0.40	0.61	0.08
The government should not control food prices	–0.07	0.73	–0.61	0.35
The government should not limit the earned wealth of citizens	–0.15	0.65	–0.58	0.35

Note: [a] In the analysis this factor has been multiplied by –1 for conceptual clarity. This manipulation allows opposition to the market to fall on the left side of the diagrams.

Table 10A.2   Nationalism attitudes – rotated factor matrix

	1995		1996	
	Factor 1[a] Anti-West	Factor 2 Anti-Union	Factor 1[a] Anti-West	Factor 2 Anti-Union
Russia should not use the experience of the West	0.62	–0.14	0.60	–0.16
The government of Russia should not decrease defence spending	0.51	0.12	0.59	0.00
The government should not adopt tariffs to protect domestic industry	–0.09	0.07	0.07	0.01
The government should not adopt tariffs to protect domestic producers in agriculture	–0.06	0.04	–0.08	0.06
The government should not intervene in the export of raw materials (oil, gas, etc.)	–0.39	0.13	–0.24	0.28
I oppose foreign investment in Russia	0.70	–0.14	0.57	–0.29
Western economic advice is not designed to weaken Russia	–0.67	0.09	–0.63	0.22
The expansion of NATO is harmful to Russia	0.21	–0.09	0.48	0.05
Breakup of the Soviet Union was detrimental	0.32	–0.46	0.33	–0.46
My homeland is not the former Soviet Union	0.00	0.67	0.04	0.67
The government should not defend Russians living in the former republics of the USSR	0.06	0.35	0.11	0.25
Russia and Ukraine should be more closely tied	0.26	–0.60	0.18	–0.62
Republics should not have the right to withdraw unilaterally from the Russian Federation	0.00	–0.21	NA	NA
The Chechen problem should be resolved by keeping Chechnya in Russia with a status equal to the other republics	–0.06	–0.03	0.00	–0.03
I support a leader who would develop Russia within its current borders not one who would restore the USSR	–0.30	0.64	–0.24	0.71

Note: [a] In the analysis this factor has been multiplied by –1 and described as 'pro-Union' in order to improve the clarity of the presentation.

Table 10A.3 Democratic attitudes – rotated factor matrix

	1995	1996
I would not support a leader who, in the name of preserving order in Russia, would establish a dictatorship	0.64	0.74
The organs of power should not break the law to defend the security of the population	0.64	0.74
Uncontrolled democracy has ruined the economy	–0.60	NA

Appendices

Appendix A1 Russian Election Results 1993-96

Table A1.1 Election to the State Duma, December 1993

	PR party list			Single-member seats		Total seats	
	Vote	Seats					
	%	N	%	N	%	N	%
Russia's Choice	15.51	40	17.8	30	13.3	70	15.6
Liberal Democratic Party	22.92	59	26.2	5	2.2	64	14.2
Communist Party	12.40	32	14.2	16	7.1	48	10.7
Agrarian Party	7.99	21	9.3	12	5.3	33	7.3
Yabloko	7.86	20	8.9	3	1.3	23	5.1
Women of Russia	8.13	21	9.3	2	0.9	23	5.1
Party of Russian Unity and Concord	6.76	18	8.0	1	0.4	19	4.0
Democratic Party of Russia	5.52	14	6.2	1	0.4	15	3.3
[5 per cent threshold]							
Civic Union	1.93	–		1	0.4	1	0.2
Democratic Reform Movement	4.08	–		4	1.7	4	0.9
Dignity and Charity	0.70	–		2	0.9	2	0.4
Russia's Future-New Names	1.25	–		1	0.4	1	0.2
Cedar	0.76	–		–		–	–
Against all	4.36	–		–		–	–
Spoiled ballots	3.10	–		–		–	–
Independents	–	–		141	62.7	141	31.3
Postponed	–			6		6	
Total		225		225		450	

Sources: Based on *Rossiiskaya gazeta*, 28 December 1993, p. 1; *Byulleten' Tsentral'noi izbiratel'noi komissii Rossiiskoi Federatsii*, 1994, No. 12, p. 67.

275

Table A1.2   Election to the State Duma, December 1995

	PR party list Vote	PR party list Seats		Single-member seats		Total seats	
	%	N	%	N	%	N	%
A. *Cleared 5 per cent threshold (4)*							
Communist Party	22.3	99	44.0	58	25.8	157	34.9
Liberal Democrats	11.2	50	22.2	1	0.4	51	11.3
Our Home is Russia	10.1	45	20.0	10	4.4	55	12.2
Yabloko	6.9	31	13.8	14	6.2	45	10.0
B. *Won single-member seats (19)*							
Agrarian Party	3.8			20	8.9	20	4.4
Power to the People!	1.6			9	4.0	9	2.0
Russia's Democratic Choice	3.9			9	4.0	9	2.0
Congress of Russian Communities	4.3			5	2.2	5	1.1
Women of Russia	4.6			3	1.3	3	0.7
Forward, Russia!	1.9			3	1.3	3	0.7
Ivan Rybkin Bloc	1.1			3	1.3	3	0.7
Pamfilova–Gurov–Lysenko Bloc	1.6			2	0.9	2	0.4
Communists–Working Russia–For the Soviet Union	4.5			1	0.4	1	0.2
Workers' Self-government	4.0			1	0.4	1	0.2
Trade Unions and Industrialists	1.6			1	0.4	1	0.2
Govorukhin Bloc	1.0			1	0.4	1	0.2
My Fatherland	0.7			1	0.4	1	0.2
Common Cause	0.7			1	0.4	1	0.2
Transformation of the Fatherland	0.7			1	0.4	1	0.2
Party of Russian Unity and Accord	0.4			1	0.4	1	0.2
Party of Economic Freedom	0.1			1	0.4	1	0.2
89 Regions of Russia	0.1			1	0.4	1	0.2
Bloc of Independents	0.1			1	0.4	1	0.2
(Independents)				77	34.2	77	17.1
C. *Won votes but no seats (20)*							
Derzhava	2.57						
Ecologists-Cedar	1.39						
Beer Lovers' Party	0.62						
Muslim Social Movement 'Nur'	0.57						
National-Republican Party of Russia	0.48						
Pre-election Bloc of Party Leaders[a]	0.47						
Association of Russian Lawyers	0.35						
For the Motherland!	0.28						
Christian Democratic Union – Christians of Russia	0.28						
Pre-election Bloc of Party Leaders[b]	0.21						
Peoples' Union Party	0.19						
Tikhonov–Tupolev–Tikhonov Bloc	0.15						
Utility Workers of Russia	0.14						
Social Democratic Party	0.13						
Russian Popular Movement	0.12						

Federal-Democratic Movement	0.12					
Stable Russia	0.12					
Duma 96	0.08					
International Union	0.06					
Generation of the Boundary	0.06					
D. *Other ballots*						
Against all lists	2.8					
Invalid vote	1.9					
Totals		225	100	225	100	450	100

Notes

Registered electorate: 107,496,856.

Total vote: 69,204,819 (valid vote 67,884,200).

Turnout (all votes as a percentage of the registered electorate): 64.4 per cent.

a Incorporating the following parties: Defence of Pensioners and Veterans, Eradication of Crime and for Law and Order, Defence of Health, Education, Science and Culture, Defence of Youth, Association of Free Trade Unions, Justice, and Defence of Nature.

b Incorporating the following parties: Defence of Children, the Russian Women's Party, the Orthodox Party, the People's Christian-Monarchist Party, Union of the Slavic Peoples, the Zemlya-Matushka Party of Rural Toilers, Defence of Invalids, and the Party of Victims and the Swindled.

Source: Derived from Tsentral'naya izbiratel'naya komissiya Rossiiskoi Federatsii, *Vybory deputatov Gosudarstvennoi Dumy. 1995. Elektoral'naya statistika (Elections of Deputies of the State Duma. 1995. Electoral Statistics)* (Moscow: Ves' mir, 1996), pp. 89–91, 154.

Table A1.3   First-round presidential election result, 16 June 1996

Candidates	Vote	
	%	N
Boris Yeltsin, *Independent*	35.3	26,665,495
Gennadii Zyuganov, *Communist*	32.0	24,211,686
Aleksandr Lebed, *no party*	14.5	10,974,736
Grigorii Yavlinskii, *Yabloko*	7.3	5,550,752
Vladimir Zhirinovskii, *Liberal Democrat*	5.7	4,311,479
Svyatoslav Fedorov, *Workers' Self-government*	0.9	699,158
Mikhail Gorbachev, *International Fund for Socioeconomic and Political Research*	0.5	386,069
Martin Shakkum, *Socioeconomic Reform*	0.4	277,068
Yuri Vlasov, *National Patriotic Party*	0.2	151,282
Vladimir Bryntsalov, *Russian Socialist Party*	0.2	123,065
Aman-Geldy Tuleev, *Communist*[a]	0.0	308
Against all candidates	1.5	1,163,921
Registered electorate		108,495,023
Total valid vote	68.7	74,515,019
Invalid ballots	1.0	1,072,120
Total turnout	69.7	75,587,139

Note: [a] Withdrew from race at last minute in favour of Zyuganov.

Source: Derived from Tsentral'naya izbiratel'naya komissiya Rossiiskoi Federatsii, *Vybory Prezidenta Rossiiskoi Federatsii. 1996. Elektoral'naya statistika (Russian Federation Presidential Election. 1996. Electoral Statistics)* (Moscow: Ves' mir, 1996), p. 128.

Table A1.4 Second-round presidential election result, 3 July 1996

Candidates	Vote	
	%	N
Boris Yeltsin, *Independent*	53.8	40,203,948
Gennadii Zyuganov, *Communist*	40.3	30,102,288
Against both candidates	4.8	3,604,462
Registered electorate		108,589,050
Total valid vote	68.1	73,910,698
Invalid ballots	0.7	780,592
Total turnout	68.8	74,691,290

Source: Derived from Tsentral'naya izbiratel'naya komissiya Rossiiskoi Federatsii, *Vybory Prezidenta Rossiiskoi Federatsii. 1996. Elektoral'naya statistika (Russian Federation Presidential Election. 1996. Electoral Statistics)* (Moscow: Ves' mir, 1996), pp. 128, 130.

Appendix A2 Contents of Companion Volume

The companion volume to the present collection, containing revised versions of other papers presented to the conference, 'Party Politics in Postcommunist Russia', held at the University of Glasgow on 23–25 May 1997, is *Party Politics in Post-communist Russia*, edited by John Löwenhardt (London: Cass, 1998); it first appeared as a special double issue of *The Journal of Communist Studies and Transition Politics* (Vol. 14, Nos 1–2, 1998). The contents are as follows:

Introduction
John Löwenhardt

Party Development in the Regions: When did Parties Start to Play a Part in Politics?
Ruth Brown

Regional Party System Formation in Russia: The Deviant Case of Sverdlovsk *Oblast*
Vladimir Gel'man and Grigorii V. Golosov

The Electoral Effects of Presidentialism in Post-Soviet Russia
Robert G. Moser

Party Platforms: Towards a Definition of the Russian Political Spectrum
Sarah Oates

Ideology, Uncertainty, and the Rise of Anti-system Parties in Post-Communist Russia
Stephen E. Hanson

Left or Right? The CPRF and the Problem of Democratic Consolidation in Russia
Richard Sakwa

Classifying Russia's Party System: The Problem of 'Relevance' in a Time of Uncertainty
Neil Robinson

Should Party in Parliament be Weak or Strong? The Rules Debate in the Russian State Duma
Moshe Haspel

Political Conflict and Institutional Design: Paths of Party Development in Russia
Thomas F. Remington

Where Now in the Study of Russian Political Parties?
Frederic J. Fleron, Jr, Richard Ahl and Finbarr Lane

The Lessons of Comparative Politics: Russian Political Parties as Independent Variables?
Paul Webb and Paul G. Lewis

Electoral Statistics, 1993–96 *compiled by Stephen White*

Subject index

283